IMAGES
of America

WESTLAKE

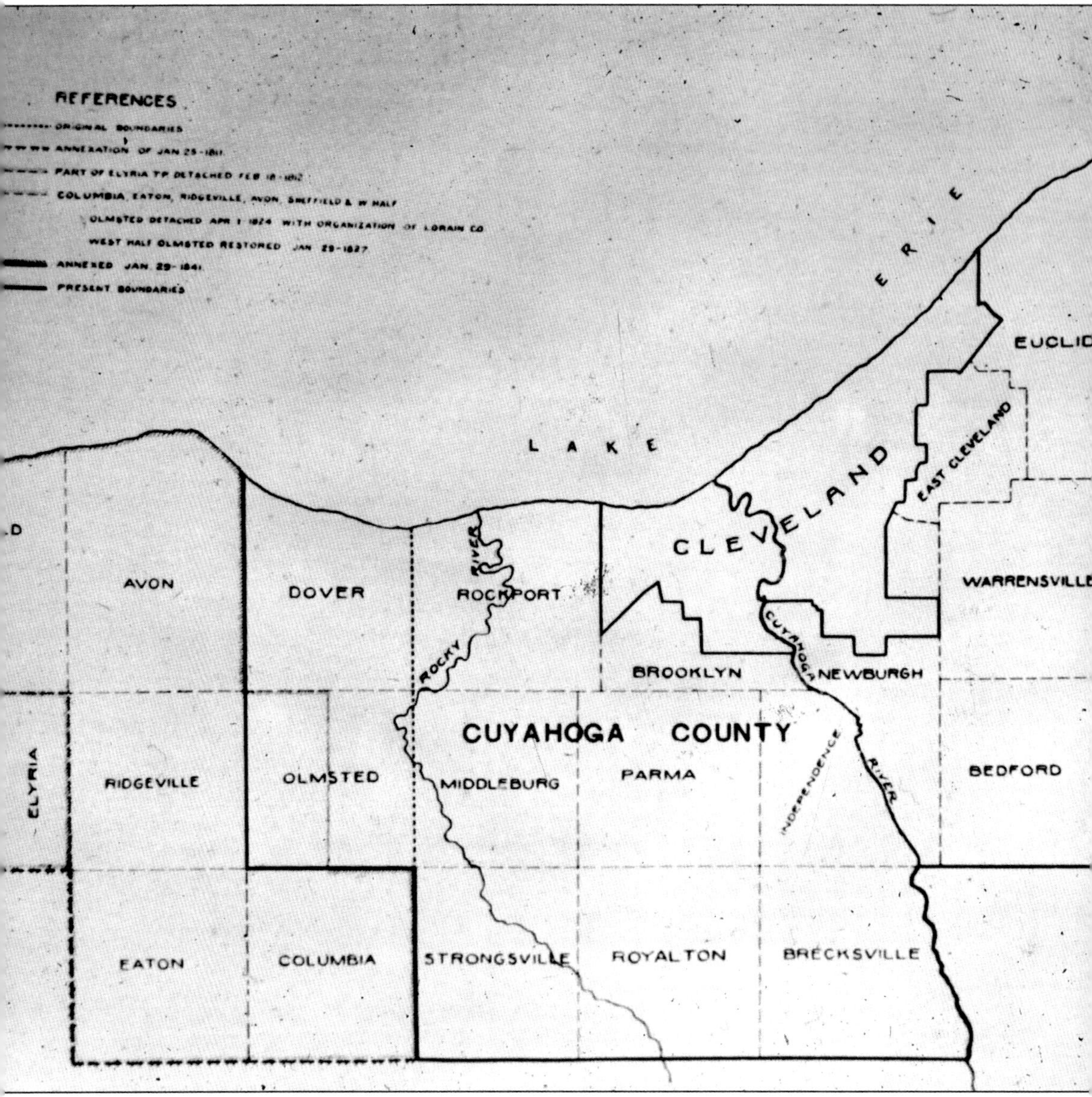

This map illustrates the boundaries of Dover as a township, officially annexed to Cuyahoga County on January 25, 1811. (Courtesy of William Robishaw Collection, Westlake Porter Public Library.)

On the cover: On May 27, 1958, Westlake was the first community in Cuyahoga County to conclude its school year. The suburb's 1,832 schoolchildren got a big jump on Cleveland youngsters, who were not out until June 13. This jubilant scene took place at Hilliard Elementary School. (Courtesy of Cleveland State University, Cleveland Memory Project, Cleveland Press Collection, Joseph E. Cole, donor.)

IMAGES
of America

WESTLAKE

Deborah S. Rossman on behalf of the Westlake Porter Public Library

ARCADIA
PUBLISHING

ISBN 978-0-7385-5203-3

Published by Arcadia Publishing
Charleston SC, Chicago IL, Portsmouth NH, San Francisco CA

Printed in the United States of America

Library of Congress Catalog Card Number: 2007941425

For all general information contact Arcadia Publishing at:
Telephone 843-853-2070
Fax 843-853-0044
E-mail sales@arcadiapublishing.com
For customer service and orders:
Toll-Free 1-888-313-2665

Visit us on the Internet at www.arcadiapublishing.com

To Melissa, Megan, and Robert, with love

Contents

ACKNOWLEDGMENTS

Hometown heritage and community spirit are ever present in the city of Westlake. From the early pioneers who settled the area to the innovative builders of today, the city is rich in pride and commitment. Thank you to all of the Westlake residents who have contributed stories and photographs to make this book possible. I am especially grateful to Roger and Lollie Cooley for their continuous efforts in historic preservation. Thanks also to Bill and Donna Nordgren for their support and assistance.

On behalf of the staff of Westlake Porter Public Library, I would like to express my gratitude to William Robishaw, a local historian, for his donation of an extensive collection of photographs and archival documentation. Before his retirement, he served as president of the Westlake Historical Society and authored two publications about Westlake: *You've Come a Long Way, Westlake and You've Got a Long Way to Go* in 1993 and *Westlake, Looking Back to Dover, a Collection of Writings* in 1980.

The following books were helpful in my research: *A History and Civics of Dover Village* by Reign Hadsell and Hazel Rutherford, published in 1930; *A History of Westlake, Ohio 1811–1961* by William Donohue Ellis and Mary Ellen Wobbecke; and *Reminiscences of Dover Pioneer Life 1810–1910* by Reuben Hall. May E. Weston's 1969 publication, *The First 100 Years of Dover Schools*, served as another excellent resource.

I appreciate the collaboration of special collections librarian Bill Barrow at Cleveland State University. Westlake Porter Public Library has partnered with Cleveland State University and other participating libraries in the area in forming the Greater Cleveland History Digital Library Consortium. Thanks to Barrow, we are able to share Westlake pictures from the *Cleveland Press* archives, spanning decades of local history and events. Thank you also to the wonderful administration and staff at Westlake Porter Public Library. Special thanks to Andrew Mangels, Mary Worthington, Susan Cozzens, Laura Ploenzke, and Susan Bennis for their assistance. I am most grateful to the Friends of Porter Public Library for making this publication possible.

Readers who are interested in local digital archives can access collections at the following sites: history.westlakelibrary.org and www.clevelandmemory.org.

INTRODUCTION

Westlake is the story of a settlement in Ohio. The village was named Westlake in 1940 and became a city in 1957, but in its beginnings it was known as Dover Township. Local residents know it as a friendly town where families live, friends gather, and dreams are fulfilled, a community where people smile and wave when they pass their neighbors on the street, where flowers spill along driveways and show the way to front doors. This is not a city known to curiosity seekers or paparazzi. Instead Westlake is special by its very nature, the warmth and welcome of home.

Following the early explorations of RenèRobert Cavelier, Sieur de La Salle, both France and England laid claim to the region along the southern shores of the Great Lakes. England won the French and Indian War in 1763, and King Charles II offered the winnings to each American colony. Connecticut was given the area extending west to the first big body of water. After the Revolutionary War, all other colonies gave up their claims, but Connecticut needed revenue to start public schools. It kept the Western Reserve for profit. Nehemiah Hubbard and Joshua Stowe, representatives of the Connecticut Land Company, sold the land to New Englanders for about $1 an acre.

Joseph and Lydia Cahoon and their eight children arrived first on October 10, 1810. Rebecca Johnson Porter, her husband, Asahel, and their two small children were the second family to arrive later the same day. The Porters were accompanied by Rebecca's brother, Leverett Johnson. Had their wagon not overturned when fording the Rocky River, the Porters may have been able to hold the title of Dover's first. As it was, these early settlers feared the sickness known as ague and the Native Americans, unaware that Lake Erie would be their most treacherous foe. The settlers faced challenges in their log homes. Harsh winters brought hardship with the drifting snow. The oak timber in Dover was five feet thick at the stump level and could tear a shoulder muscle loose from the bone before the axe cut through. But the settlers were tenacious. They made the township their home.

Ohio pioneers compensated for hardships with friendships and social gatherings. It is easy to imagine how much Rebecca Porter wanted to go to a wedding in Cleveland in 1814; and it is easy to picture the scene that April 1. Rebecca held her one-month-old son, Dennis, in an open boat, accompanied by Noah Crocker and George Smith. She probably wore her fanciest dress, giddy with anticipation of the grand celebration. A storm overtook the party upon their return, and the boat capsized at the mouth of Rocky River. Only Crocker survived the incident. Rebecca's worn gravestone remains at Lakeside Cemetery almost 200 years later. Regardless of the rumor to the contrary, the lake was far more deadly than the ague. In truth, the disease rarely killed. It only made people wish they were dead.

The township's oldest celebrity, conservationist and naturalist Jack Miner, was born in Dover Village in 1865. He lived in a small weather-beaten house with a leaky roof just south of the area where Jenkins Funeral Chapel now stands. His father formed bricks for a living and sold them for the sum of $3.50 per thousand. Jack's red hair and freckles made him the brunt of teasing as a boy, so much so that he played hooky from school and roamed the woods near his family home. The creek that ran near Dover Center Road became both Jack's play yard and his laboratory. He studied the creatures that inhabited the area and learned the lessons of bird life that formed a foundation for his life's work. Miner's innovative bird banding recorded Canadian geese migration.

The city claims bragging rights to another celebrity. Robert Overmyer, a 1954 Westlake High School graduate, became commander of the seven-man crew of the space shuttle *Challenger* that was launched from Cape Canaveral in April 1985.

Westlake is an opportunity to glimpse not only the past events in the city of Westlake but also the lives of the people who call Westlake home. Sometimes the pictures tell their own stories, such as the tintype of the Civil War soldier who entered the military with lofty aspirations but never returned home, or the photographs on the lawn outside the schoolhouse of boys in baggy pants with slicked-down hair and girls wearing ruffled dresses and bows with their gap-toothed smiles. These children went on to live, love, laugh, and have families of their own, many never traveling very far from the place where they were born.

One of these children was Doris Weston, who traced her roots to the George Weston family of Dover Village settlers in 1854. George bought 120 acres of farmland on the east side of Hall Road in 1872. He and his wife, Rhoda, had three sons, Asa, Arthur, and Frank. Doris remembered her father, Arthur, the clerk-treasurer of the Dover Village School Board, and her brother, Walter, a promising young scholar and athlete, whose plane was shot down in World War II. Residents who attended Doris's memorial services were lucky to find a seat in the Dover Congregational Church. It was packed with relatives and friends who loved her, teachers who worked with her, and members of the Westlake Historical Society who admired her.

As a local historian, Doris may have told the story about Dover in 1900, the year the township broke in two, and the wealthy summer residents from Cleveland who formed their own Bay Village community, taking the railroad with them. For the next three decades, the 15.9-square-mile area of Dover Village was primarily a community of farmers raising grapes and grain; then the population shifted after World War II and changes soon followed.

The phenomenal growth rate led to the prestigious city of Westlake with an award-winning 75,000-square-foot library and a new first-rate city hall. Westlake has a population of approximately 33,000 people, who enjoy a recreation center, a senior center, beautiful homes, office buildings, and a mixed-use town square with retail, office, and housing space known as Crocker Park. What was once a prime farming settlement is now a thriving community in the new millennium.

The collection of photographs within the pages that follow tells time in skips and gaps. From a family's lovingly arranged scrapbook collection to the historical archives of a Cleveland newspaper that stopped the presses in 1982, individual stories mark the passage of time in brief glances. While reading, reminisce, compare journeys, and imagine the lives of those who came before. The past and present residents of the city of Westlake are more than astronauts, conservationists, farmers, teachers, business owners, or librarians. They are important people with tales to tell.

One

Back in the Day

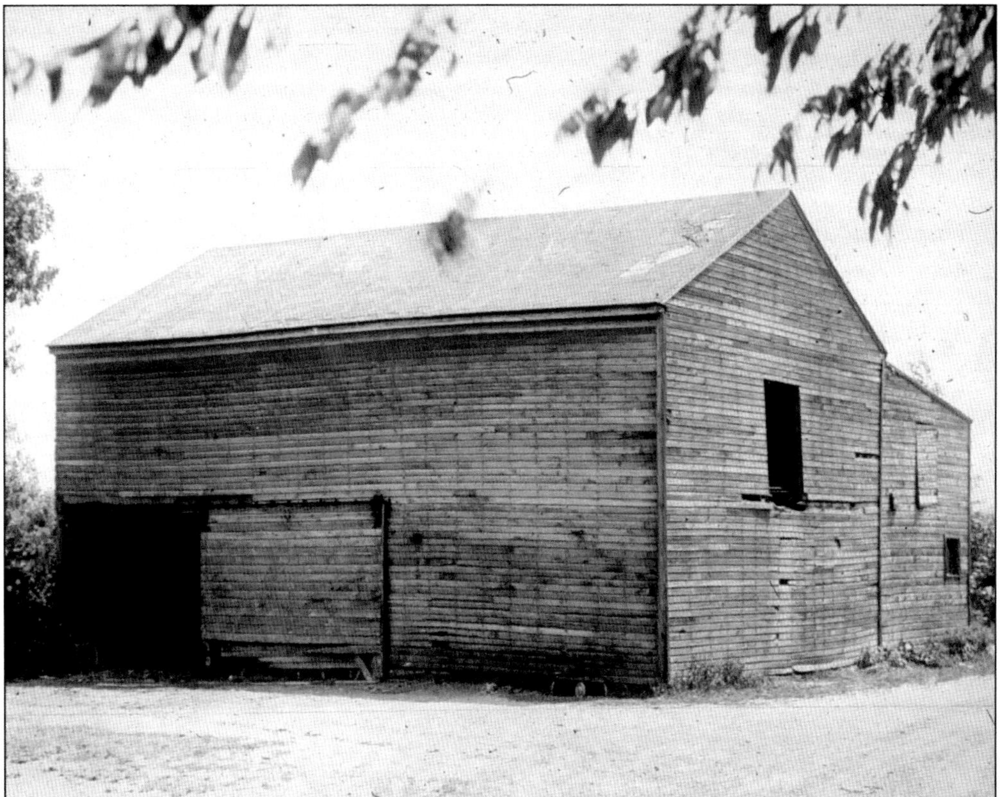

This barn served as the Sperry Inn, built in 1824 on Center Ridge Road, east of Clague Road. The inn had five enormous fireplaces, a first-floor barroom, and an upstairs ballroom. The back part of the Sperry Inn accommodated patrons in sleeping rooms. Three barns near the tavern were used to keep horses and store hay and grain. (Courtesy of William Robishaw Collection, Westlake Porter Public Library.)

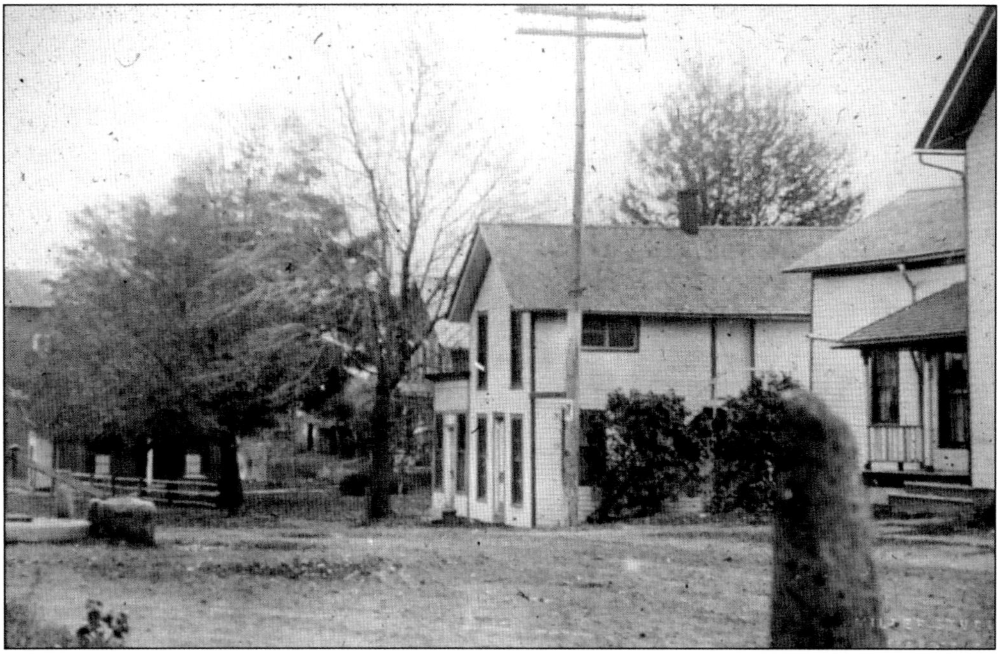

The center of town at the intersection of Dover Center and Center Ridge Roads shows, from left to right, Old Rublin Mill, Dr. George Lathrop's office and house, Powers' Butcher Shop, Pease Funeral Home, Clotz house, and the town pump and a horse trough (foreground). William Ziska owned the corner barbershop. Across the street lived Dr. Christopher Stall, and a few doors up the street stood the blacksmith shop of John Ehele, the Chapple homestead, and the morgue. (Courtesy of William Robishaw Collection, Westlake Porter Public Library.)

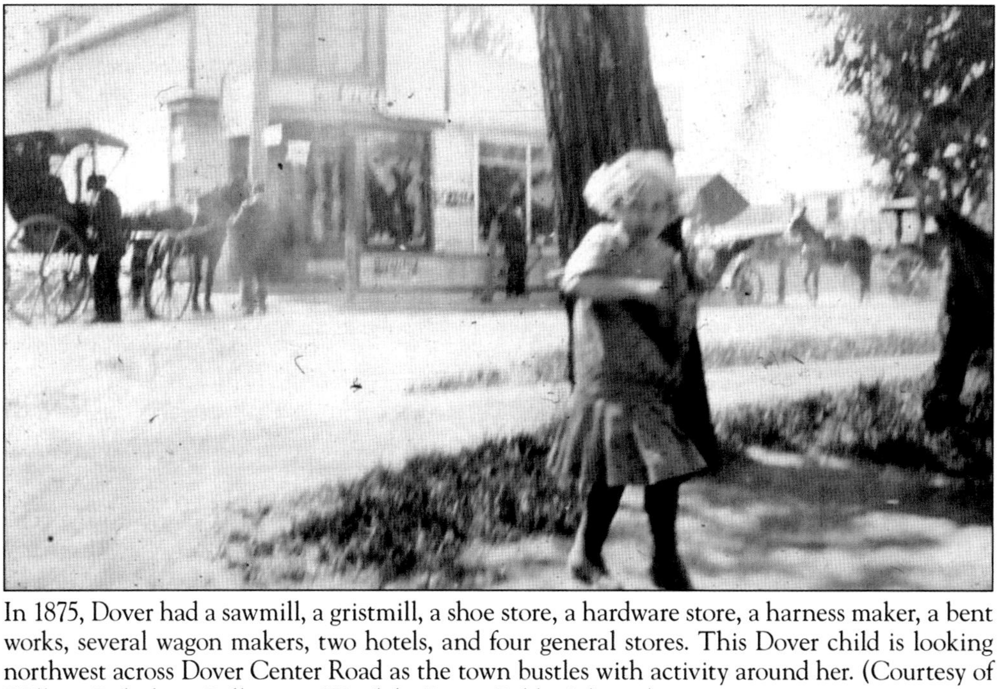

In 1875, Dover had a sawmill, a gristmill, a shoe store, a hardware store, a harness maker, a bent works, several wagon makers, two hotels, and four general stores. This Dover child is looking northwest across Dover Center Road as the town bustles with activity around her. (Courtesy of William Robishaw Collection, Westlake Porter Public Library.)

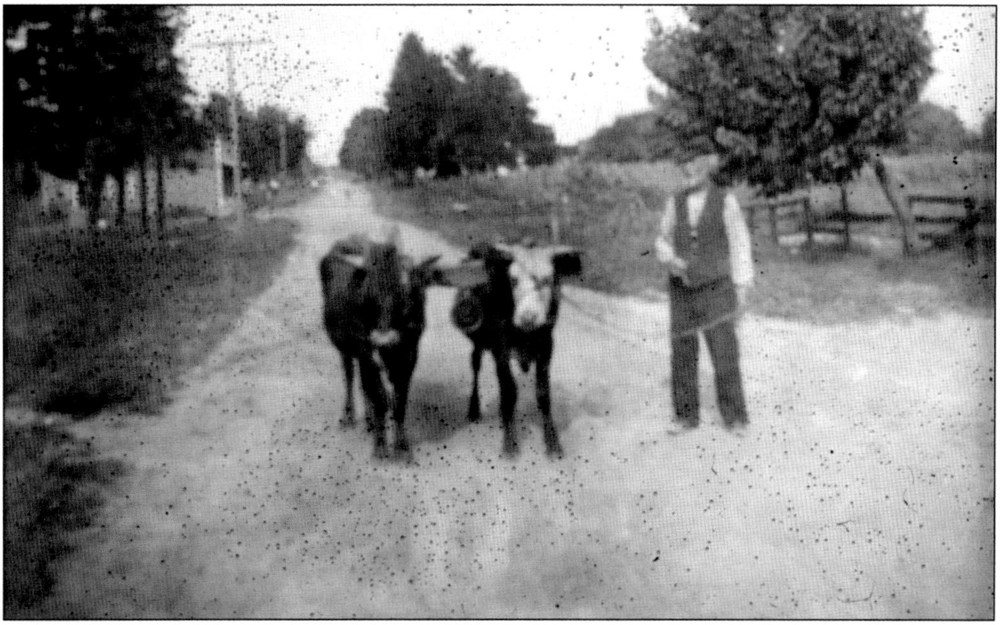

Lorenzo Bement and his team of oxen stand for a picture on Bradley Road. (Courtesy of William Robishaw Collection, Westlake Porter Public Library.)

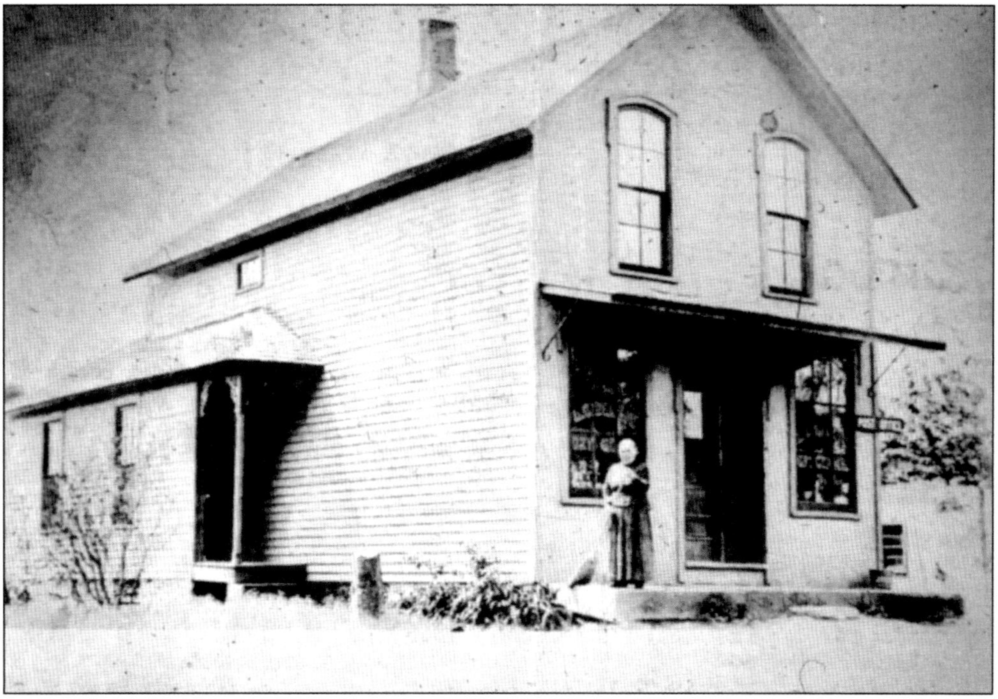

Ann Bement, Lorenzo's wife, poses in front of Bement's country store in 1874. Bement's store housed the West Dover Post Office and was located on the southwestern corner of Bradley and Center Ridge Roads. According to May E. Weston's book, *The First 100 Years of Dover Schools*, the stagecoach left mail once or twice a week at Bement's Corners. (Courtesy of William Robishaw Collection, Westlake Porter Public Library.)

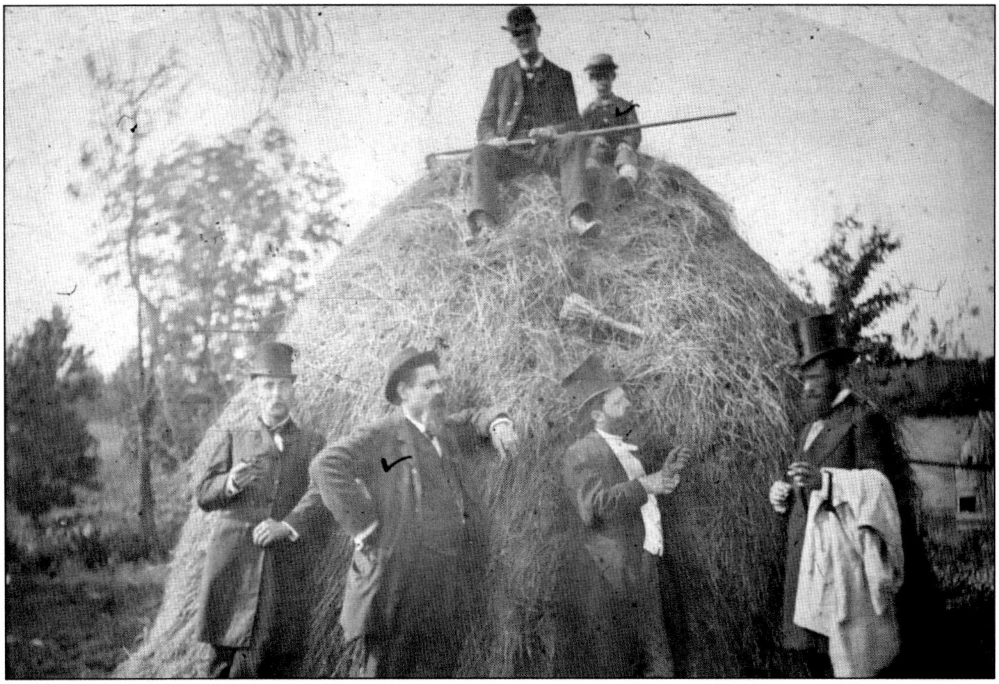

Gentlemen gather around the haystack on Brennan's farm in 1876. This picture appeared in the *Cleveland Press* in 1976. (Courtesy of William Robishaw Collection, Westlake Porter Public Library.)

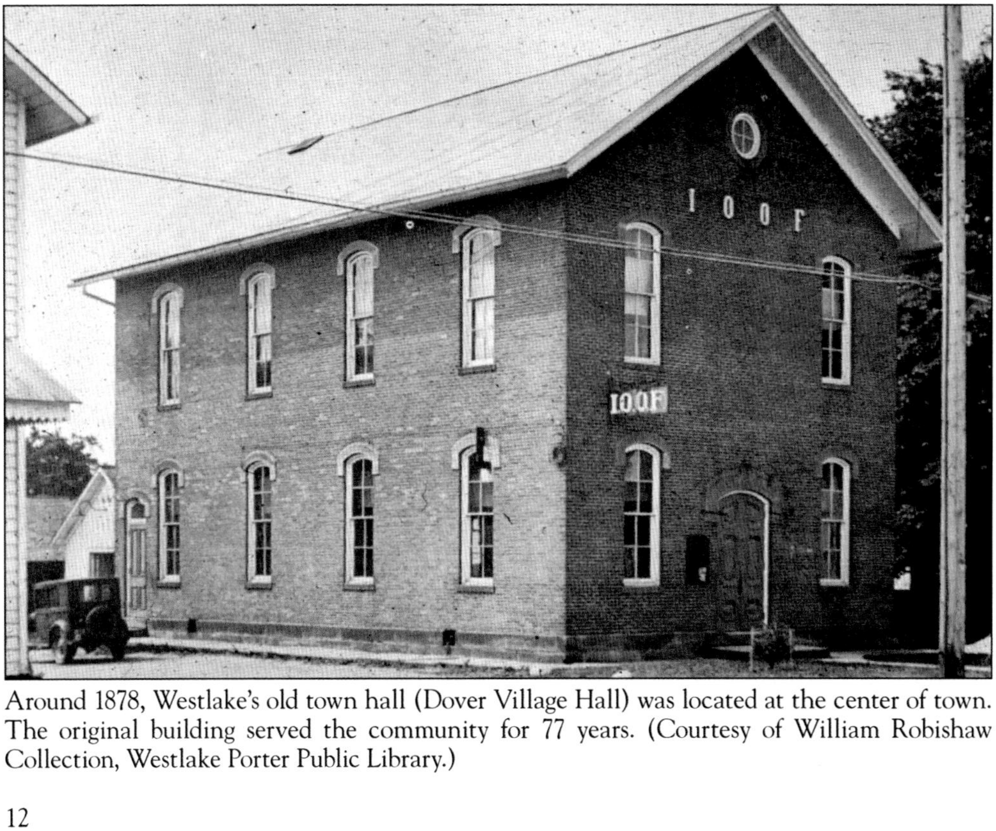

Around 1878, Westlake's old town hall (Dover Village Hall) was located at the center of town. The original building served the community for 77 years. (Courtesy of William Robishaw Collection, Westlake Porter Public Library.)

According to a 1932 article in the *Cleveland Sunday News*, the frame building that housed the Porter library was originally used as a saloon. "Way back in the [18]80's, the gay young blades of Dover thronged the building for a drink of this, that or the other. Many a night the good townsfolk were kept awake by the roisterers. Then a literary society decided to take matters in hand. The saloon was a menace that had to be dealt with drastically." Leonard G. Porter willed his private library to establish a community library and left a fund to keep it going. Porter Library was born in 1882. The brass rail and barrels were replaced with books. The minutes of a Dover Literary Society meeting in 1886 stated that a building was purchased to house the library in December of that year. (Courtesy of Westlake Porter Public Library Collection.)

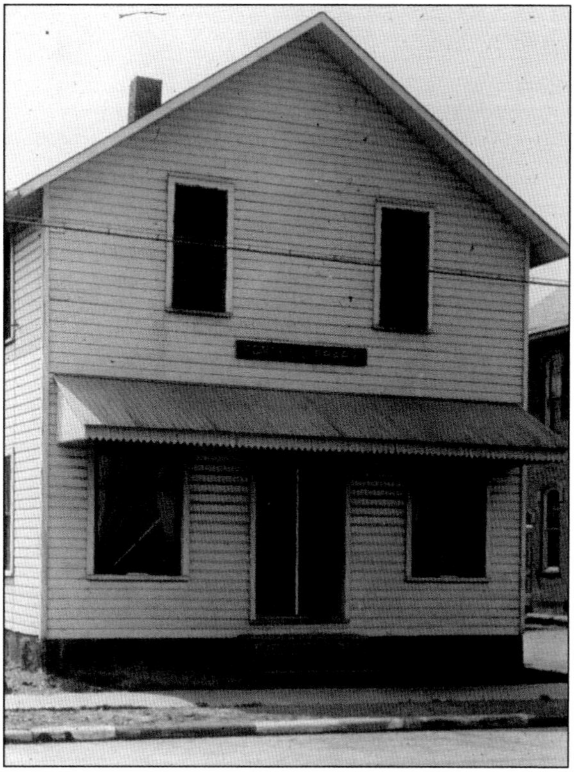

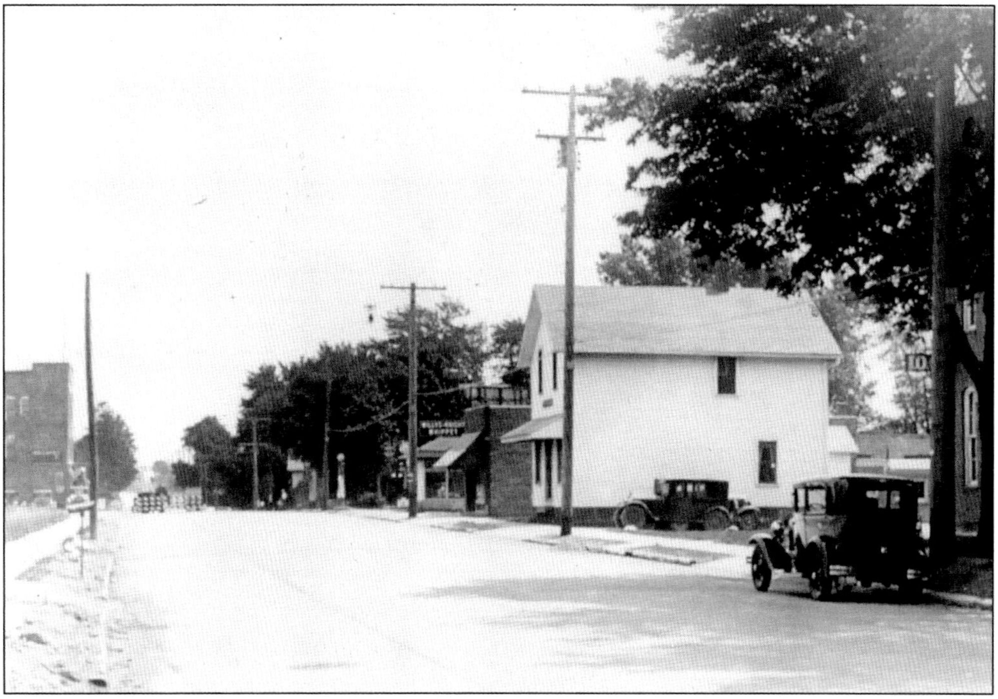

The original Westlake Porter Public Library, known as Porter Library, was located on Center Ridge Road beside the town hall building. (Courtesy of Westlake Porter Public Library Collection.)

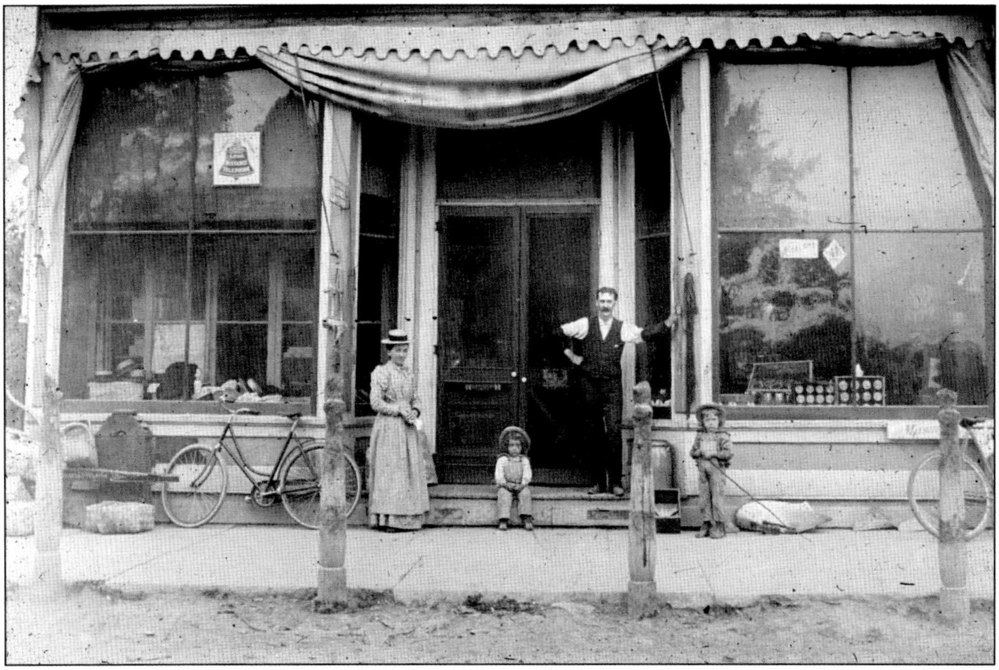

James D. Hurst, Lyda Hurst, and their sons Russell (left) and Lloyd (right) are pictured in front of the family's general store on the northwest corner of Dover Center and Center Ridge Roads in 1895. (Courtesy of William Robishaw Collection, Westlake Porter Public Library.)

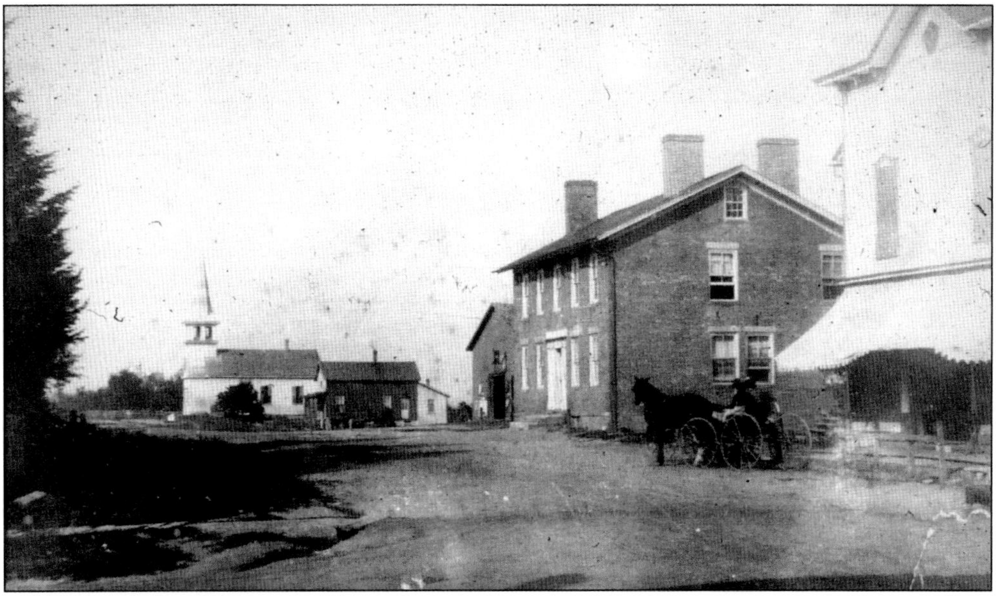

This view looks west along Center Ridge Road from the Dover Center Road intersection around 1899. The five buildings visible from left to right are the former Methodist church, a house (owner unknown), a barn belonging to the Phillips Hotel, the Phillips Hotel, and the general store. (Courtesy of William Robishaw Collection, Westlake Porter Public Library.)

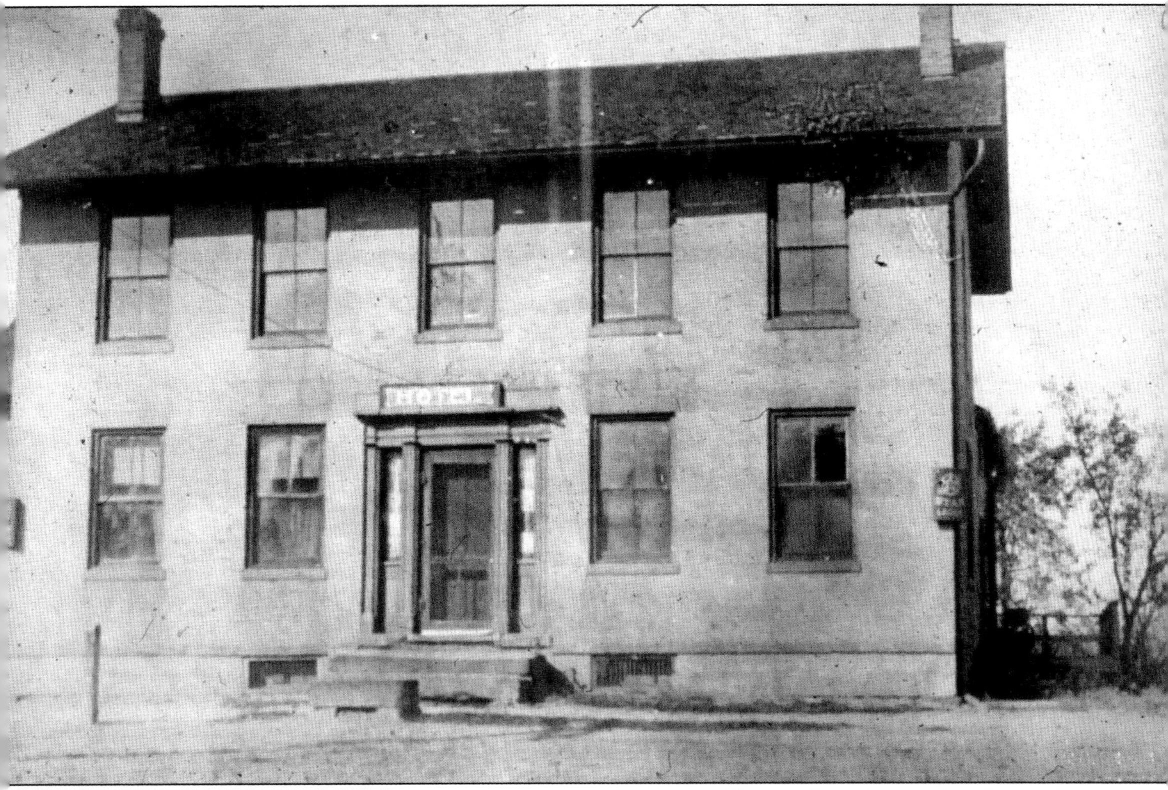

The Phillips Hotel and barn were once a stagecoach stop and horse-changing station located on Center Ridge Road at the Dover Center Road intersection. The hotel had a popular dance floor. The building accommodated three chimneys. In 1906, when the owner tried to start a kitchen fire with suet, the hotel turned to flames. The Dover Township Methodist Church bell clanged long and hard. Everyone able rushed to the scene, and the Dover Bucket Brigade was formed. A supply of spirits was stored in the basement of the hotel, and the volunteer firefighters made every effort to save the stash. Although the fire won the match, the spirits were somehow rescued. As a result, several members of the bucket brigade salvaged their own spirits as soon as the fire was out. (Courtesy of William Robishaw Collection, Westlake Porter Public Library.)

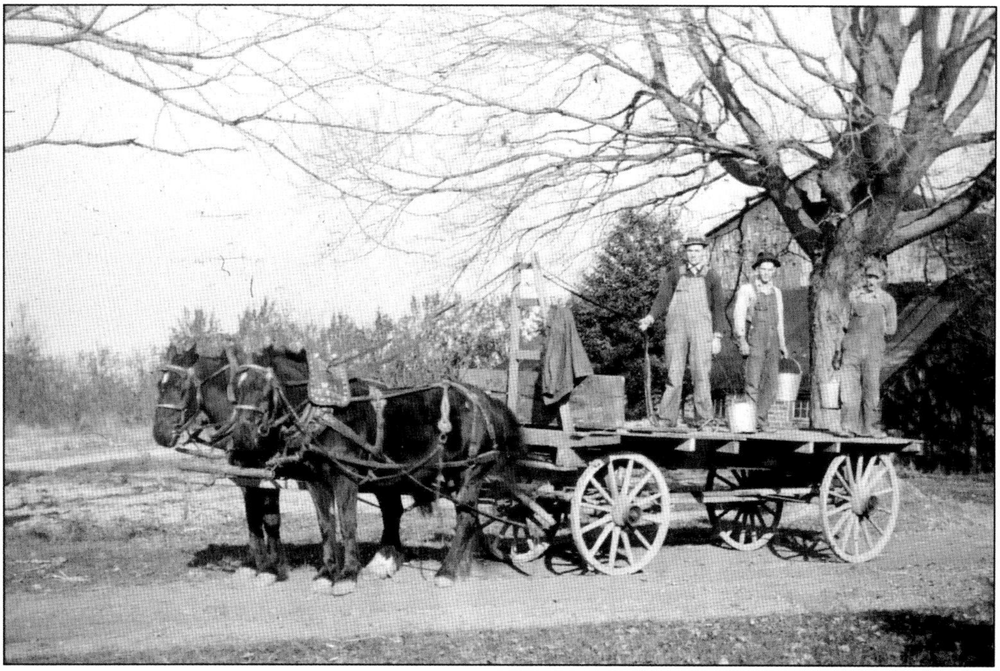

A few of the Dover firefighting volunteers in the bucket brigade wagon pulled by horses are shown here. The brigade was the earliest organized group for putting out fires. (Courtesy of William Robishaw Collection, Westlake Porter Public Library.)

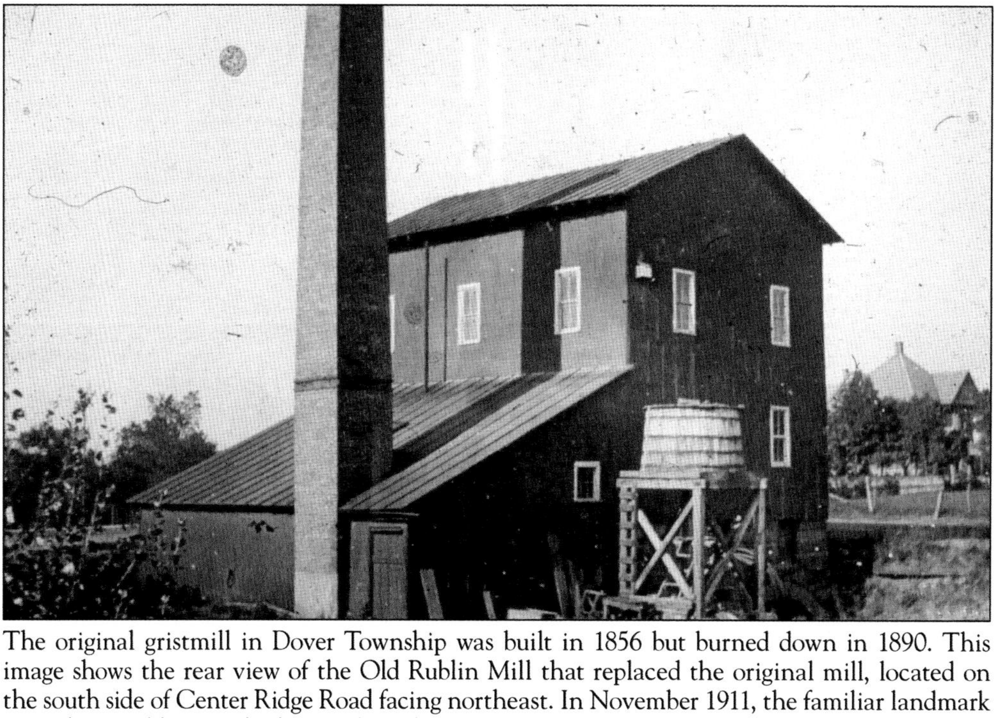

The original gristmill in Dover Township was built in 1856 but burned down in 1890. This image shows the rear view of the Old Rublin Mill that replaced the original mill, located on the south side of Center Ridge Road facing northeast. In November 1911, the familiar landmark turned to smoldering ash, despite the valiant efforts of the bucket brigade. (Courtesy of William Robishaw Collection, Westlake Porter Public Library.)

Two

Hard Work and Determination

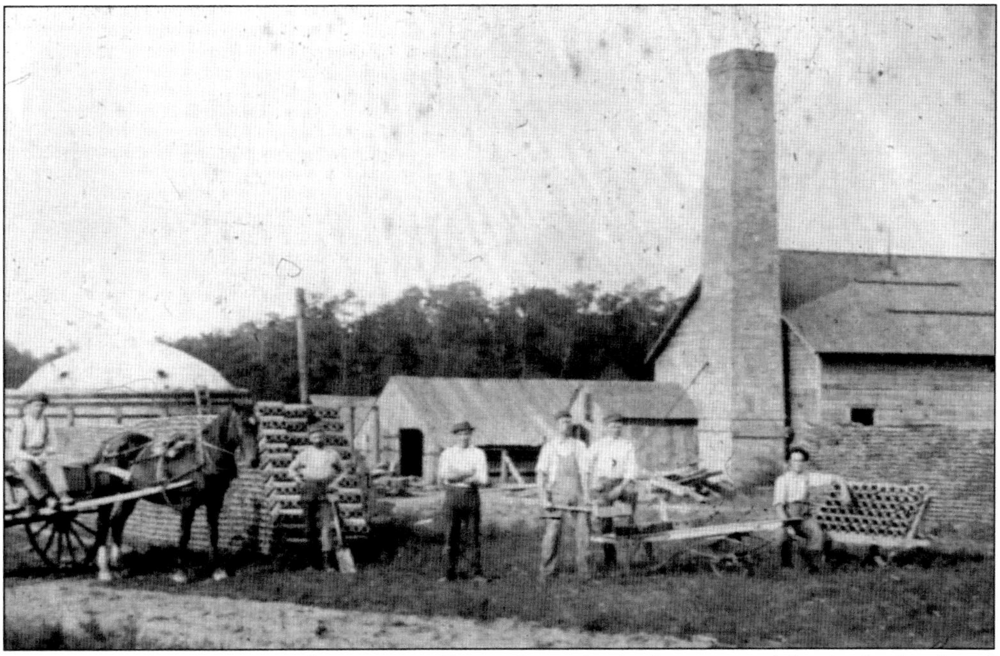

Clay was an abundant natural resource in Dover. Isaac Asplin Jr., owner of the Asplin brickyard on Detroit Road, operated a brick and tile kiln and supplied the bricks to many buildings in the area, including the town's one-room schoolhouse. Pictured from left to right about 1900 are two unidentified men, Fred Asplin, John Bailey, Louis Hamsler, and Charles Lewis. (Courtesy of William Robishaw Collection, Westlake Porter Public Library.)

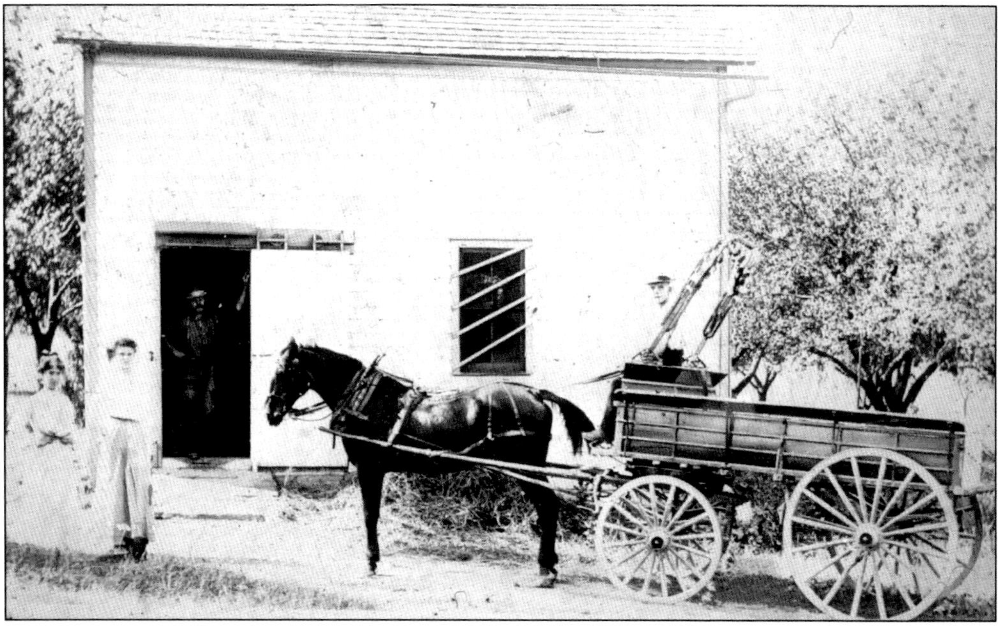

Dover was primarily an agricultural community. At the dawn of the 20th century, horse-drawn wagons were used to transport produce to markets in downtown Cleveland. Farmers hitched the horses to the wagons early in the morning and set out for the 15-mile journey. This picture was taken on Center Ridge Road near Columbia Road in 1890. (Courtesy of William Robishaw Collection, Westlake Porter Public Library.)

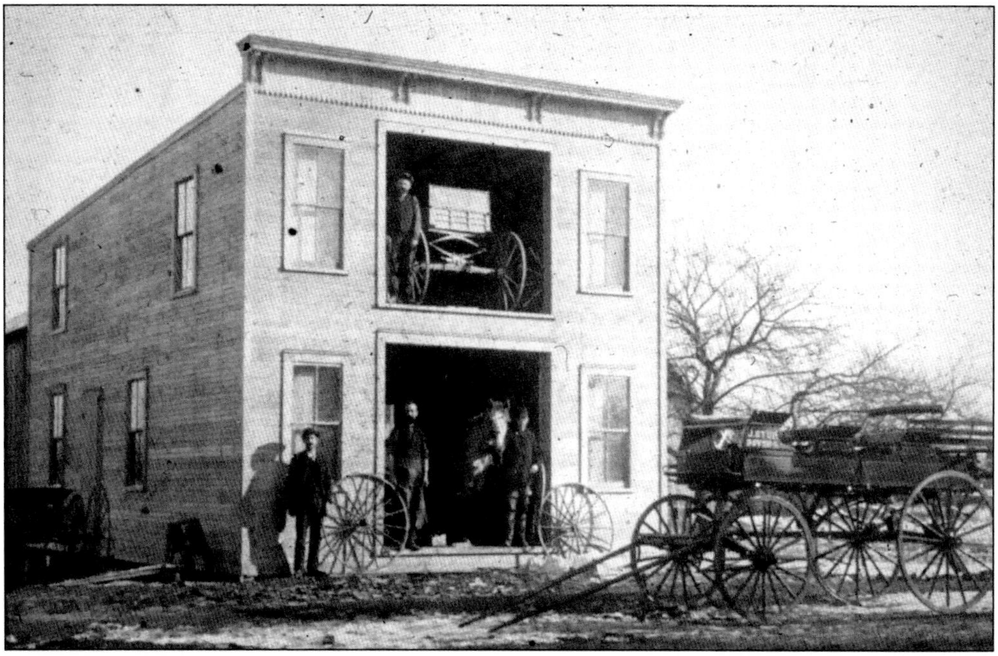

Located on Dover Center Road just a few hundred feet from the center of town, the wagon works store employed those who possessed great skill in the trades of blacksmithing and carriage building. By 1884, carriages became so fancy that they had lanterns inside and out. (Courtesy of William Robishaw Collection, Westlake Porter Public Library.)

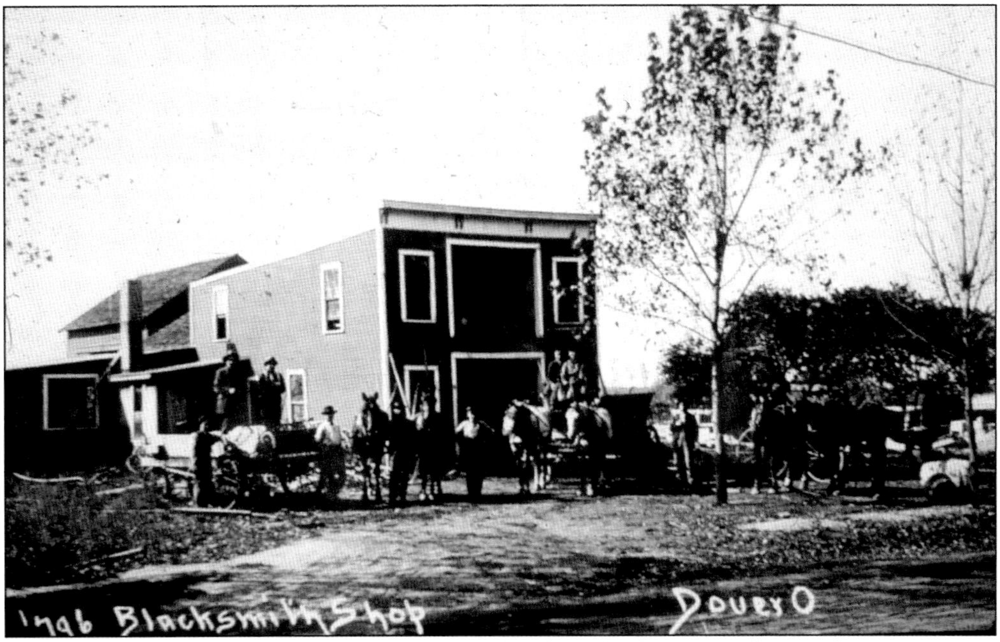

In 1914, Amos "Hank" Mitchell opened this blacksmith shop near the northeast corner of Clague and Center Ridge Roads. He continued to operate the shop for over 42 years. (Courtesy of William Robishaw Collection, Westlake Porter Public Library.)

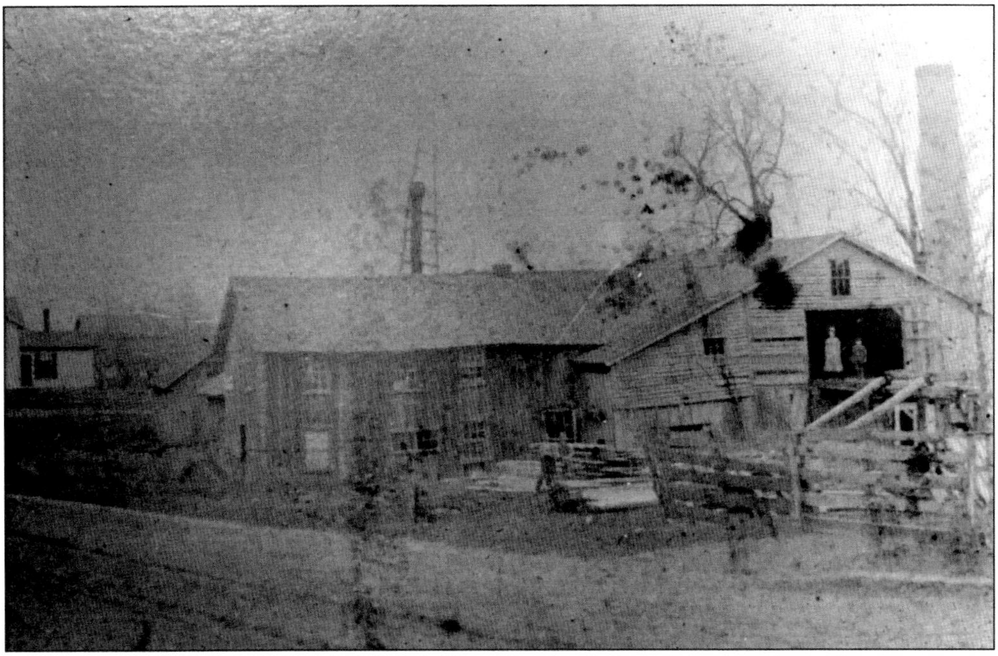

Fauver and Hurst Brothers constructed a bending factory and a sawmill, employing six men to manufacture felloes, sleigh runners, and shafts. The bending works was located near the intersection of Bailus and Center Ridge Roads. (Courtesy of William Robishaw Collection, Westlake Porter Public Library.)

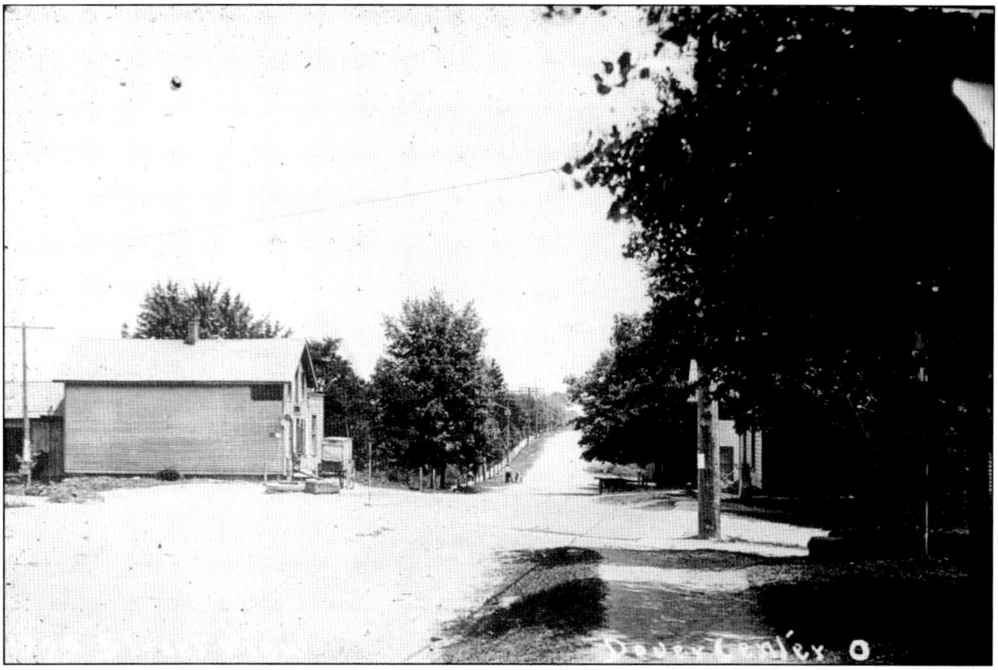

This view of the Francis Egger store, located on the northeastern corner of Dover Center and Center Ridge Roads, dates from 1905. (Courtesy of William Robishaw Collection, Westlake Porter Public Library.)

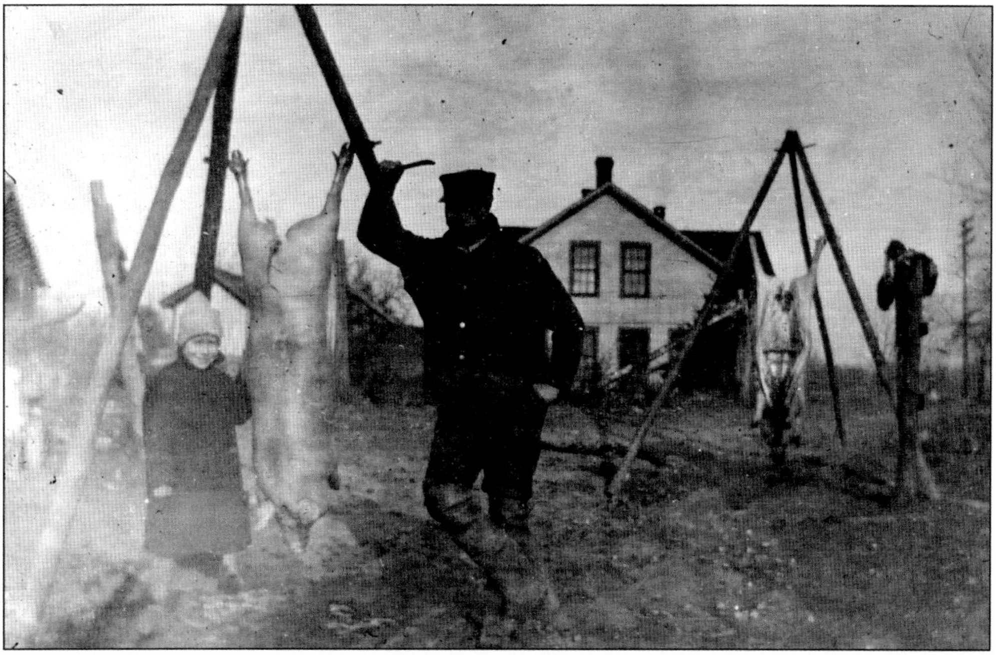

Hog butchering on the Parfitt farm was done in the cold weather. After the hog was killed and bled, it was hung as pictured so the insides could be cut out. Hams, shoulders, and sides of bacon were prepared. These pieces were salted. The meat was cured for days in the smoke of a hickory wood fire. (Courtesy of William Robishaw Collection, Westlake Porter Public Library.)

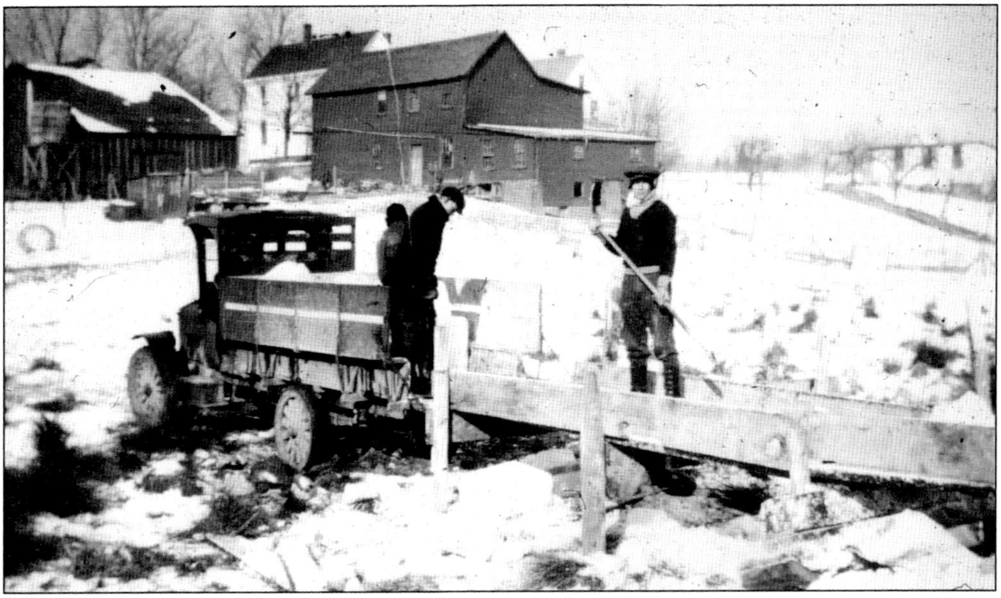

Around 1910, the Tanners cut ice on their pond and sold it to Boone's Meat Market and General Store to preserve meats the following summer. Boone's was located west of Dover Center Road. (Courtesy of William Robishaw Collection, Westlake Porter Public Library.)

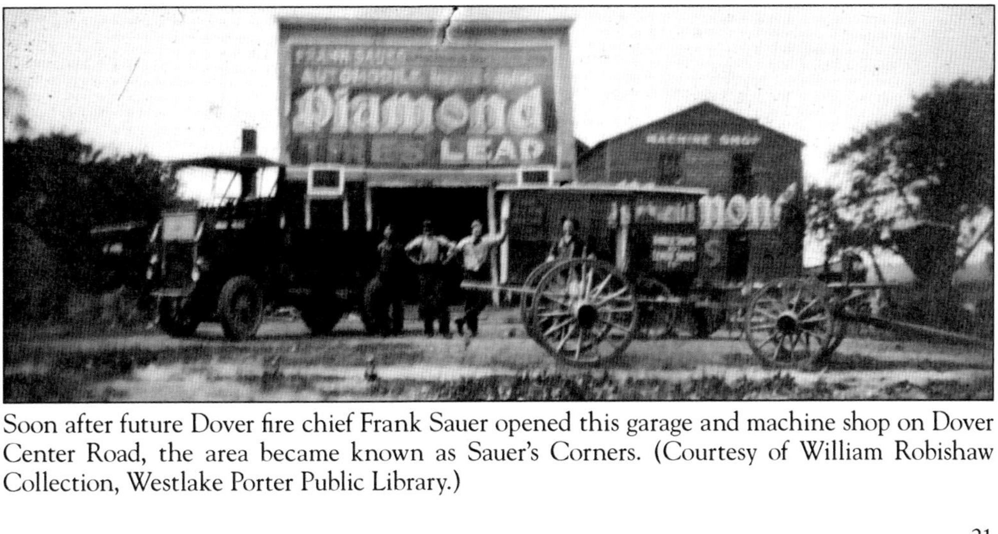

Soon after future Dover fire chief Frank Sauer opened this garage and machine shop on Dover Center Road, the area became known as Sauer's Corners. (Courtesy of William Robishaw Collection, Westlake Porter Public Library.)

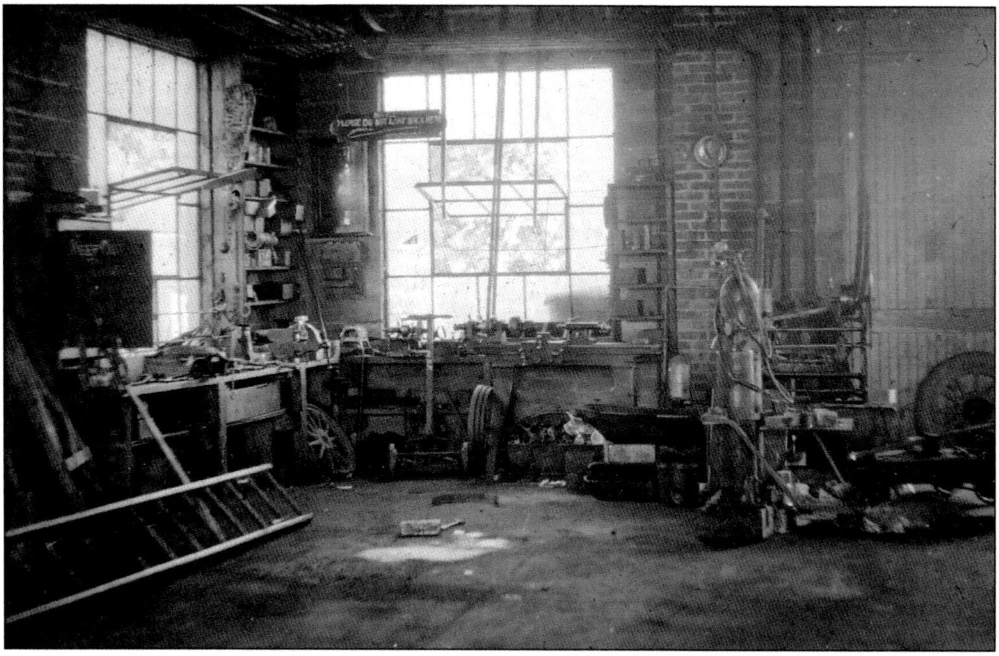

The inside view of Frank Sauer's garage and machine shop located at Sauer's Corners on Dover Center Road around 1928 shows an assortment of tools and equipment. Sauer built the first fire engine in Dover Township from a Cadillac chassis. (Courtesy of William Robishaw Collection, Westlake Porter Public Library.)

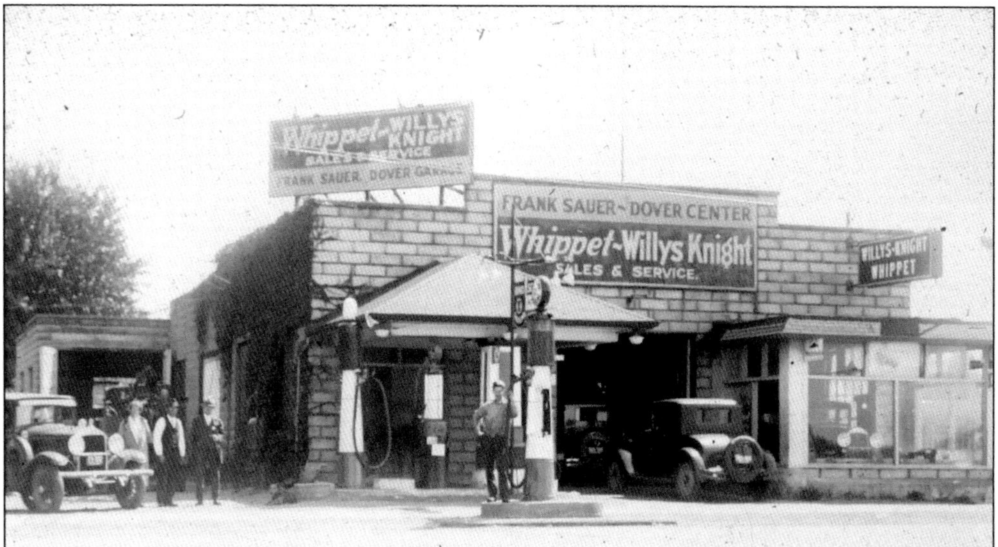

Sauer's Whippet-Willys Knight Sales and Service was located on Dover Center Road. From 1912 to 1918, John North Willys became the second-largest automobile producer in the United States. The Whippet had four-wheel brakes, water pump cooling, and pressurized lubrication. The styling was European, with a compact yet roomy body and low center of gravity. (Courtesy of William Robishaw Collection, Westlake Porter Public Library.)

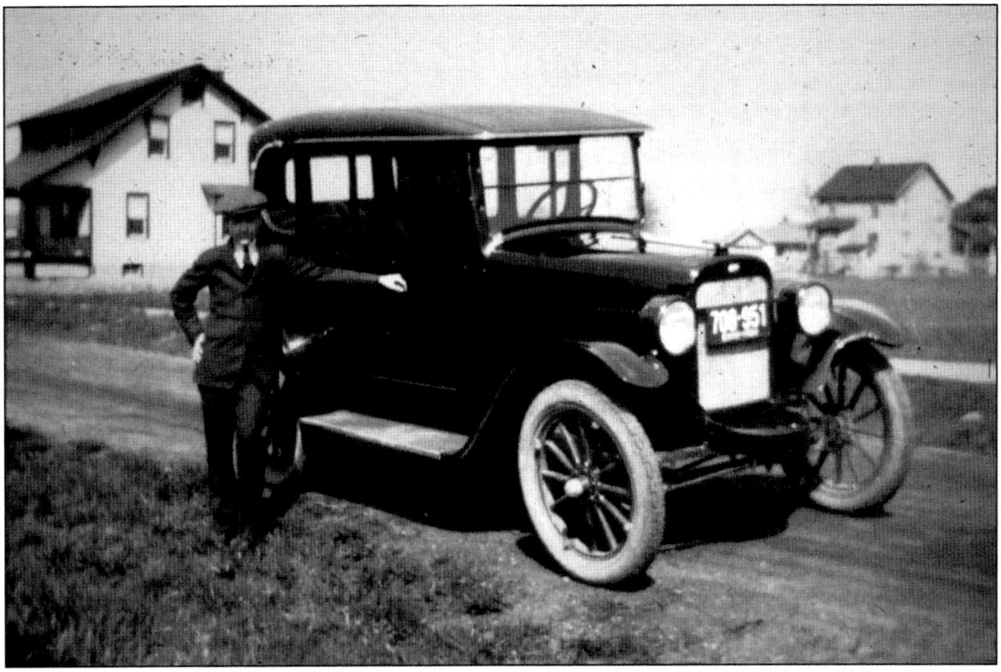

The Willys-Overland Motor Company made both cars and trucks. This Willys-Overland automobile is shown in Dover around 1926. (Courtesy of William Robishaw Collection, Westlake Porter Public Library.)

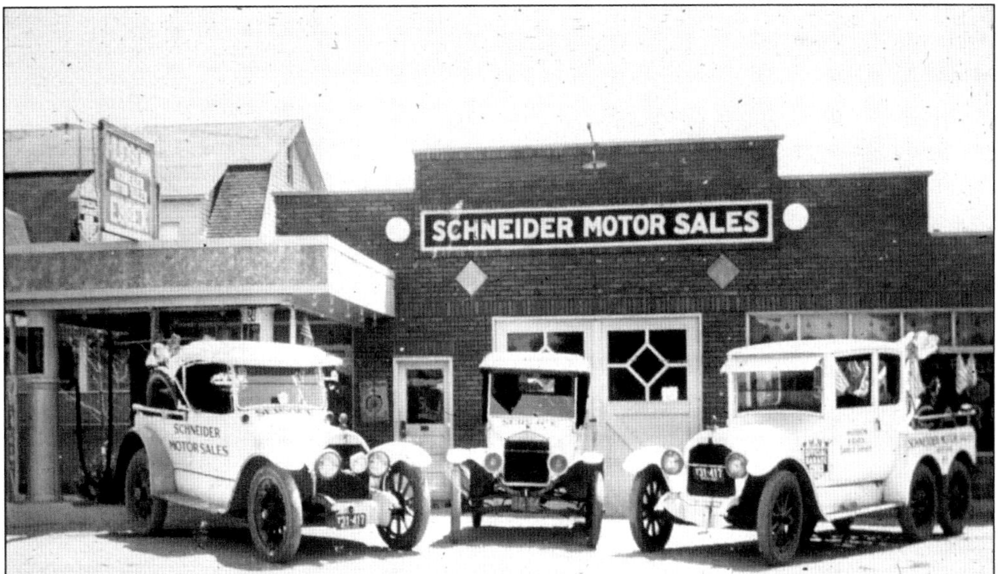

John A. Schneider built a tow truck and opened a garage in Dover to rescue stranded passengers on Center Ridge Road. His businesses grew to later include a motel, a car dealership, restaurants, a nightclub, a barbecue, a tourist camp, cottages, and campgrounds in the area. Schneider Motor Sales, pictured here in 1920, sold Hudson-Essex vehicles and later Chevrolets. (Courtesy of William Robishaw Collection, Westlake Porter Public Library.)

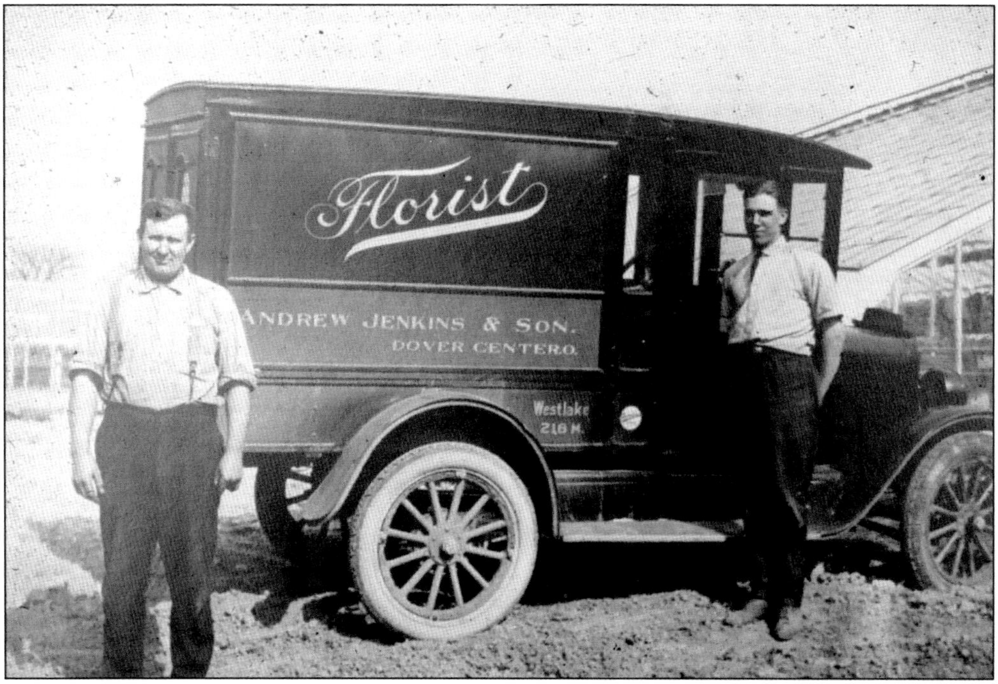

Andrew Jenkins and his son Melvin owned a prosperous florist business located on the corner of Dover Center Road and Westown Boulevard around 1924. (Courtesy of William Robishaw Collection, Westlake Porter Public Library.)

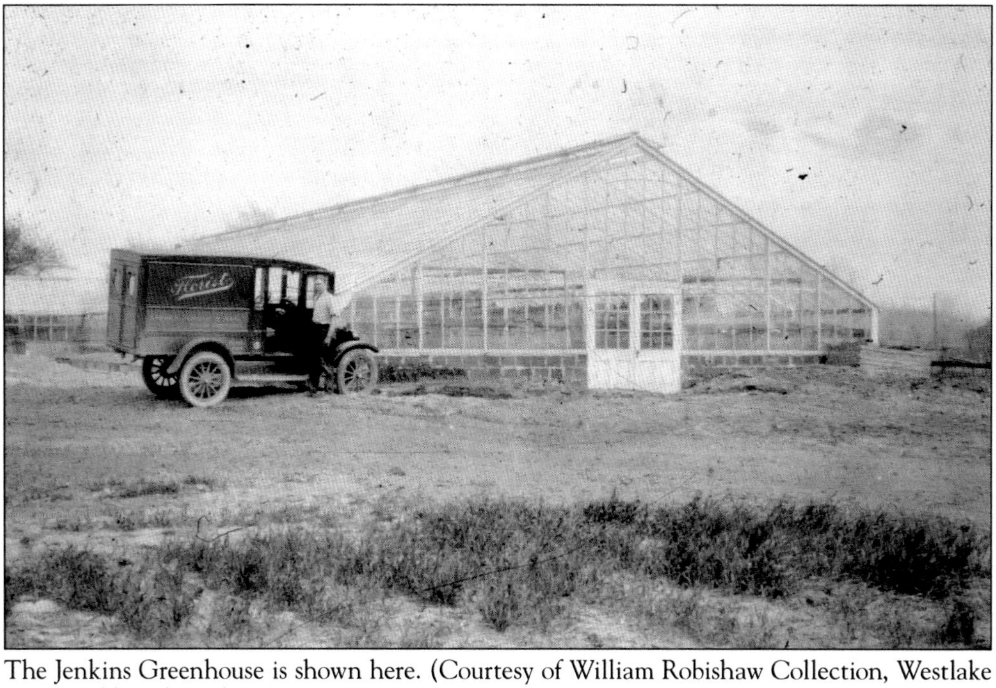

The Jenkins Greenhouse is shown here. (Courtesy of William Robishaw Collection, Westlake Porter Public Library.)

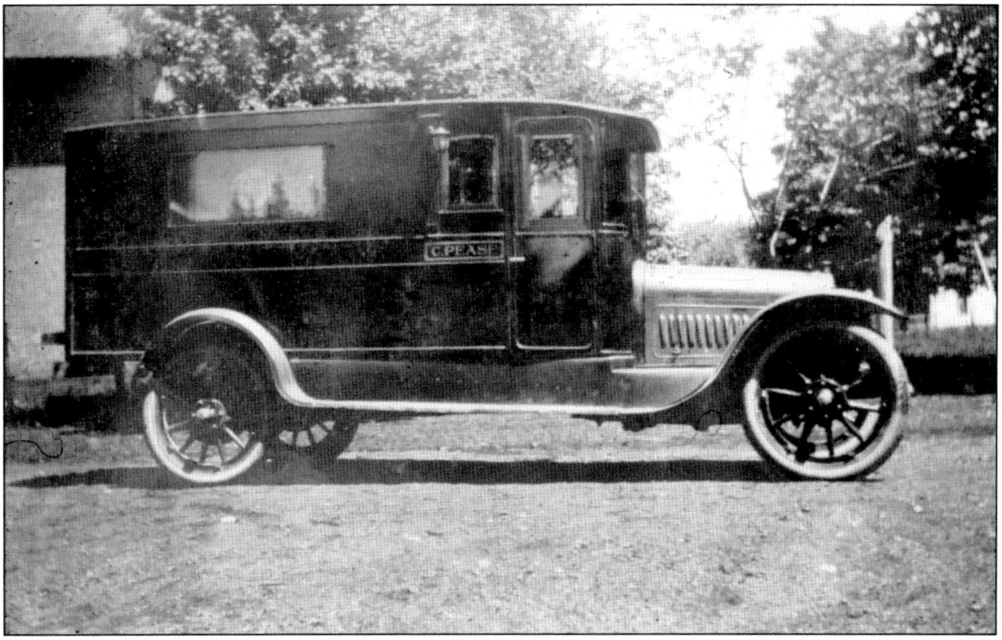

Clifford Pease owned the funeral home on Dover Center Road. His Dodge hearse is pictured around 1920. The funeral home had been the Dover Center School building. In 1924, Pease lowered the roof and renovated the building. (Courtesy of William Robishaw Collection, Westlake Porter Public Library.)

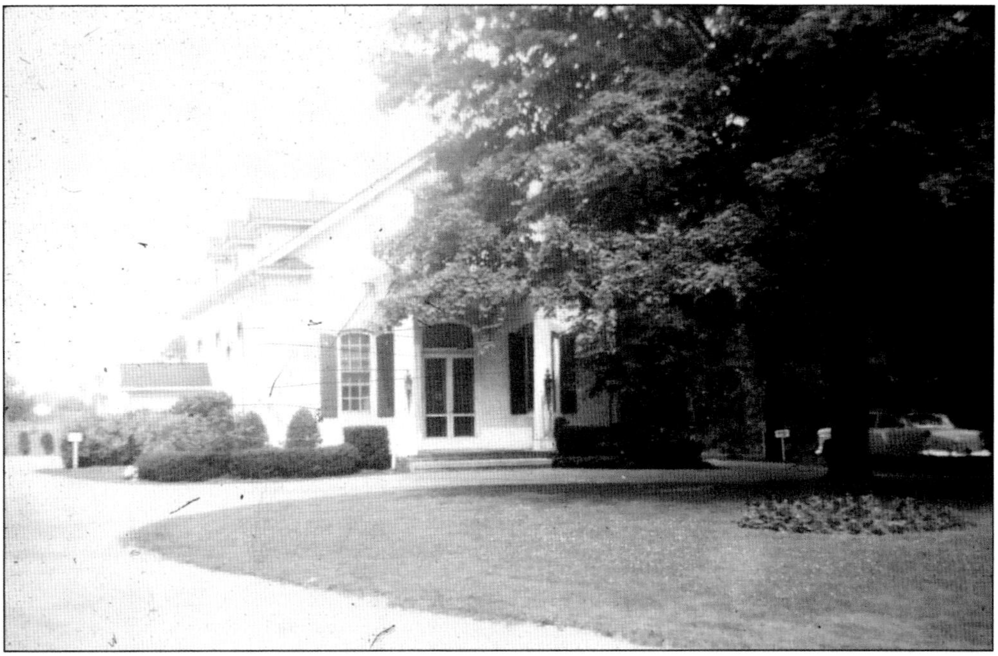

Pease sold the funeral chapel in 1955 to the Jenkins family. (Courtesy of William Robishaw Collection, Westlake Porter Public Library.)

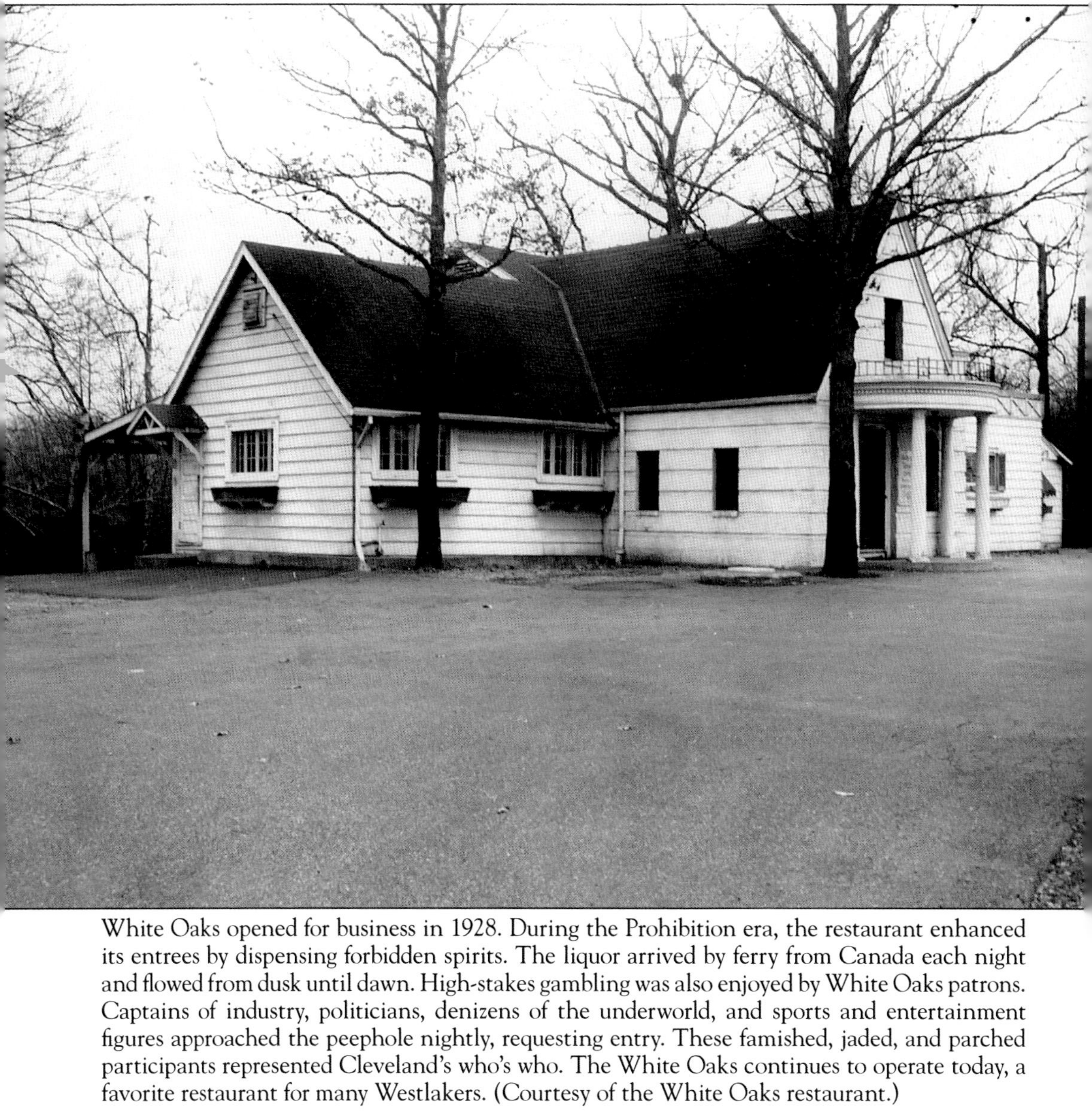

White Oaks opened for business in 1928. During the Prohibition era, the restaurant enhanced its entrees by dispensing forbidden spirits. The liquor arrived by ferry from Canada each night and flowed from dusk until dawn. High-stakes gambling was also enjoyed by White Oaks patrons. Captains of industry, politicians, denizens of the underworld, and sports and entertainment figures approached the peephole nightly, requesting entry. These famished, jaded, and parched participants represented Cleveland's who's who. The White Oaks continues to operate today, a favorite restaurant for many Westlakers. (Courtesy of the White Oaks restaurant.)

Roadside fruit stands were a familiar sight in Westlake Village in the 1950s. The Herbkersman stand sold fruits, vegetables, homemade canned goods, and fresh flowers. Russell Herbkersman owned a 2.5-acre peach orchard at 3987 Porter Road. The fruit trees bloomed in May, and the peaches were ready to harvest in early August. (Courtesy of William Robishaw Collection, Westlake Porter Public Library.)

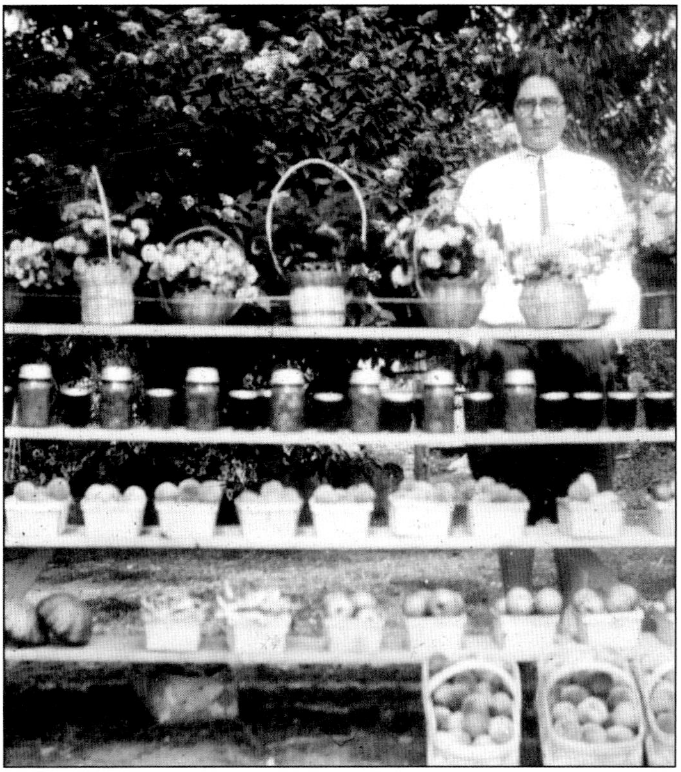

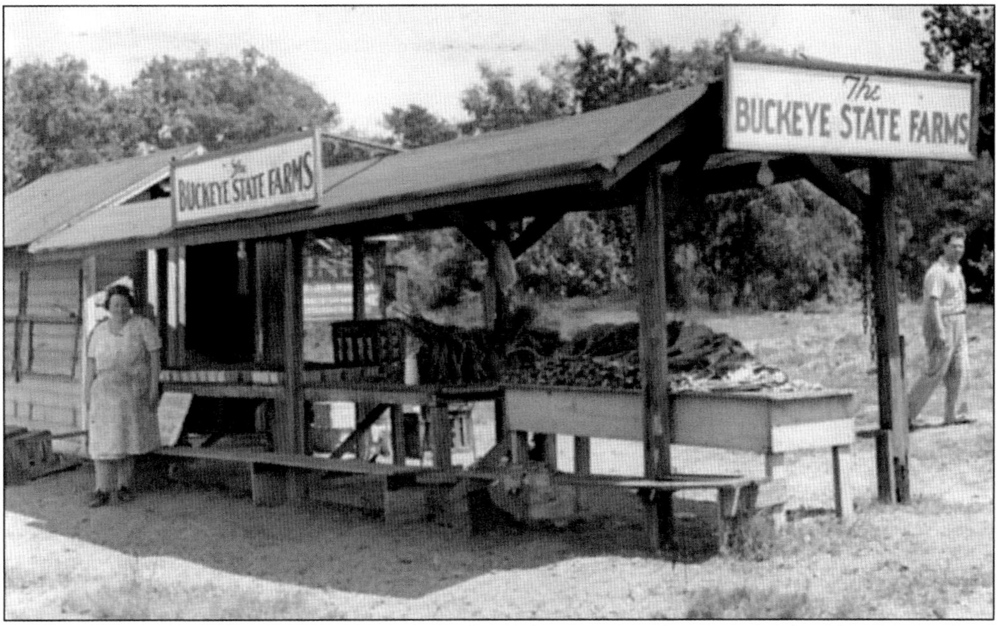

The Buckeye State Farms stand was located on the corner of Detroit and Cahoon Roads in 1942. Farms dotted the landscape in Westlake Village, and grapes were the primary crop. Traffic congestion along Detroit Road sometimes became problematic due to the many fruit and vegetable stands in the area. (Courtesy of Cleveland State University, Cleveland Memory Project, Cleveland Press Collection, Joseph E. Cole, donor.)

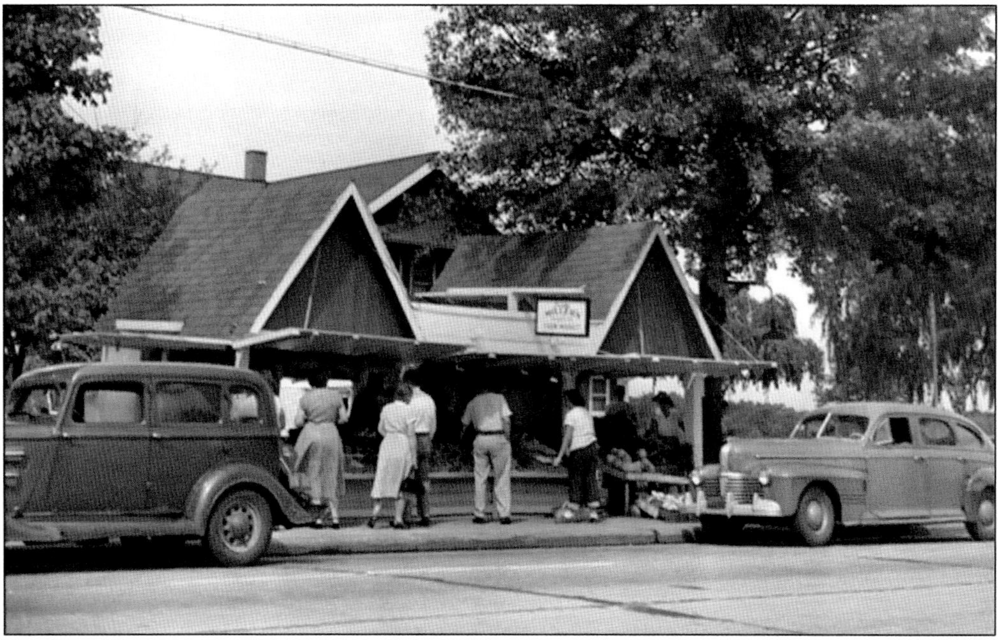

Dusty Miller's farm market was located at 24976 Center Ridge Road in 1962. (Courtesy of Cleveland State University, Cleveland Memory Project, Cleveland Press Collection, Joseph E. Cole, donor.)

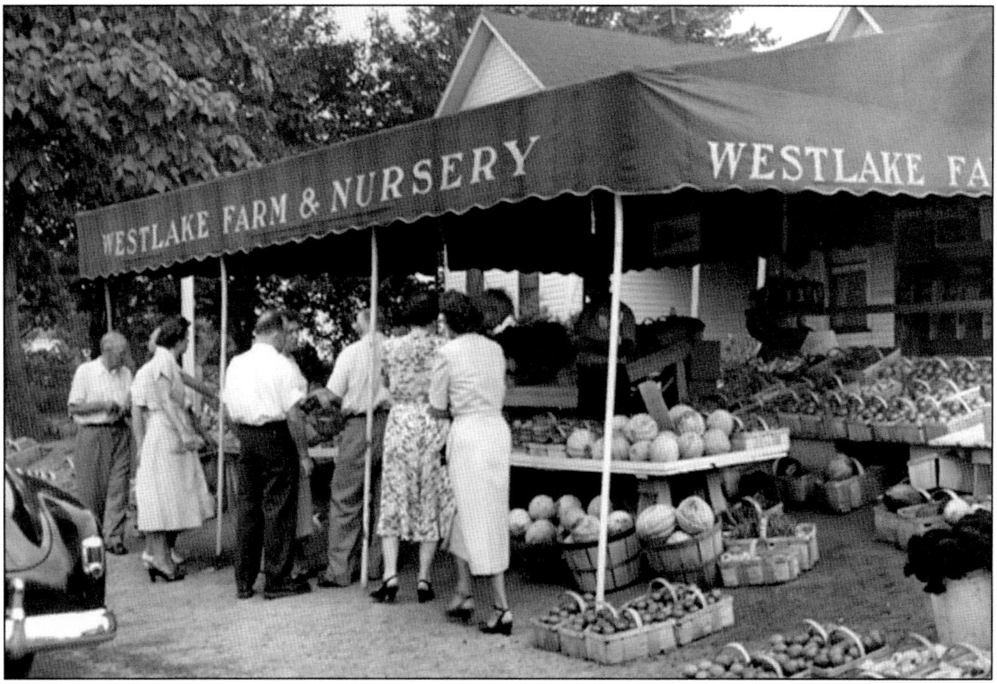

Westlake Farm and Nursery was owned by Harry Kassouf and was located at 25700 Detroit Road. (Courtesy of Cleveland State University, Cleveland Memory Project, Cleveland Press Collection, Joseph E. Cole, donor.)

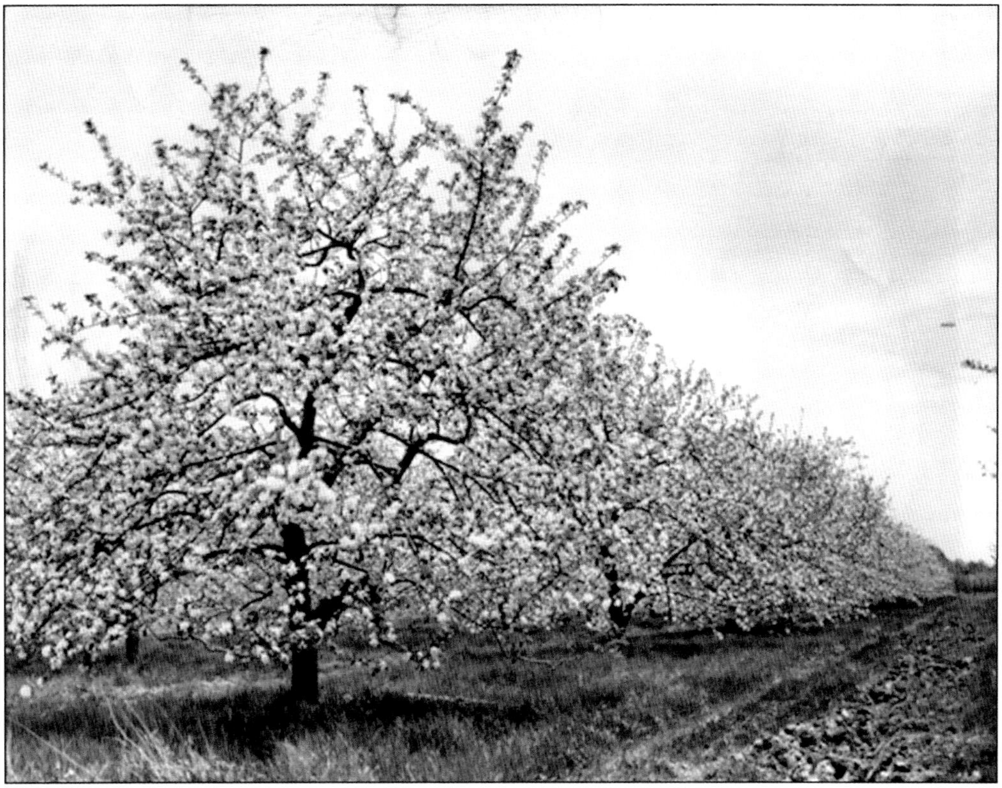

Lehman's Orchard was located at 24961 Detroit Road in Westlake and is shown at apple blossom time on May 16, 1958. (Courtesy of Cleveland State University, Cleveland Memory Project, Cleveland Press Collection, Joseph E. Cole, donor.)

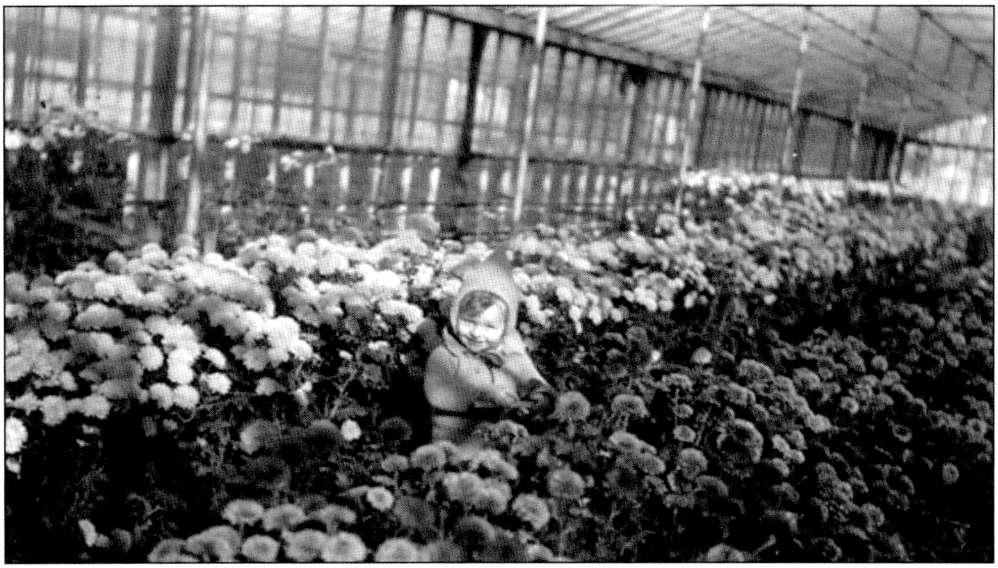

Dana Perkins co-owned a greenhouse in Westlake. Dana's son Gerald is pictured with chrysanthemums in the greenhouse. (Courtesy of Robert Perkins and Judy Dobbs.)

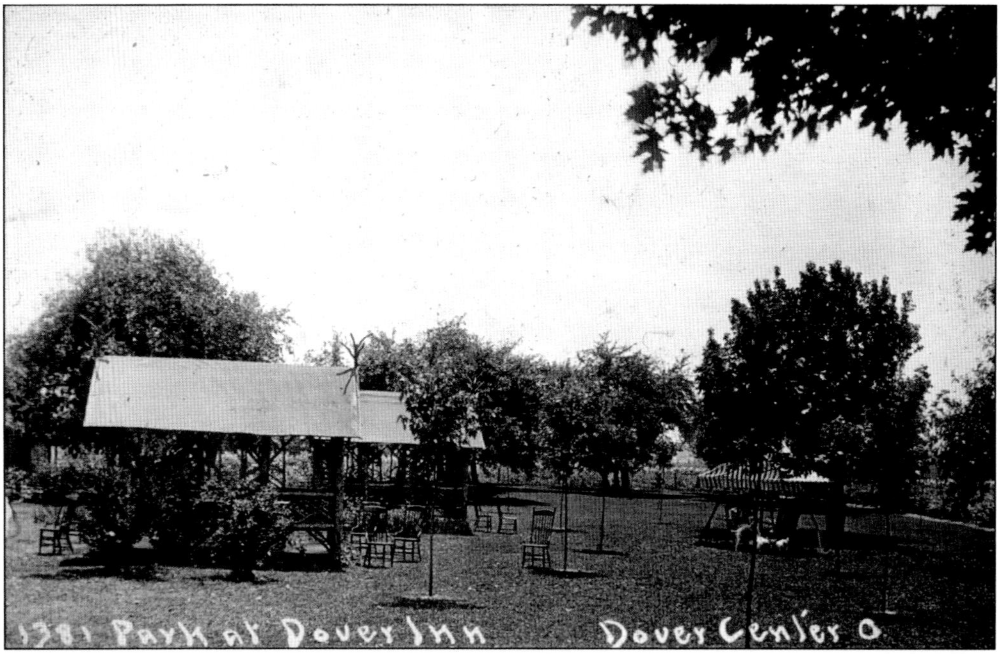

The Dover Inn and Park was located on Center Ridge Road, west of Dover Center Road. The cottages provided accommodations to weary travelers. The park operated without incident until 1937, when a young couple staying in one of the cabins met with a tragic end. The couple died due to asphyxiation from the fumes from the gas heater in their cottage. (Courtesy of William Robishaw Collection, Westlake Porter Public Library.)

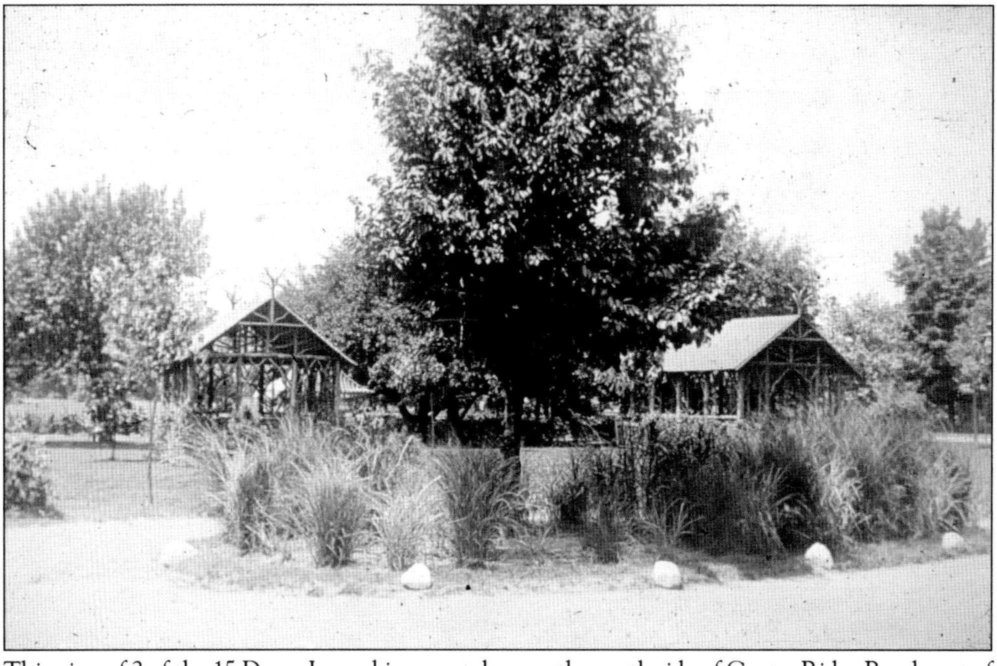

This view of 2 of the 15 Dover Inn cabins was taken on the south side of Center Ridge Road west of Dover Center Road. (Courtesy of William Robishaw Collection, Westlake Porter Public Library.)

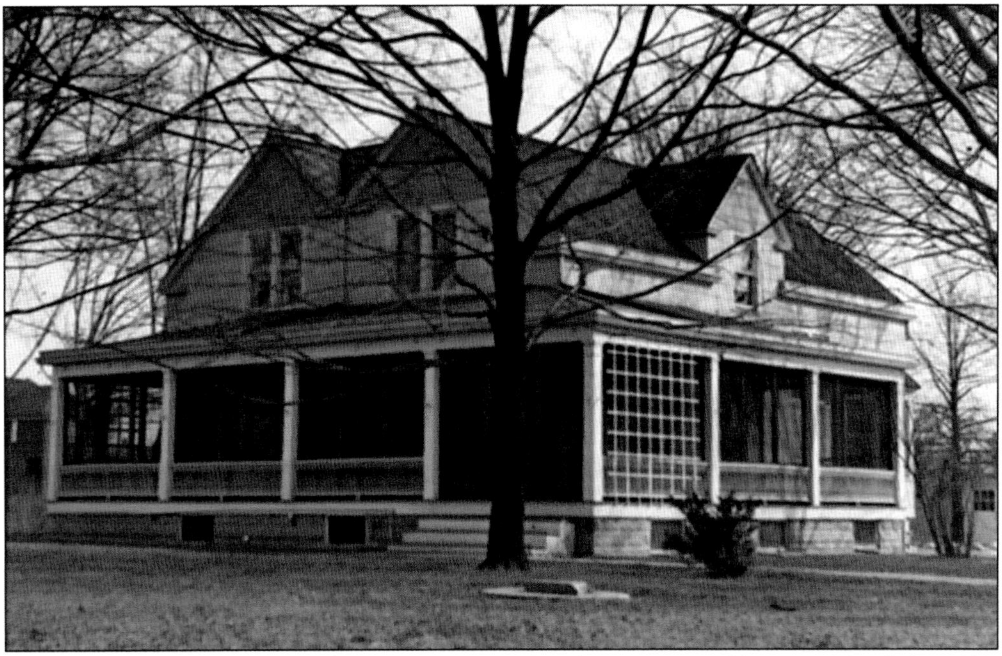

The Elzona Tavern was located at 23575 Detroit Road. It is pictured here on March 29, 1939, when a man tried to shoot his ex-girlfriend during an argument. A Dover police officer shot the gunman, not wounding him seriously. (Courtesy of Cleveland State University, Cleveland Memory Project, Cleveland Press Collection, Joseph E. Cole, donor.)

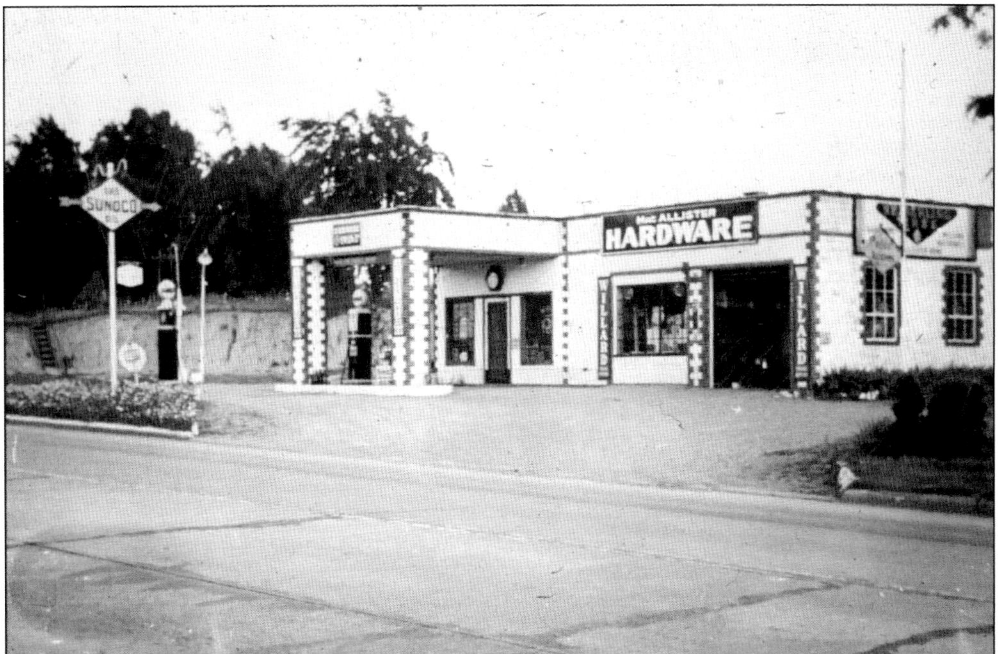

McAllister's Gas Station and Hardware later became Michael's Town and Country Store at 23355 Center Ridge Road. (Courtesy of William Robishaw Collection, Westlake Porter Public Library.)

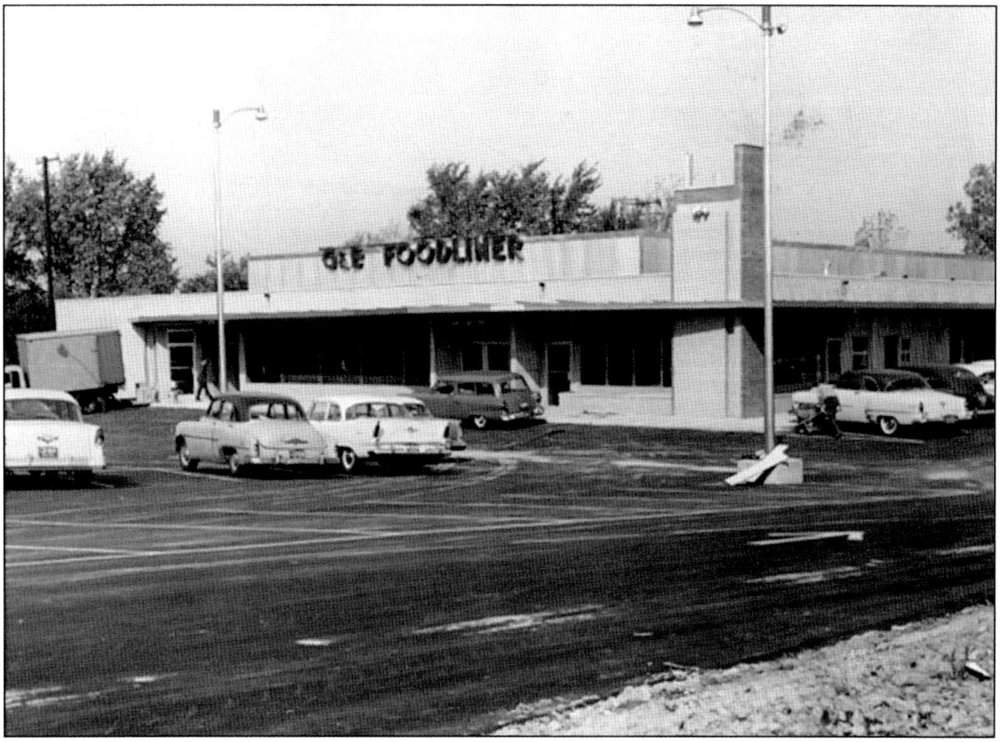

This picture of G and E Foodliner grocery store, located at 24350 Center Ridge Road in Westlake, was taken on October 12, 1956. (Courtesy of Cleveland State University, Cleveland Memory Project, Cleveland Press Collection, Joseph E. Cole, donor.)

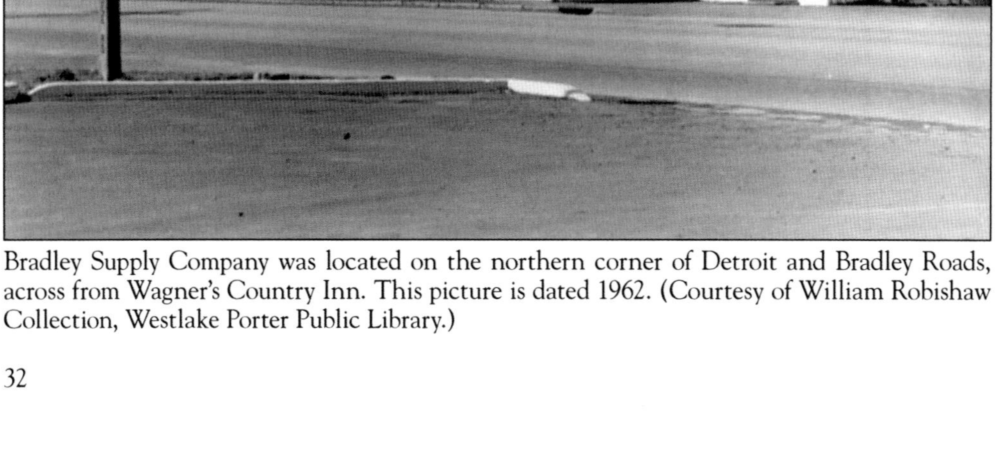

Bradley Supply Company was located on the northern corner of Detroit and Bradley Roads, across from Wagner's Country Inn. This picture is dated 1962. (Courtesy of William Robishaw Collection, Westlake Porter Public Library.)

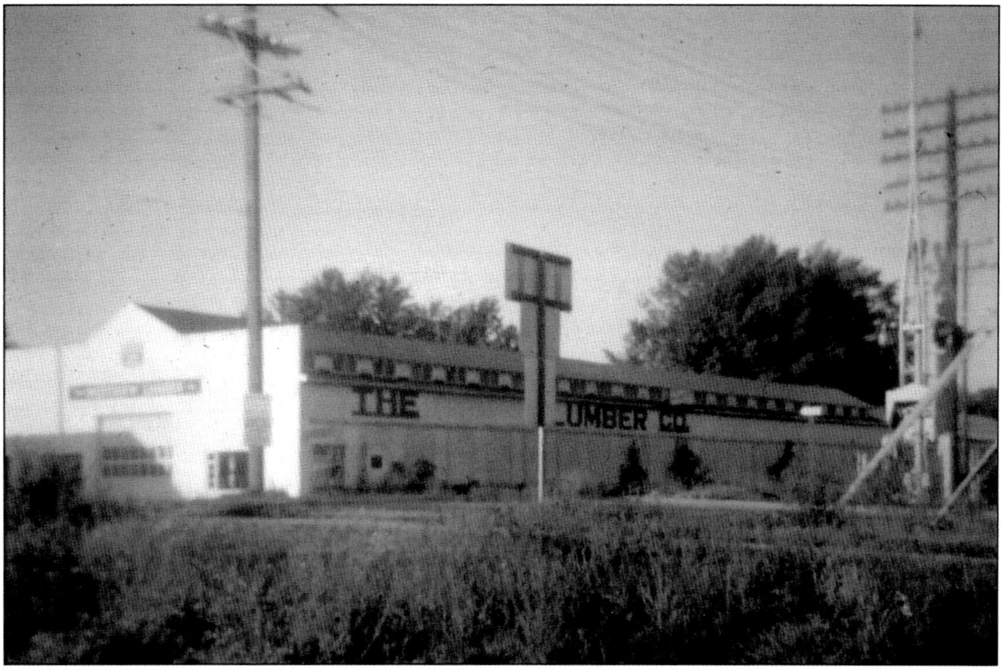

The Dover Lumber Company was located on Dover Center Road, just south of the railroad tracks. Freight trains stopped to unload lumber at the Dover Center Road crossing. (Courtesy of William Robishaw Collection, Westlake Porter Public Library.)

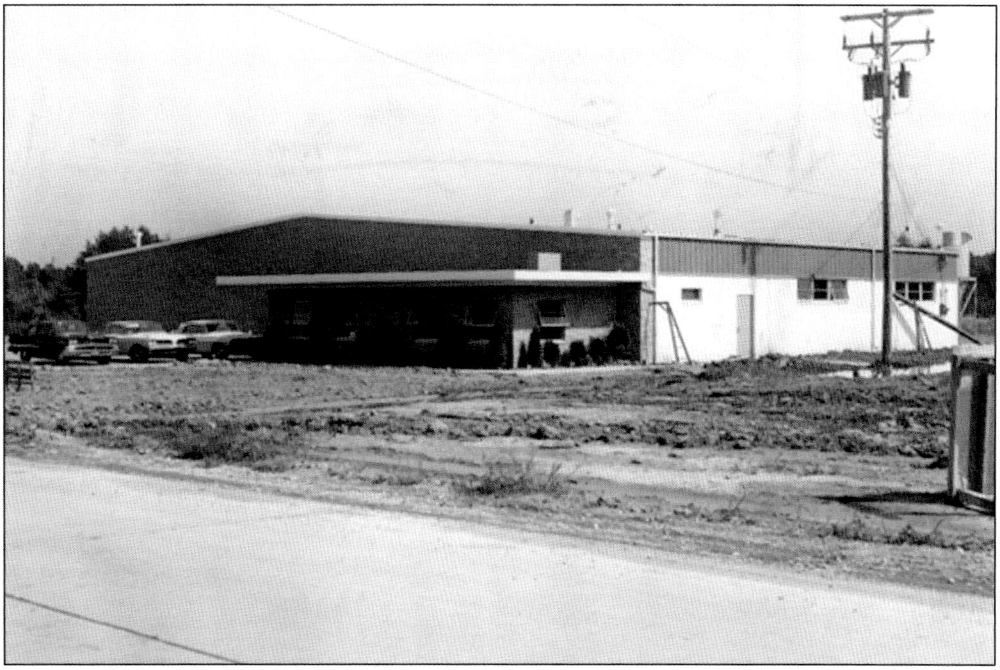

Steamway Products was located on Sharon Drive, shown here in 1962. (Courtesy of Cleveland State University, Cleveland Memory Project, Cleveland Press Collection, Joseph E. Cole, donor.)

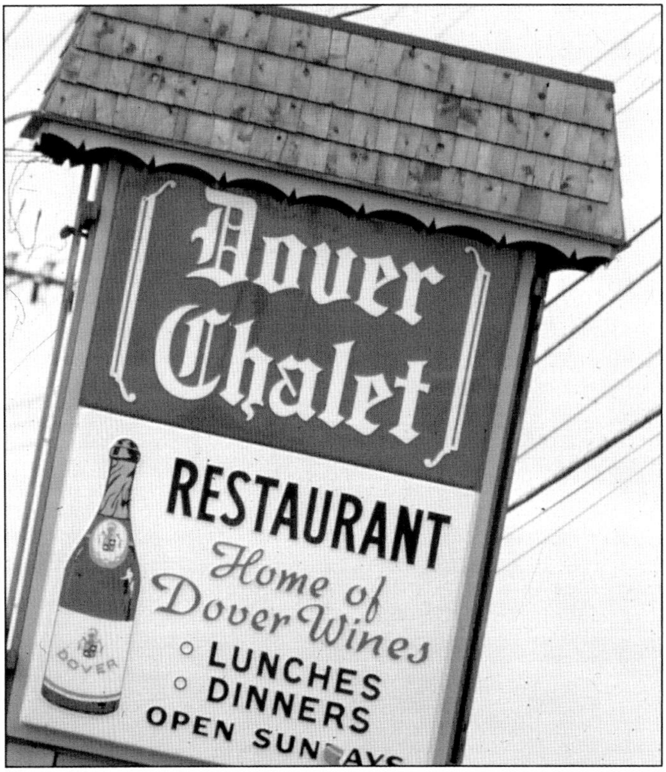

The Dover Chalet opened in 1920 on the south side of Detroit Road, east of Columbia. The restaurant was demolished in 1965 and rebuilt. (Courtesy of William Robishaw Collection, Westlake Porter Public Library.)

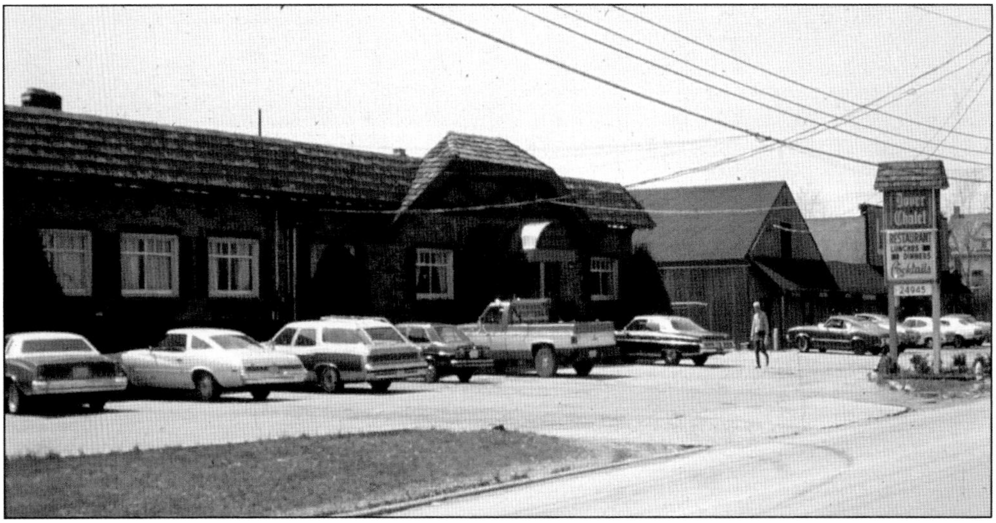

The Dover Chalet restaurant served sweet Dover wines with house specialties such as chicken paprikash. (Courtesy of William Robishaw Collection, Westlake Porter Public Library.)

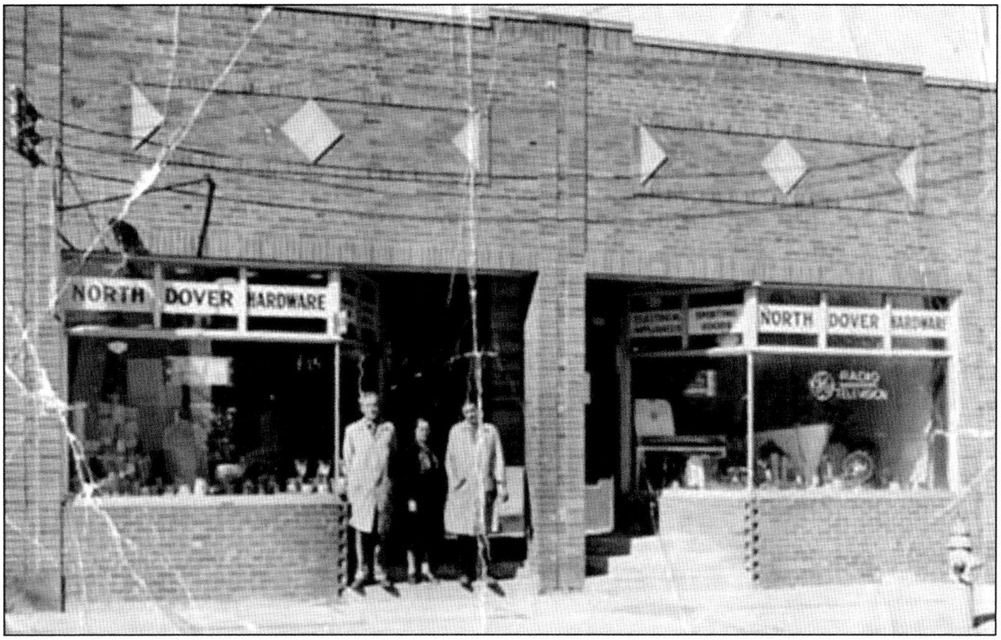

Ollie Dietz, Gertie Bell Ferguson, and Boots Poyer pose in front of the North Dover Hardware store. (Courtesy of Bill Dietz and Susan and Herman Jachnick.)

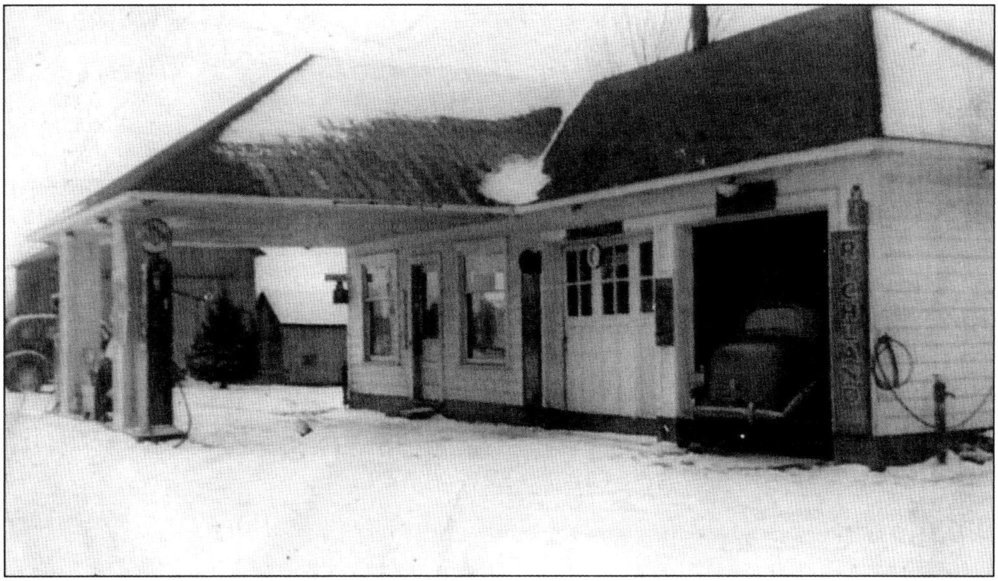
Ollie Dietz ran the gas station on the northwest corner of Bradley and Center Ridge Roads around 1940. (Courtesy of Bill Dietz.)

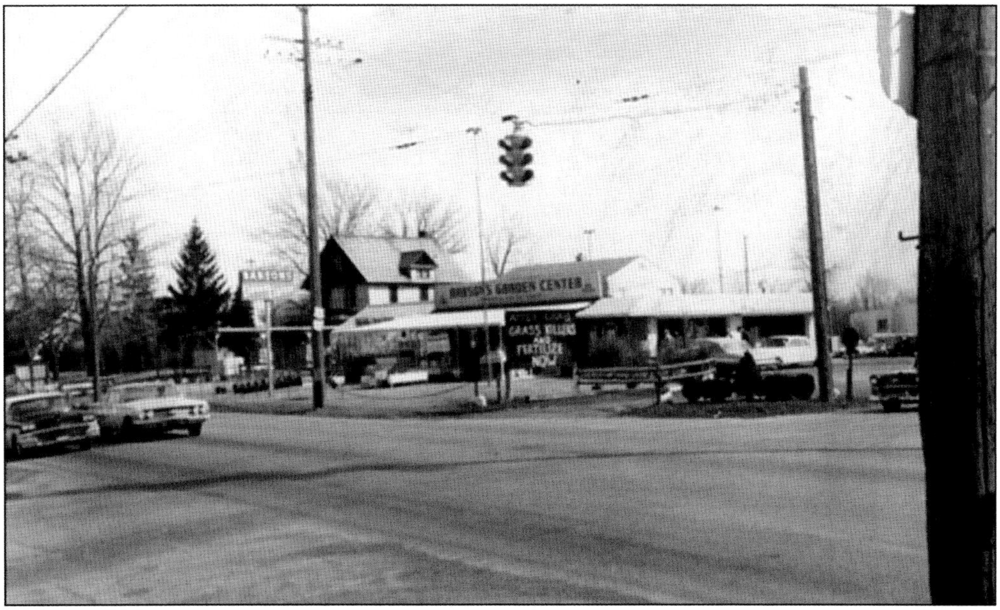

Babson's Garden Center was located on the busy southeast corner of Center Ridge and Clague Roads. Bob Ferda served as general manager of Babson's from 1972 to 1979. (Courtesy of Cleveland State University, Cleveland Memory Project, Cleveland Press Collection, Joseph E. Cole, donor.)

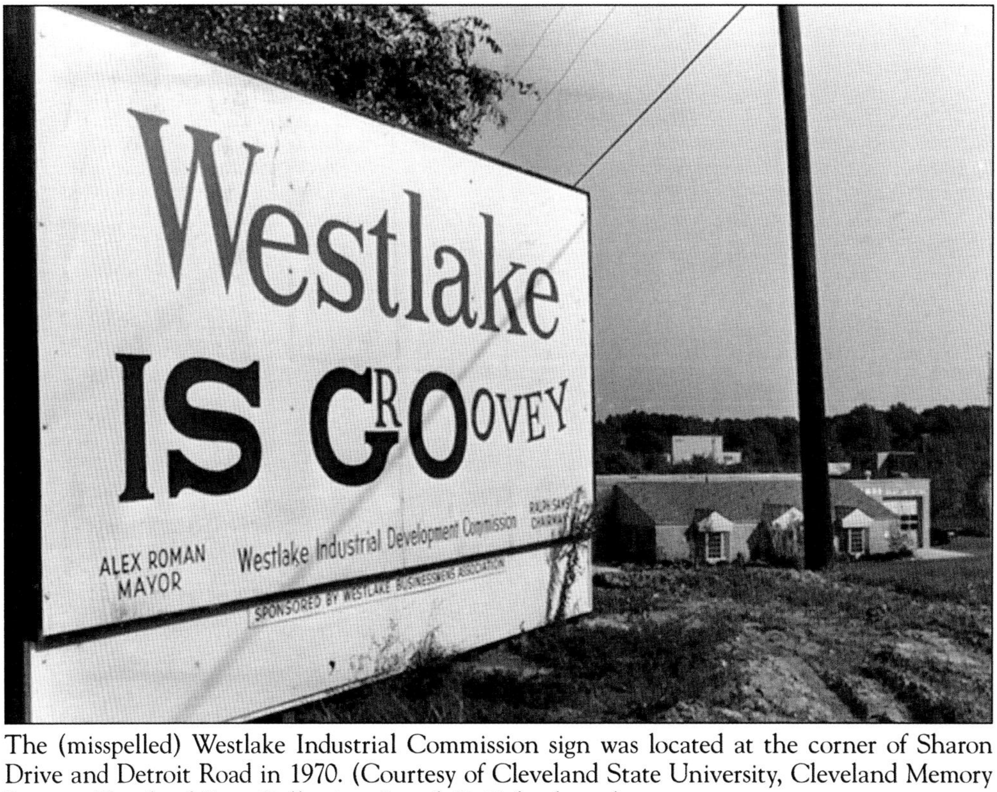

The (misspelled) Westlake Industrial Commission sign was located at the corner of Sharon Drive and Detroit Road in 1970. (Courtesy of Cleveland State University, Cleveland Memory Project, Cleveland Press Collection, Joseph E. Cole, donor.)

Three

DOVERITES AND WESTLAKERS

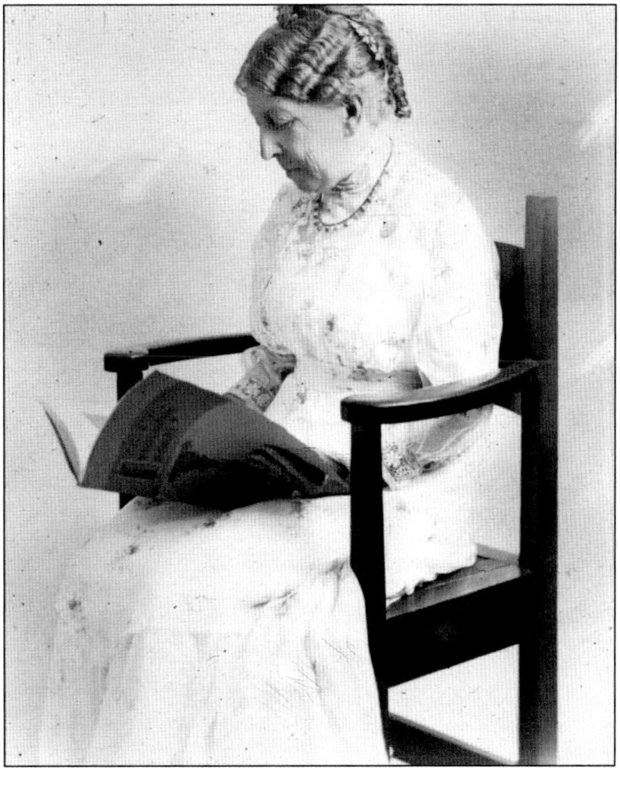

Lydia Cahoon arrived in Dover with her husband, Joseph, and their children to settle on lot 95 in Dover Township on October 10, 1810. Lydia lived to be 84 years old. (Courtesy of Elton Studio, Westlake Porter Public Library archives.)

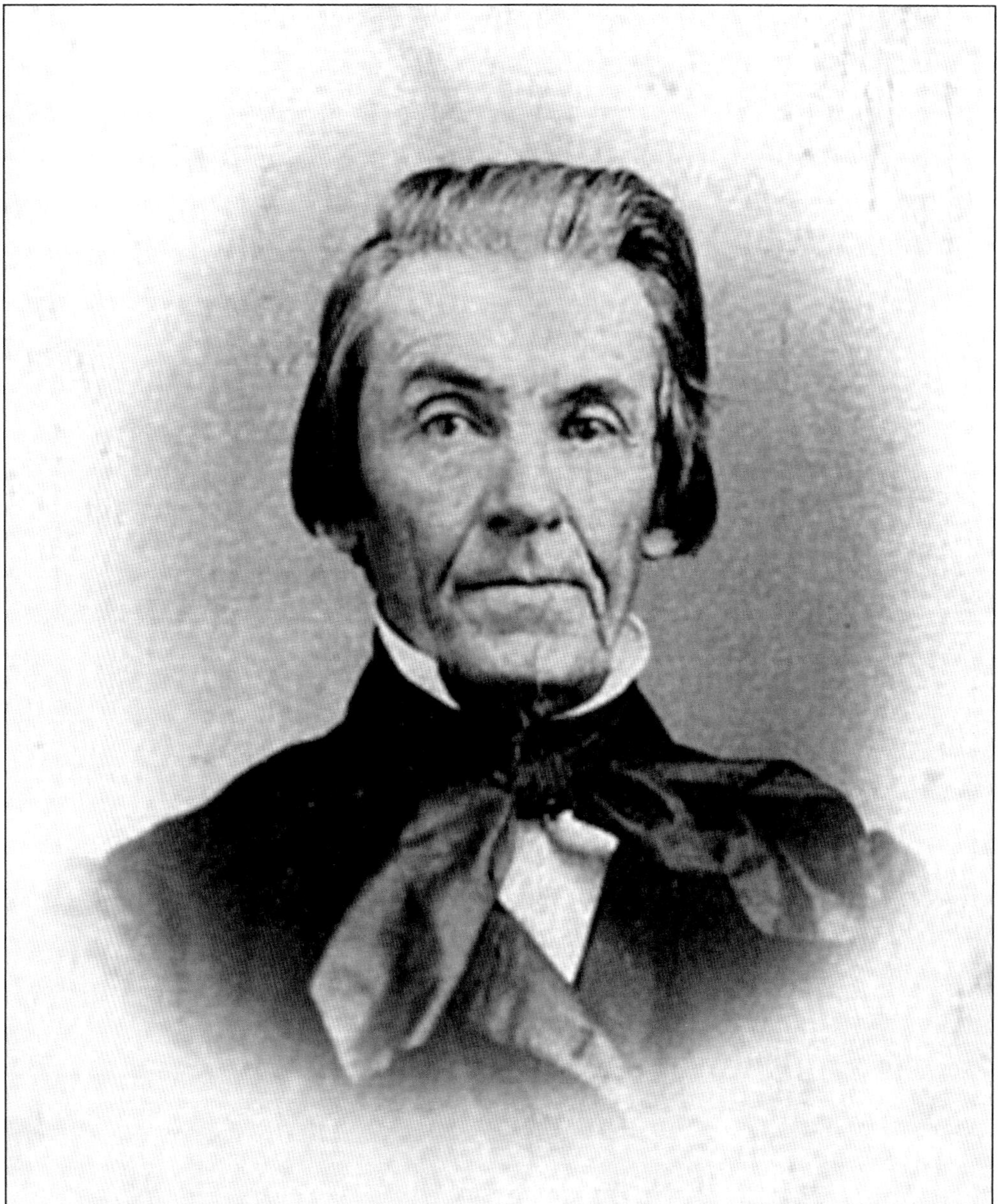

Leonard G. Porter (1806–1884), the 10th born of 11 children, was a pioneer at home among town builders. He held public offices, serving as trustee of the township and justice of the peace. Porter taught at Dover Academy. His wife, Catherine Stevens, was the daughter of the minister of the Dover Congregational Church. Porter lived across the street from the church and served as Sunday school superintendent and the leader of the church choir. The Porters' only child died in infancy, and Catherine passed away a few years later. Porter devoted his life to the citizens of Dover. A provision in his will allotted the sum of $1,000 to the establishment of a public library in Dover and a collection of books to be housed within. (Courtesy of Westlake Porter Public Library archives.)

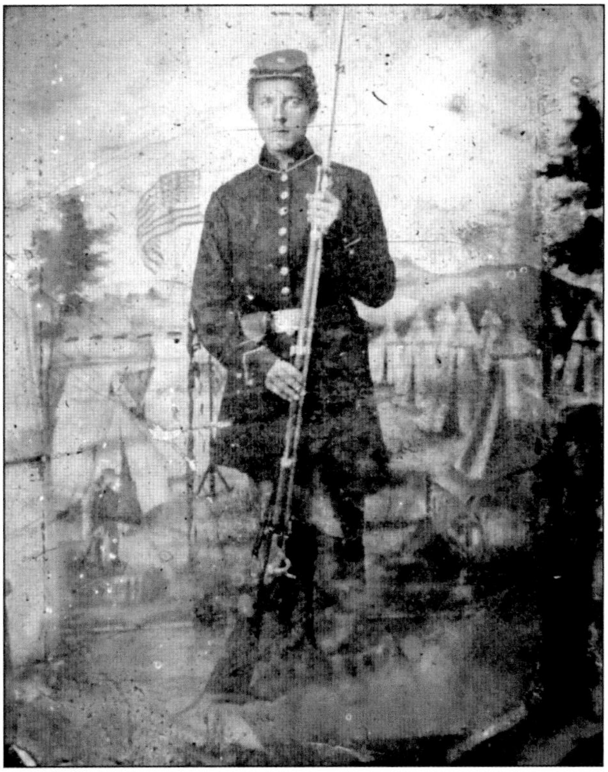

Dover soldiers enlisted in the Civil War in the 103rd Regiment Ohio Volunteer Infantry, the 124th Regiment Ohio Volunteer Infantry, and the 42nd Regiment Ohio Volunteer Infantry. Of those who enlisted from the area, 11 brave men lost their lives in service. An unidentified Dover soldier is pictured. (Courtesy of William Robishaw Collection, Westlake Porter Public Library.)

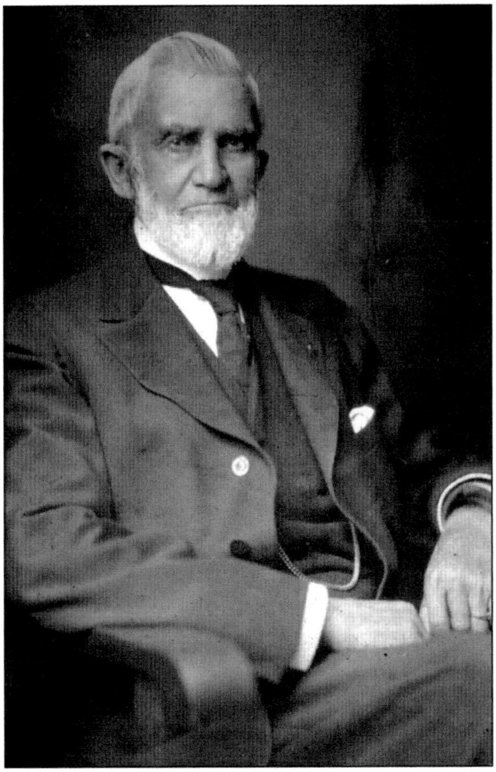

Reuben Hall, grandson of early settler Moses Hall, was born in Dover in 1821. He married Matilda Lilly and lived his life in the area, eventually recording his memories in the book *Reminiscences of Dover Pioneer Life (1810–1910)*. (Courtesy of William Robishaw Collection, Westlake Porter Public Library.)

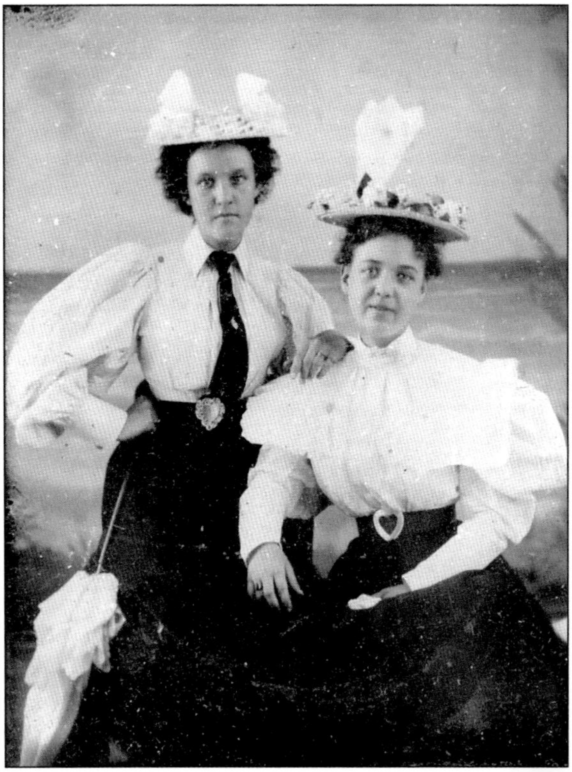

Stylish women of the era, Cora Simonson and Alice Rose Mason enjoyed a game of tennis or a stroll along the beach at the Lake Erie shore around 1876. Perhaps they frequented the Dover-Bay Country Club. (Courtesy of the Mason Family Collection, Westlake Porter Public Library.)

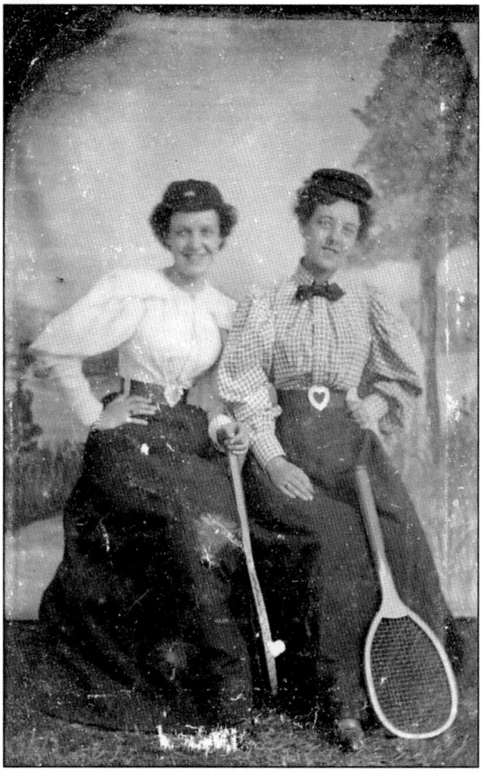

This photograph of Cora Simonson and Alice Rose Mason shows the women holding tennis racquets. (Courtesy of the Mason Family Collection, Westlake Porter Public Library.)

Pictured here is Francis Edgar Mason, a member of the Mason family, who were early residents of Dover. (Courtesy of the Mason Family Collection, Westlake Porter Public Library.)

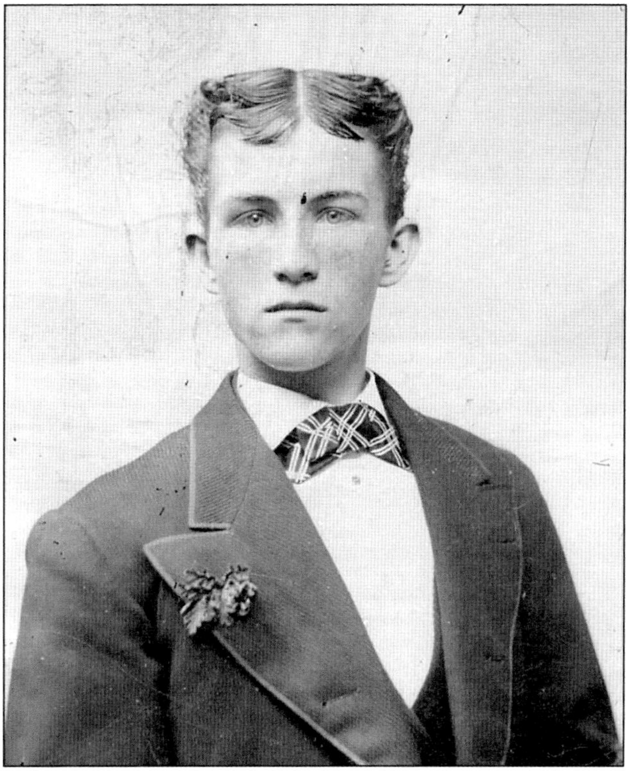

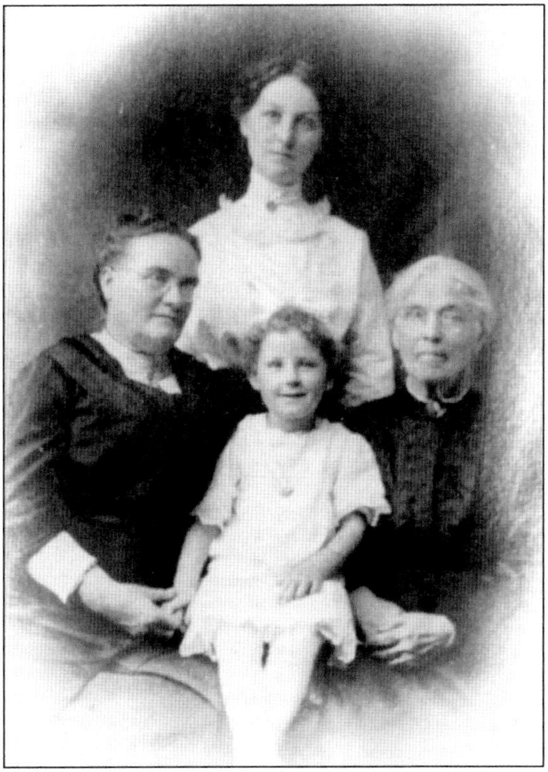

Four generations of the Sperry family are pictured around 1913. From left to right are Augusta Sperry Laughlin, Mabel R. Laughlin Balch (center, top), Violet Elizabeth Balch (center, bottom), and Rachel Sperry. Violet was born on November 4, 1909, and later married a member of the Mason family. (Courtesy of the Mason Family Collection, Westlake Porter Public Library.)

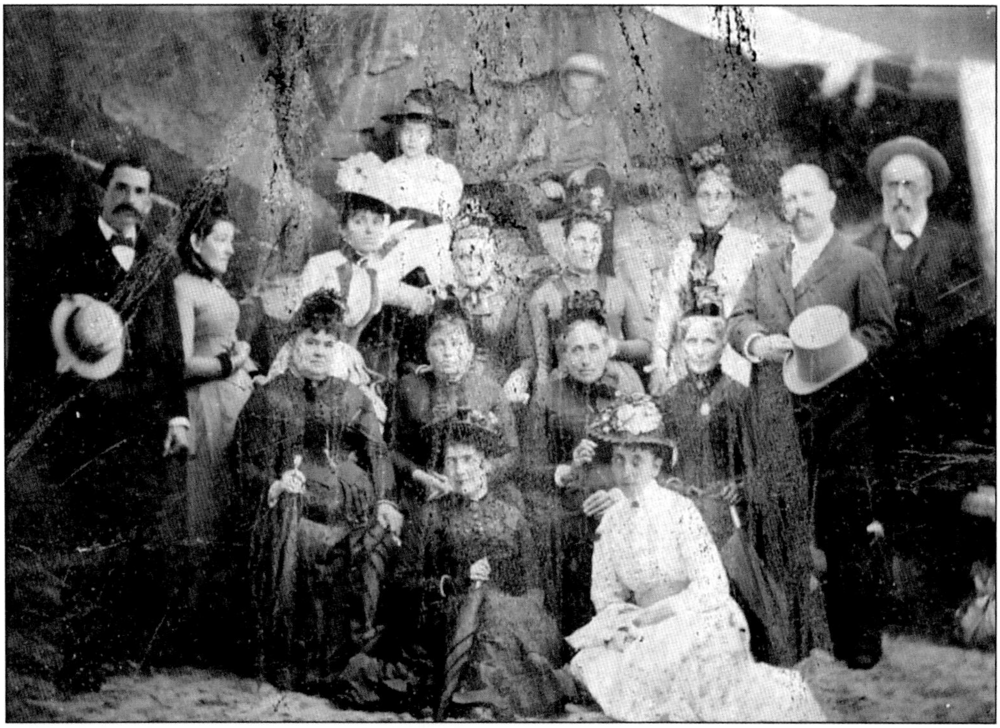

Here is a group picture of the Sands and Cooper families. Hiram Cooper is holding his hat on the far left. (Courtesy of the Mason Family Collection, Westlake Porter Public Library.)

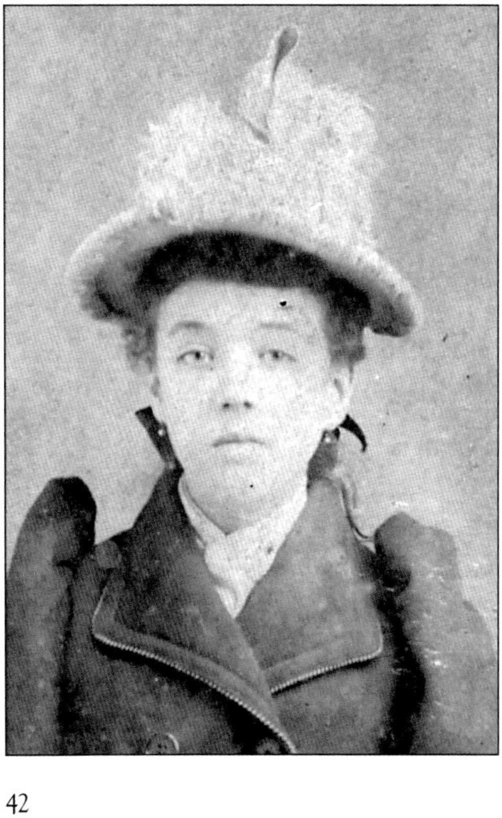

Alice Cooper, daughter of Hiram Cooper, poses in this photograph during her teenage years. She wears a stylish hat. (Courtesy of the Mason Family Collection, Westlake Porter Public Library.)

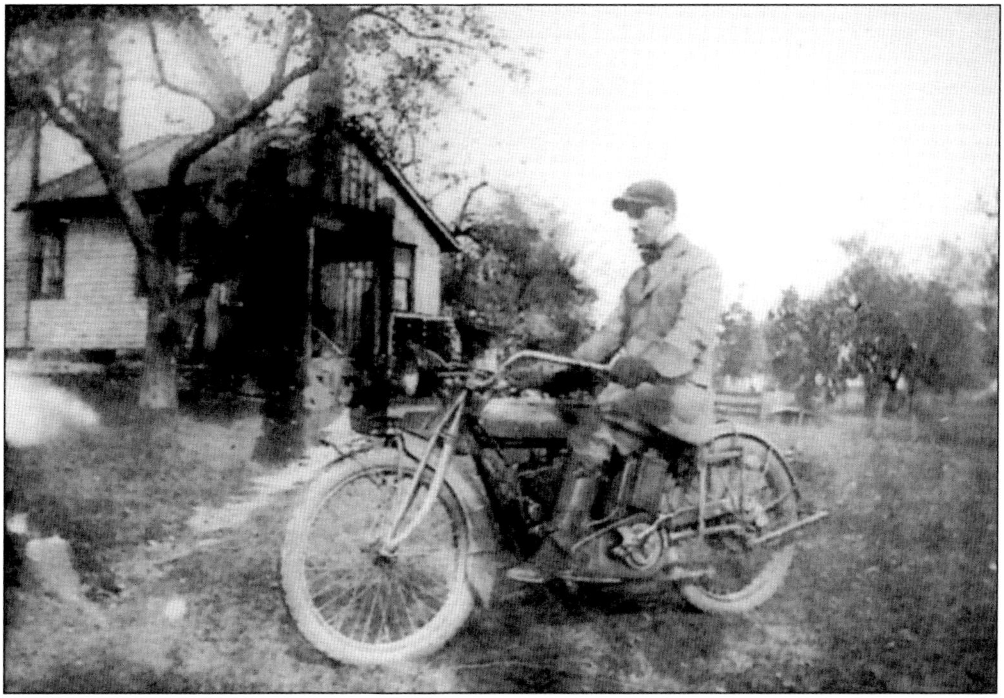

Edward Oster, son of George Oster, is pictured on a motorcycle in front of his father's home. Edward was killed in 1917 in an automobile accident. (Courtesy of Diane Oster.)

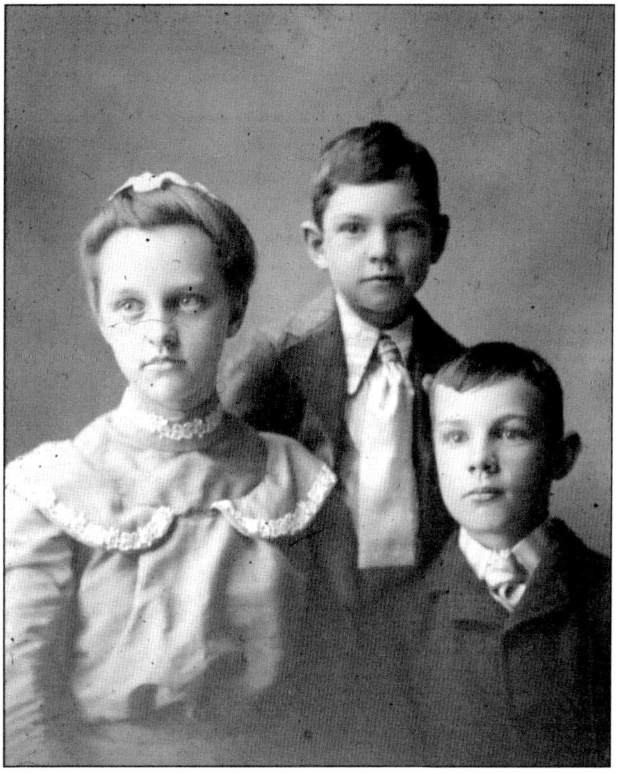

In 1855, George Weston settled in Dover with his wife, Rhoda, farming the land on Center Ridge Road west of Dover Center and then moving to the east side of Hall Road. Weston's son Arthur was a skilled carpenter and clerk of the Dover Village School Board in the 1920s. He had three children, Lucy, Charles, and Bert Weston, pictured here. (Courtesy of William Robishaw Collection, Westlake Porter Public Library.)

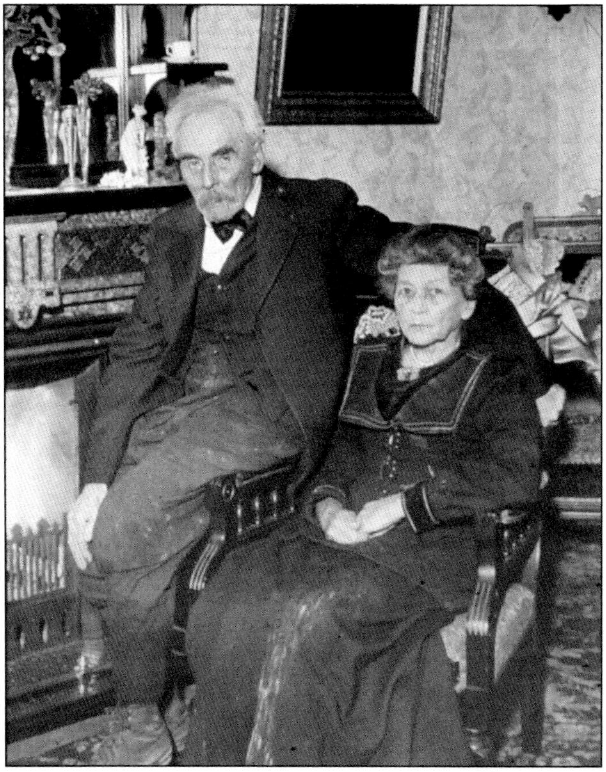

In 1835, Robert and Margaret Clague left the Isle of Man with their daughter Ruth in tow, to travel to America and to Dover. They farmed 78 acres on Clague Road and prospered there, having eight more children. The last surviving children, Walter and his sister Sophronia, are pictured here. On October 12, 1929, Walter and Sophronia presented the Village of Dover with parkland from their farm. "We hope that the Park will be a place where the people of Dover can relax both mentally and physically with sufficient space to play and a place that eventually will become a natural beauty spot in Dover," Sophronia said. Her wish came true. (Courtesy of William Robishaw Collection, Westlake Porter Public Library.)

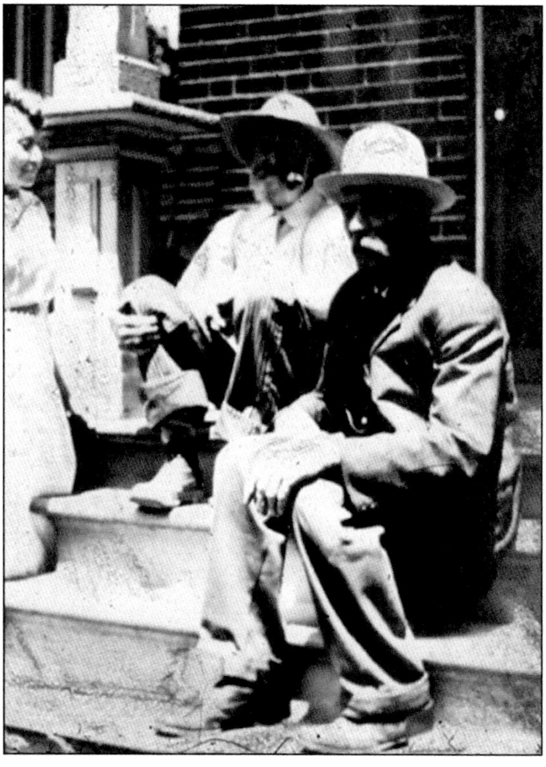

Sophronia and Walter Clague are shown here on the steps of the Clague House with an unidentified man. (Courtesy of William Robishaw Collection, Westlake Porter Public Library.)

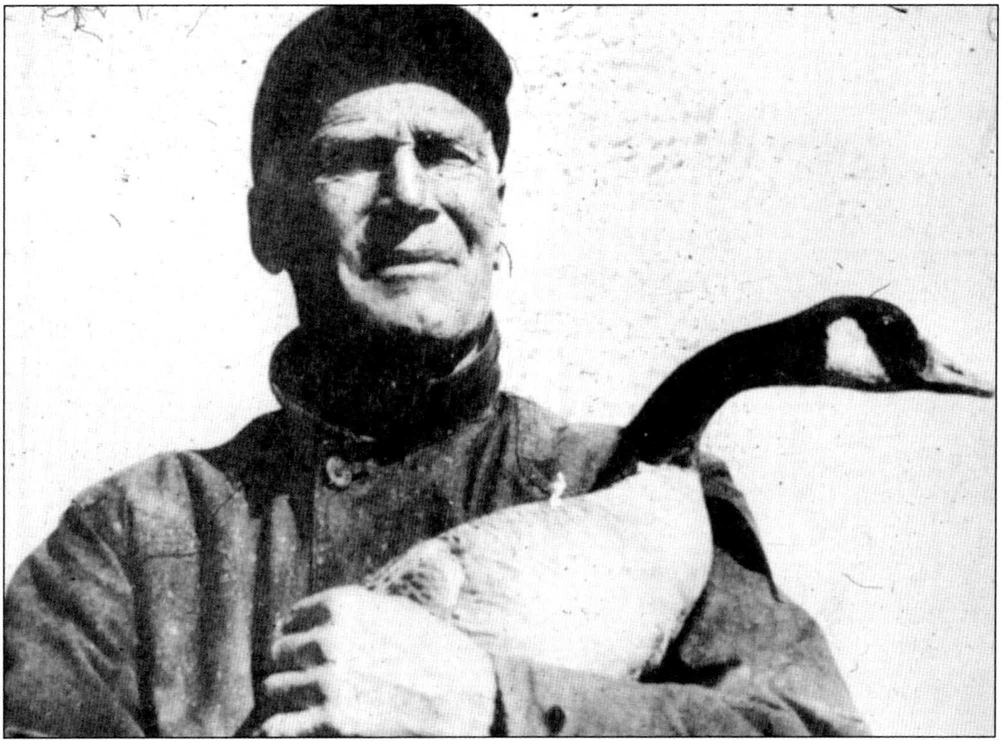

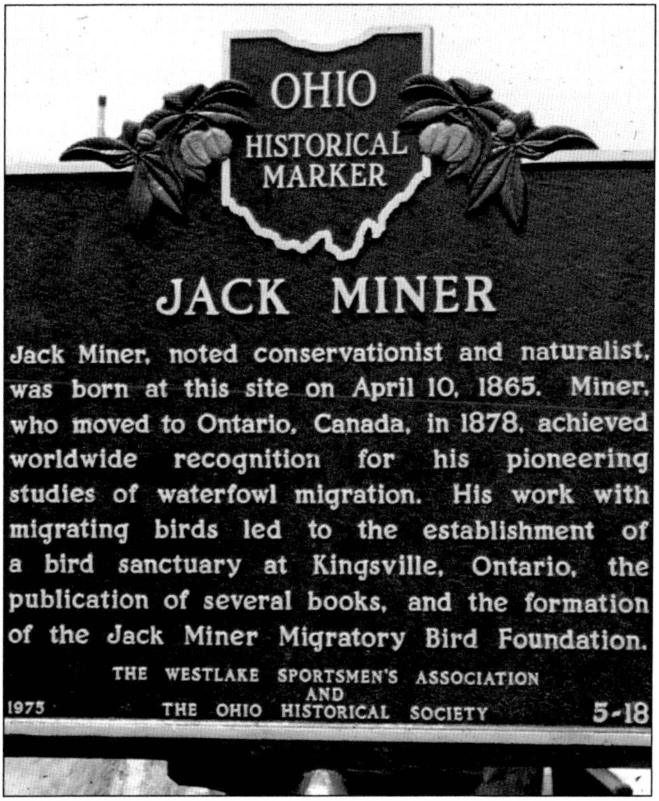

Jack Miner, noted naturalist, author, and lecturer, was born in Dover Village in 1865. The creek that ran near Dover Center Road became Miner's play yard and his laboratory. He studied the creatures that inhabited the area and learned the lessons of bird life that formed the foundation for his life's work. By banding more than 50,000 ducks between 1910 and 1915, he made the first complete banding records of North American birds. In 1931, his friends established the Jack Miner Migratory Bird Foundation to ensure the continuation of his work. Kirk Miner continues to maintain the bird sanctuary in Kingsville, Ontario, in memory of his grandfather. (Courtesy of Kirk Miner, William Robishaw Collection, Westlake Porter Public Library.)

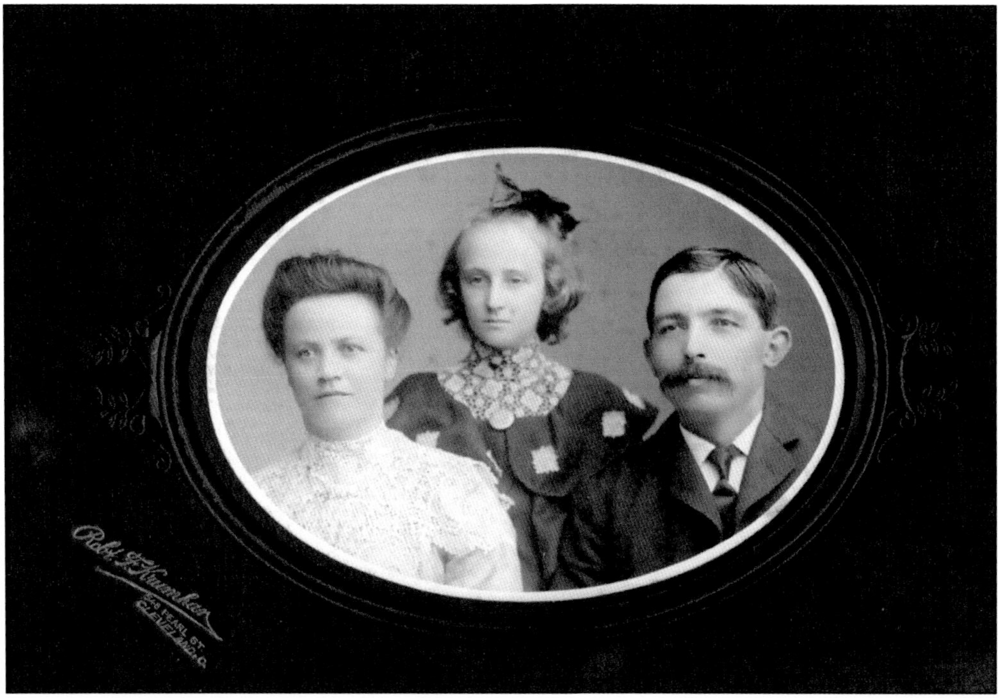

Mary and Alfred Yaeger with their daughter Anna are pictured here. (Courtesy of Susan and Herman Jachnick.)

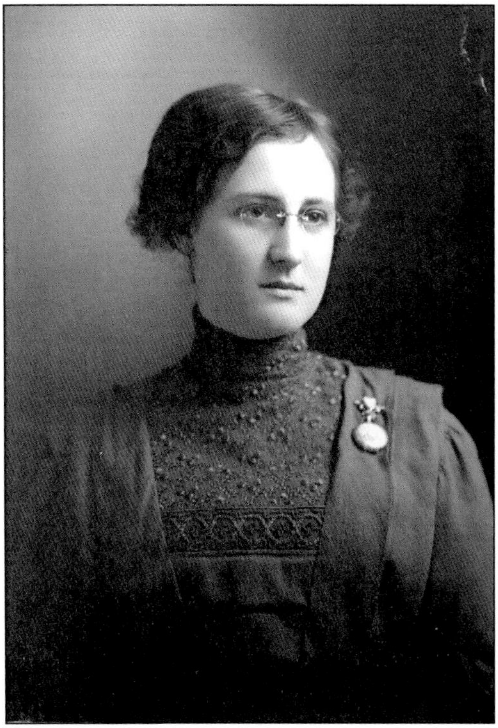

Anna resembles both of her parents as a grown-up. She became one of the first telephone operators in Dover. (Courtesy of Susan and Herman Jachnick.)

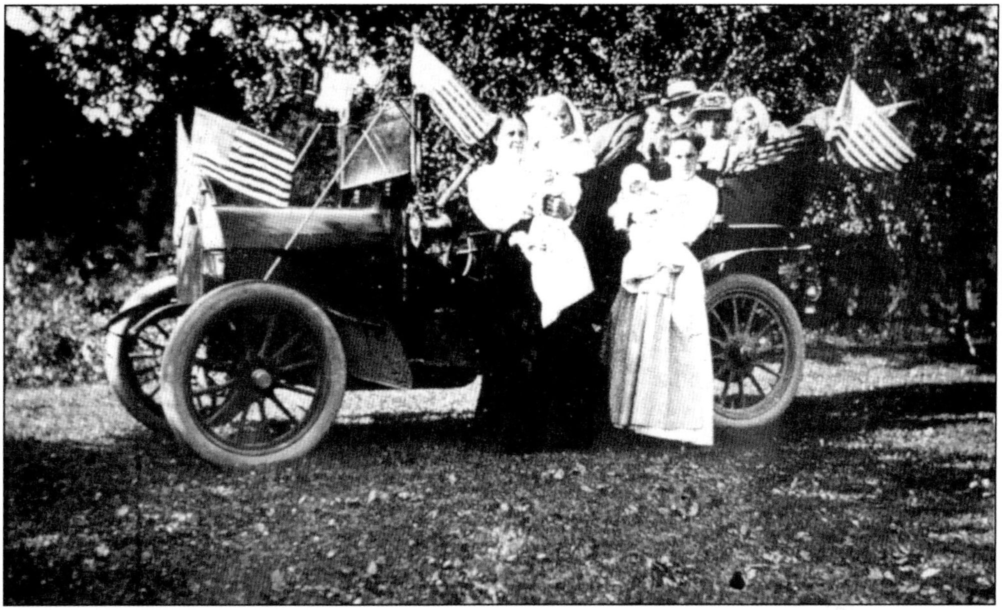

Although the individuals pictured are unidentified, there is no mistaking this Dover family's enthusiasm for the 1915 Fourth of July celebration. (Courtesy of William Robishaw Collection, Westlake Porter Public Library.)

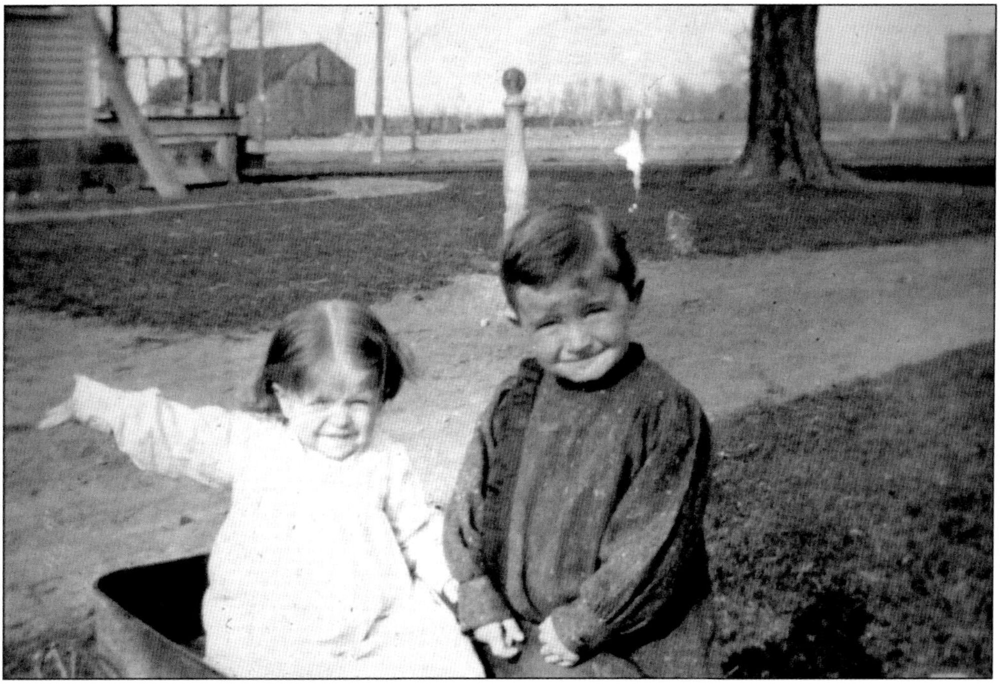

Asher Cooley arrived in Dover with his wife, Lydia Smith Cooley, and five children on October 19, 1818. They had five more children for a total of seven sons and three daughters. Members of the family still live in Westlake. Reuben Cooley and his sister Esther Cooley are shown here in 1905 in the Cooley yard on the west side of Dover Center Road. (Courtesy of William Robishaw Collection, Westlake Porter Public Library.)

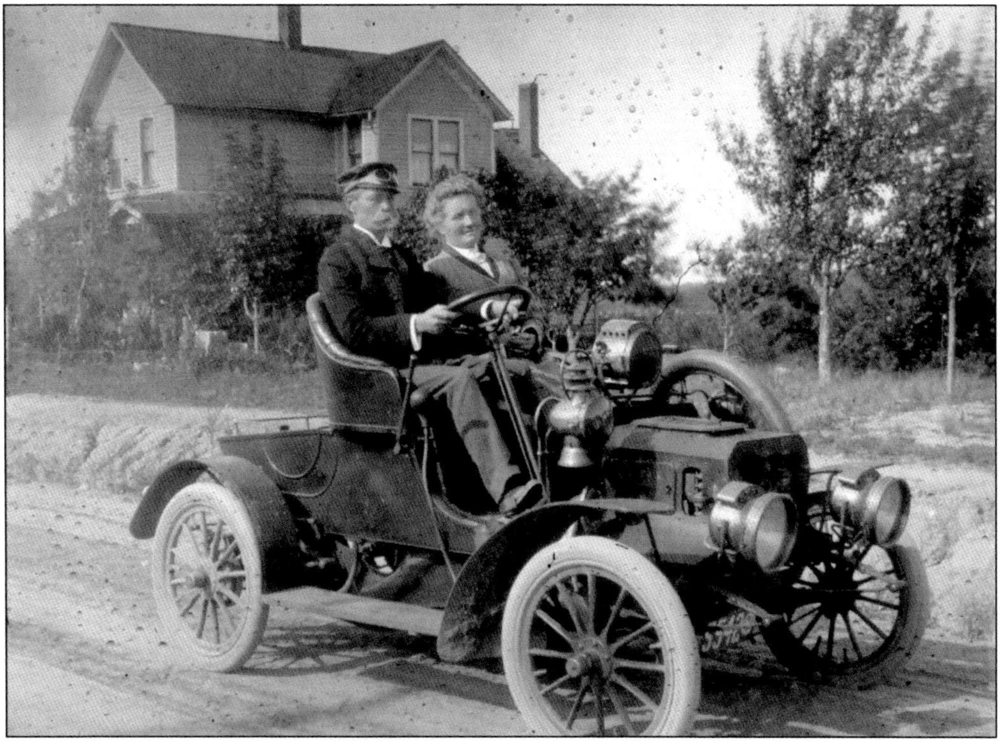

James and Mary E. May, Detroit Road residents, enjoy a spin in a stylish, new touring car. (Courtesy of William Robishaw Collection, Westlake Porter Public Library.)

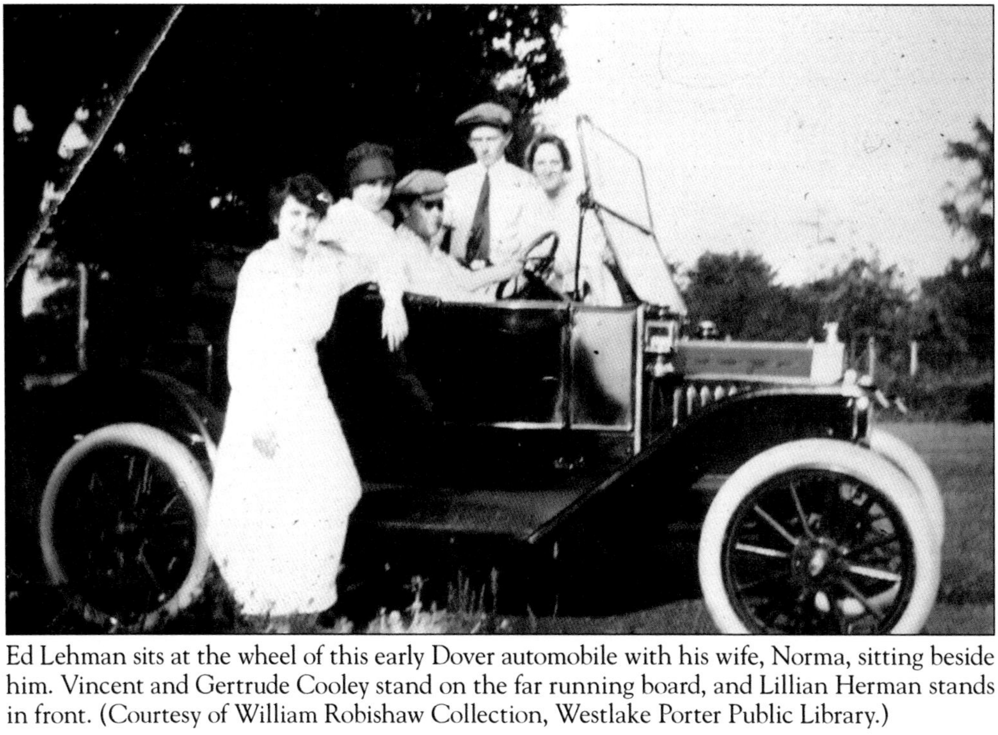

Ed Lehman sits at the wheel of this early Dover automobile with his wife, Norma, sitting beside him. Vincent and Gertrude Cooley stand on the far running board, and Lillian Herman stands in front. (Courtesy of William Robishaw Collection, Westlake Porter Public Library.)

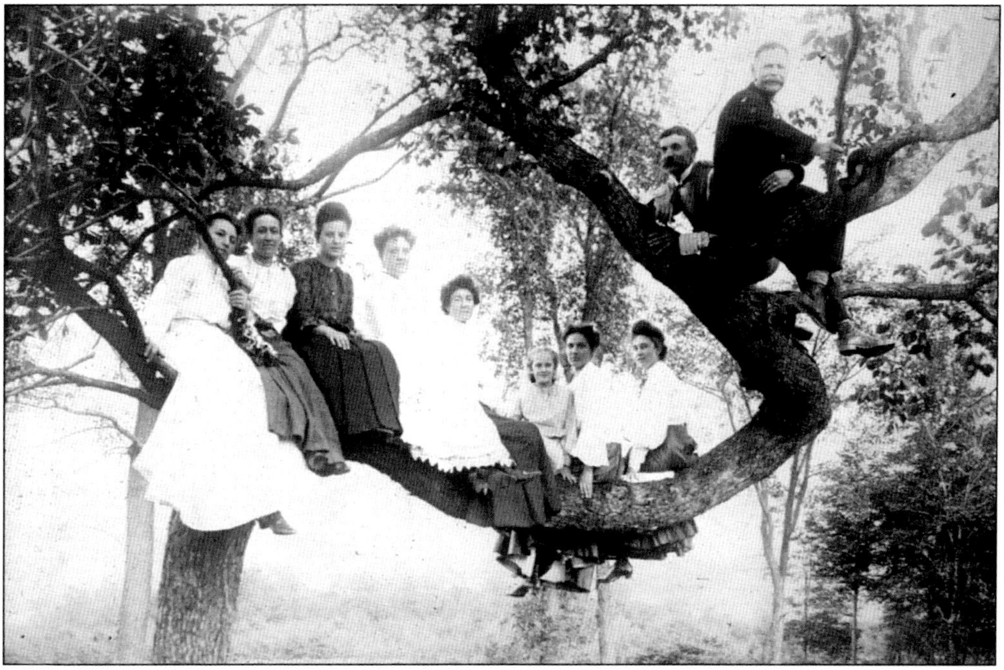

The Lewis family farm was located at 24629 Detroit Road. The signal tree on the farm was a curiosity to Dover residents, who wondered if it was shaped by accident, by a greater power, or by a human hand. (Courtesy of William Robishaw Collection, Westlake Porter Public Library.)

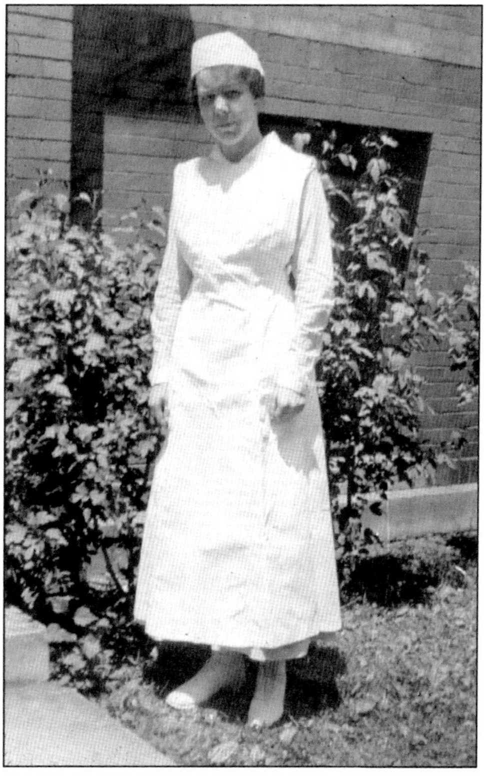

This picture of May E. Weston was taken to commemorate her 1918 graduation from the Ohio University. Weston was the author of *The First 100 Years of Dover Schools*. She taught in the old Mitchell district one-room school in Dover, then in the Cleveland school system. (Courtesy of William Robishaw Collection, Westlake Porter Public Library.)

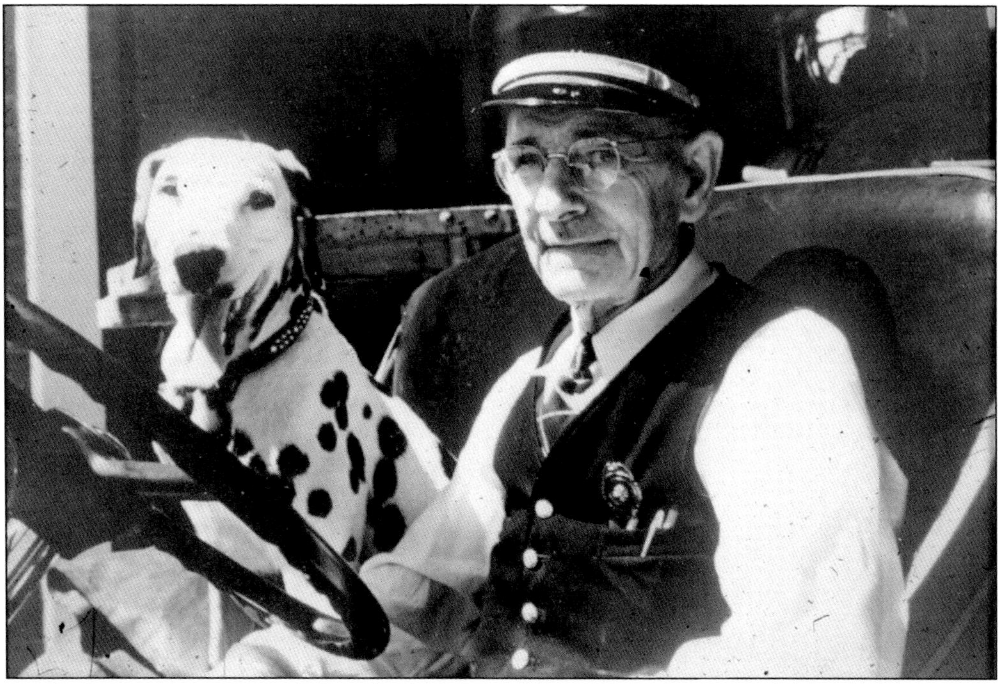

Frank Sauer was appointed fire chief of Dover in 1937 and remained in the position for 20 years. He is pictured here with the fire department's mascot, a dalmatian. (Courtesy of William Robishaw Collection, Westlake Porter Public Library.)

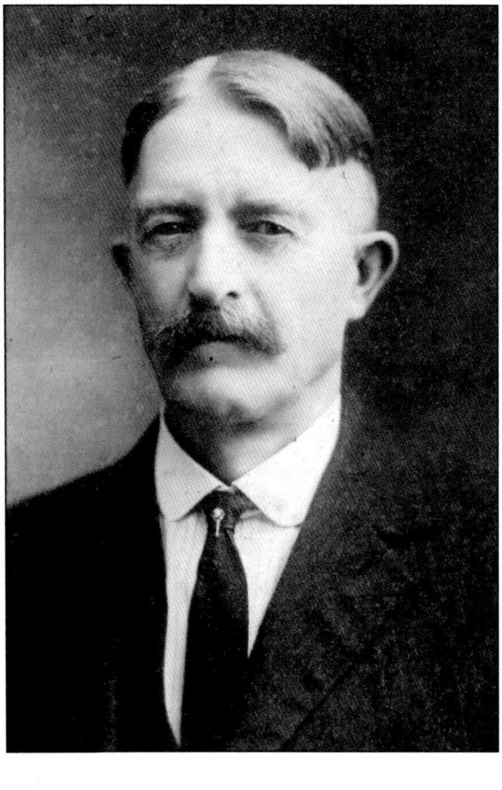

George Cooley was born in Dover on January 14, 1861. He attended Ohio Northern University and then returned to Dover to become active in civic affairs. Cooley was chairman of the county farm bureau when it united with local improvement associations to form the Ohio Farm Bureau Federation. Cooley served as the first president of the newly created federation. (Courtesy of William Robishaw Collection, Westlake Porter Public Library.)

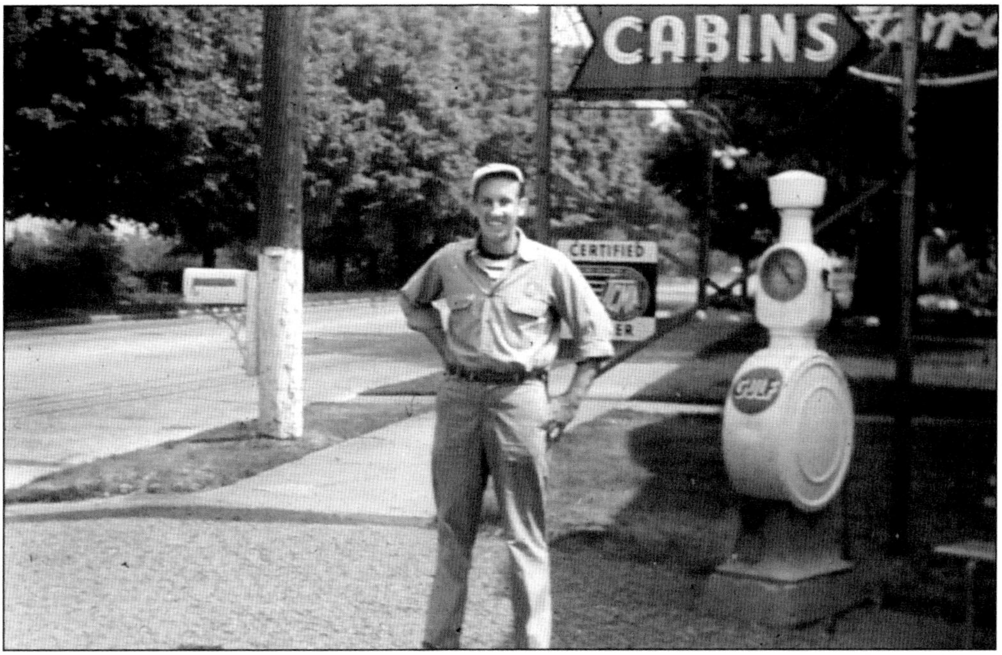

Clark D. Schneider stands in front of a gasoline pump. Clark Parkway was later built on the Schneider family's original property and named after Schneider. Clark Parkway is located between Westwood Road and Rose Road, parallel to Dover Center Road. (Courtesy of William Robishaw Collection, Westlake Porter Public Library.)

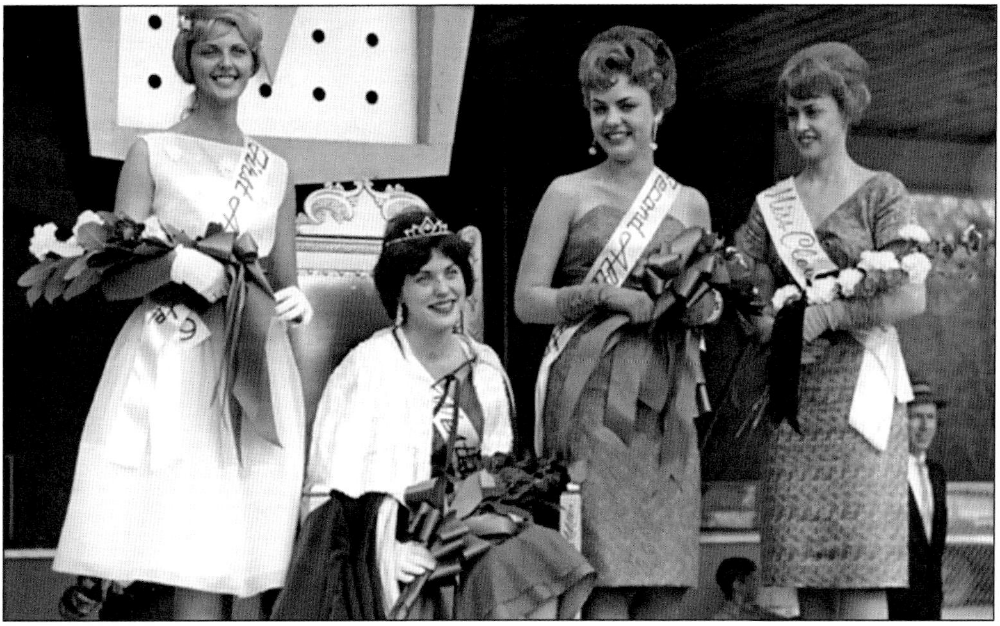

Judy Frank (seated on throne) of Lorain was elected Miss Westlake 1962. First runner-up was Barbara Sakowski of Lorain (left of throne). Second runner-up was Joann Maskow of Westlake (right of throne). Miss Cleveland 1961, Margaret Pae, is also shown (right). (Courtesy of Cleveland State University, Cleveland Memory Project, Cleveland Press Collection, Joseph E. Cole, donor.)

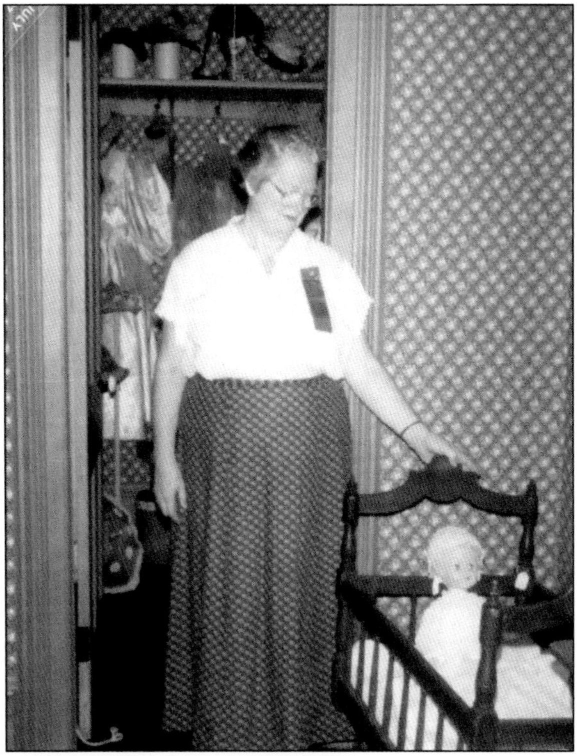

Doris Weston, a longtime resident of Westlake, was devoted to the area and active in the Westlake Historical Society and the Dover Congregational Church. She attended Westlake Public Schools, where she excelled in her studies and became an elementary school teacher. Weston taught in North Olmsted and in Chardon. After retirement, she volunteered at Fairview Hospital and continued her work with the Westlake Historical Society. Shown here in the Clague House Museum, she could always be counted on for a warm and delightful account about the history of Westlake. (Courtesy of the Westlake Historical Society, Doris Weston Collection, Westlake Porter Public Library.)

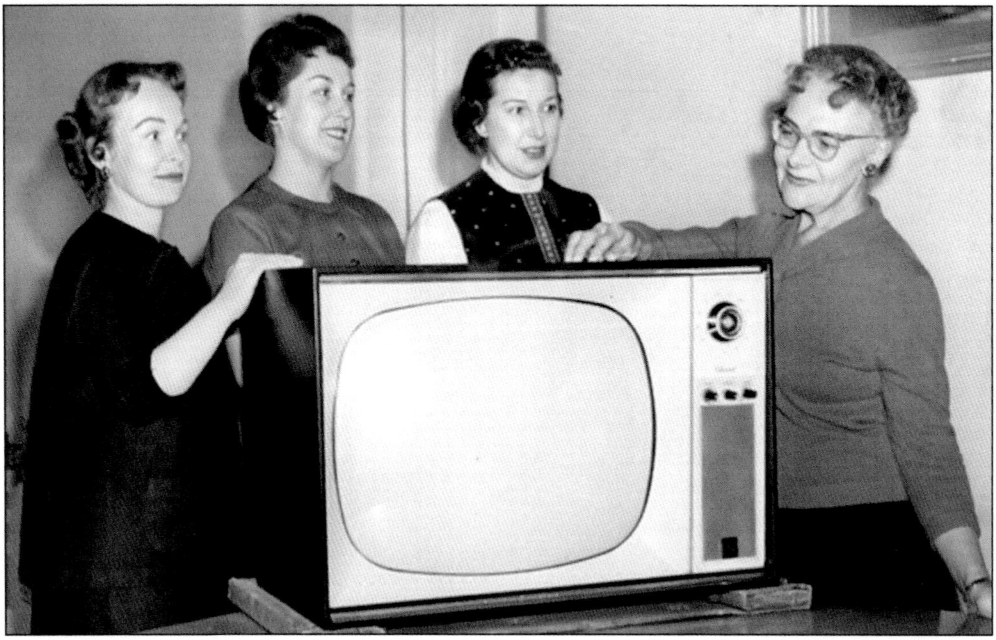

As part of a mental health welfare project in 1959, the Westlake Junior Women's Club donated a television set to the state hospital. Pictured making the presentation at the hospital, from left to right, are Jo Radice, Lois Sweany, Ruth Roesinger, and Rose Rhulaman. (Courtesy of Cleveland State University, Cleveland Memory Project, Cleveland Press Collection, Joseph E. Cole, donor.)

Four

Reading, Writing, and Arithmetic

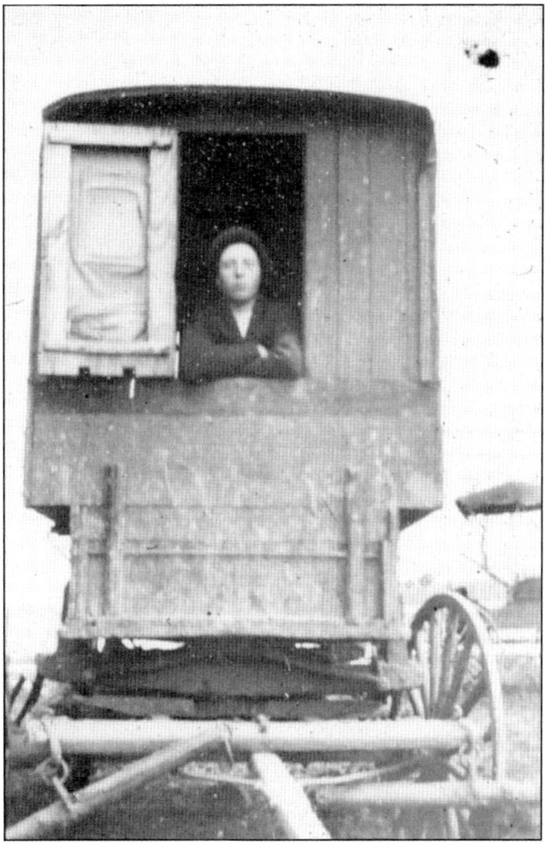

Reuben Osborn gave land on the Lake Erie shore near the western end of the township for Dover's first school. Betsy Crocker, daughter of Jedediah and Sarah Crocker, became Dover's first schoolteacher at the age of 14 around 1816 in a one-room log schoolhouse heated by a large fireplace. Reading, writing, arithmetic, and spelling were taught. Polite behavior was part of the curriculum. The first kind of school bus, a kid wagon, is pictured here. Howard Tanner is the only passenger. (Courtesy of William Robishaw Collection, Westlake Porter Public Library.)

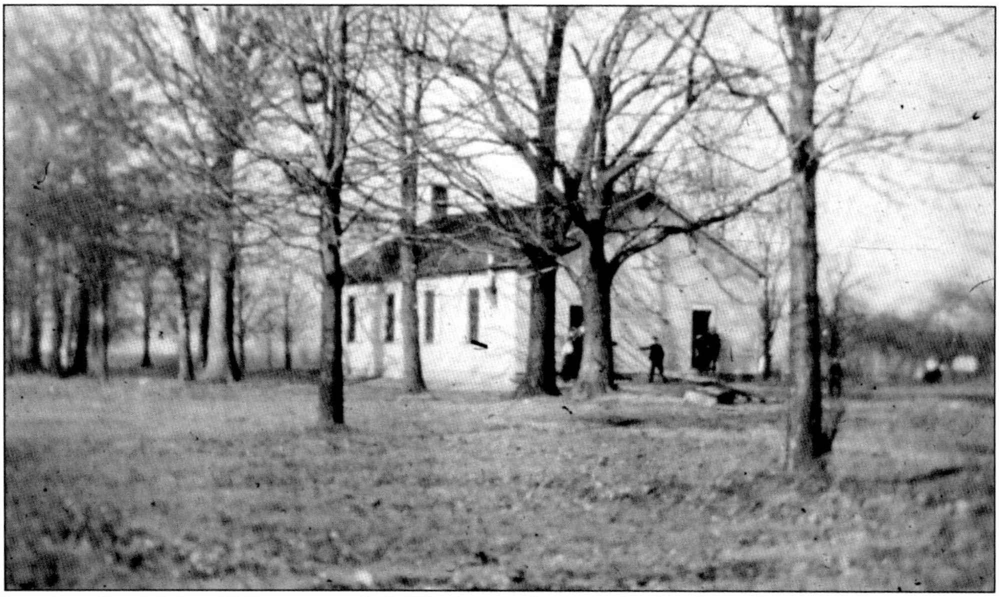

In 1844, Prof. John Wilson attended Oberlin College to further his education. Returning to Dover in 1845, he formed the Dover Academical Society for higher education. Three directors, Leverett Johnson, Leonard G. Porter, and Benjamin Reed, were appointed. In 1852, the Dover Academy, pictured here, was relocated on the west side of Dover Center Road on land donated by Leonard Porter. The academy served the community until 1862. (Courtesy of William Robishaw Collection, Westlake Porter Public Library.)

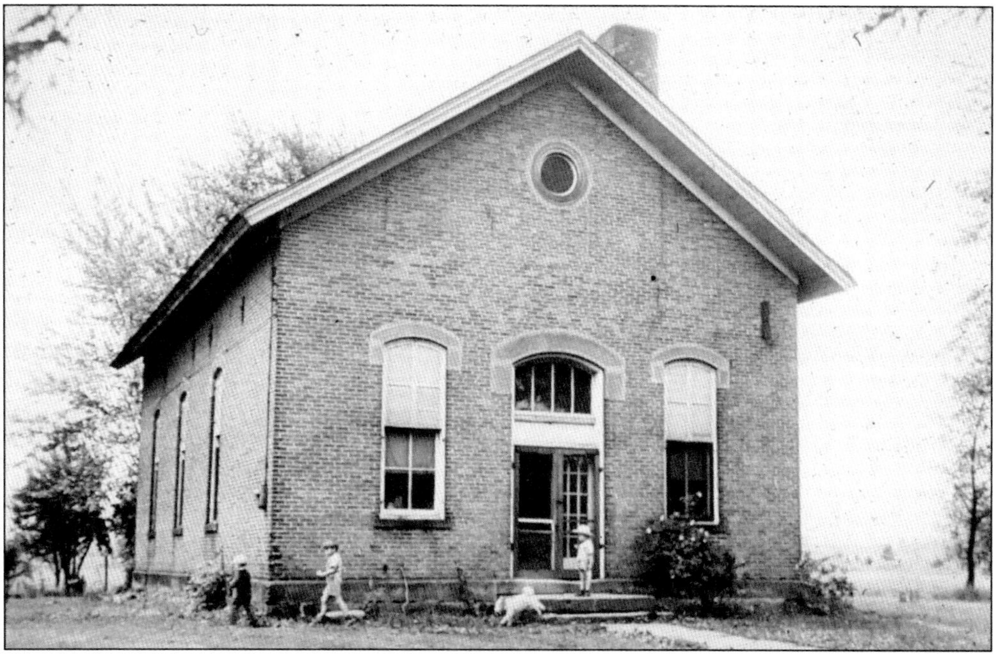

Nettie E. Lotner taught at Westlake's little red schoolhouse, Zothner School, for 44 years. Built around 1890, the school usually held 30 to 35 pupils. This picture was taken on December 18, 1943. The school was located on Detroit Road, west of Bassett Road. (Courtesy of Cleveland State University, Cleveland Memory Project, Cleveland Press Collection, Joseph E. Cole, donor.)

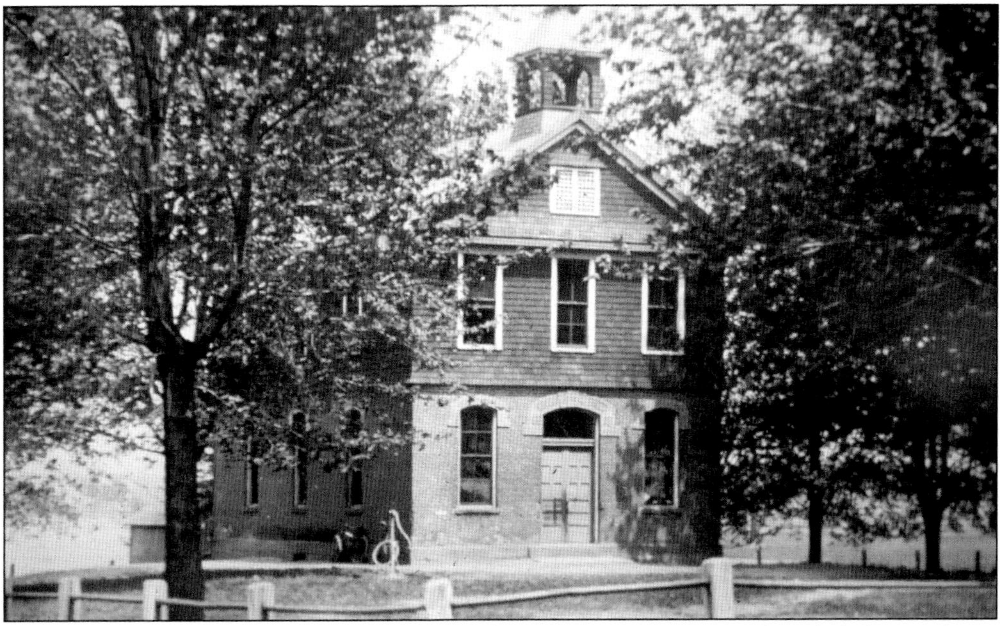

In 1823, Judge Asher Coe arrived from Middletown, Connecticut, and settled the southeast section of Dover Township. Coe School was built in 1878 at the corner of Lorain and Columbia Roads and served the Austin, Spencer, Olmstead, and Coe families. The two-story building surrounded by several additions became part of the North Olmsted School District in 1908. (Courtesy of William Robishaw Collection, Westlake Porter Public Library.)

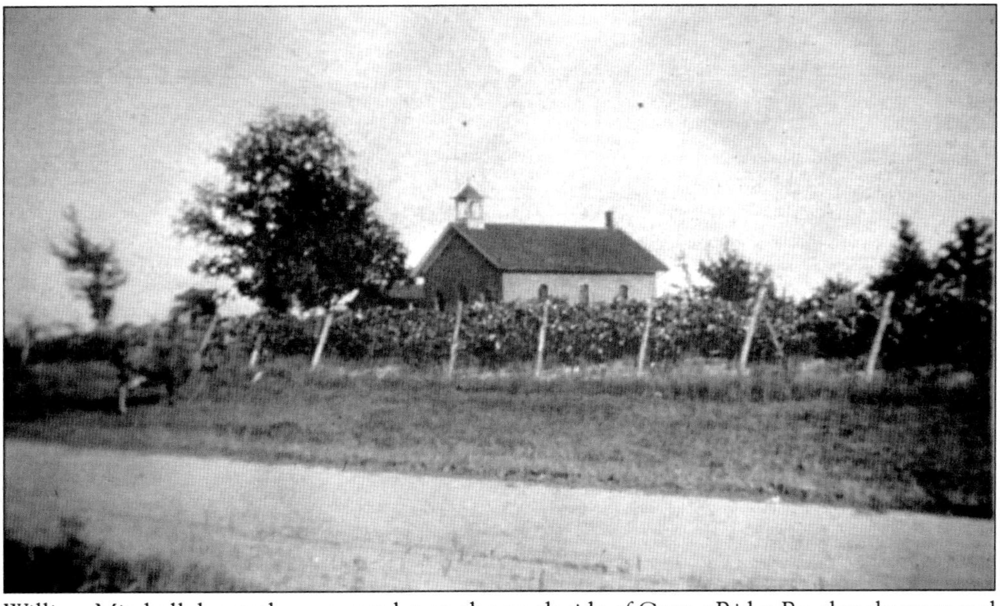

William Mitchell donated a one-acre lot on the south side of Center Ridge Road at the west end of his farm for a schoolhouse, a one-story brick building with a sandstone foundation. Two doors opened into the front hallway. The boys sat on the east side of the building, and the girls sat on the west side. Between the doors was a window to the teacher's platform. Above the platform, a bell hung in the belfry. In the front peak of the roof, an American eagle perched on the Liberty Bell. (Courtesy of William Robishaw Collection, Westlake Porter Public Library.)

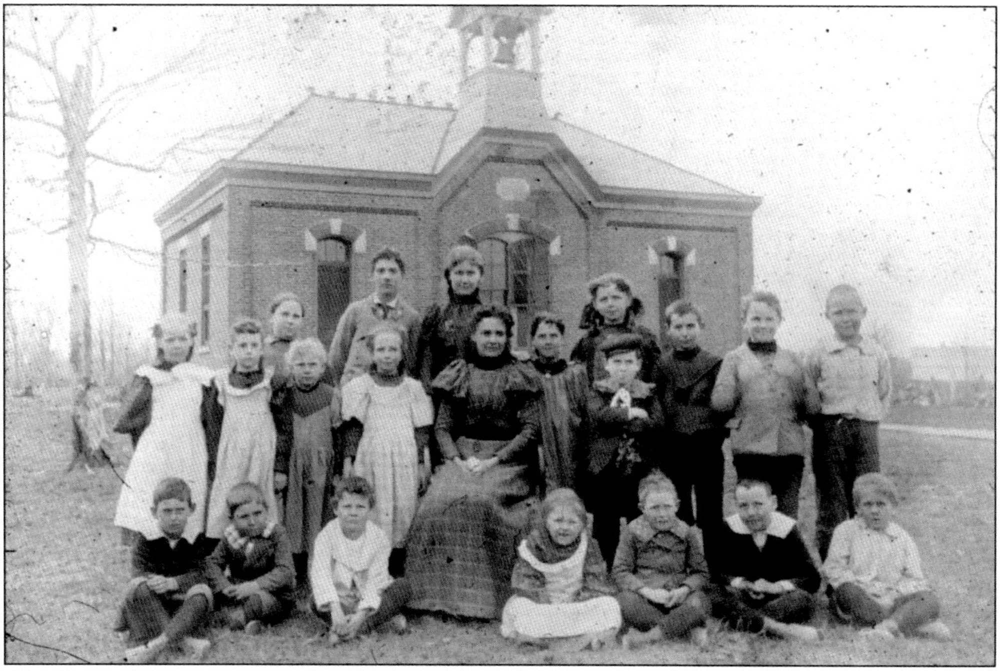

The Depot School was located at 760 Dover Center Road around 1900. William Yaeger, pictured at lower right, later bought his former school and made it his home. (Courtesy of William Robishaw Collection, Westlake Porter Public Library.)

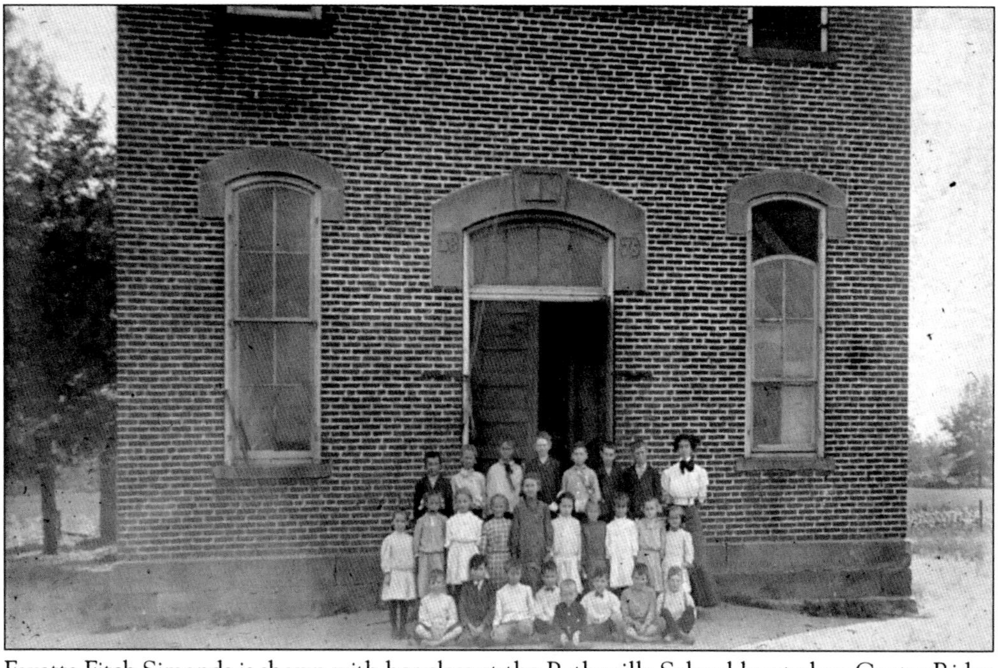

Fayette Fitch Simonds is shown with her class at the Putheville School located on Center Ridge Road near Bailus Road. The school building was the first to be torn down when Dover schools were centralized in the early 1900s. (Courtesy of William Robishaw Collection, Westlake Porter Public Library.)

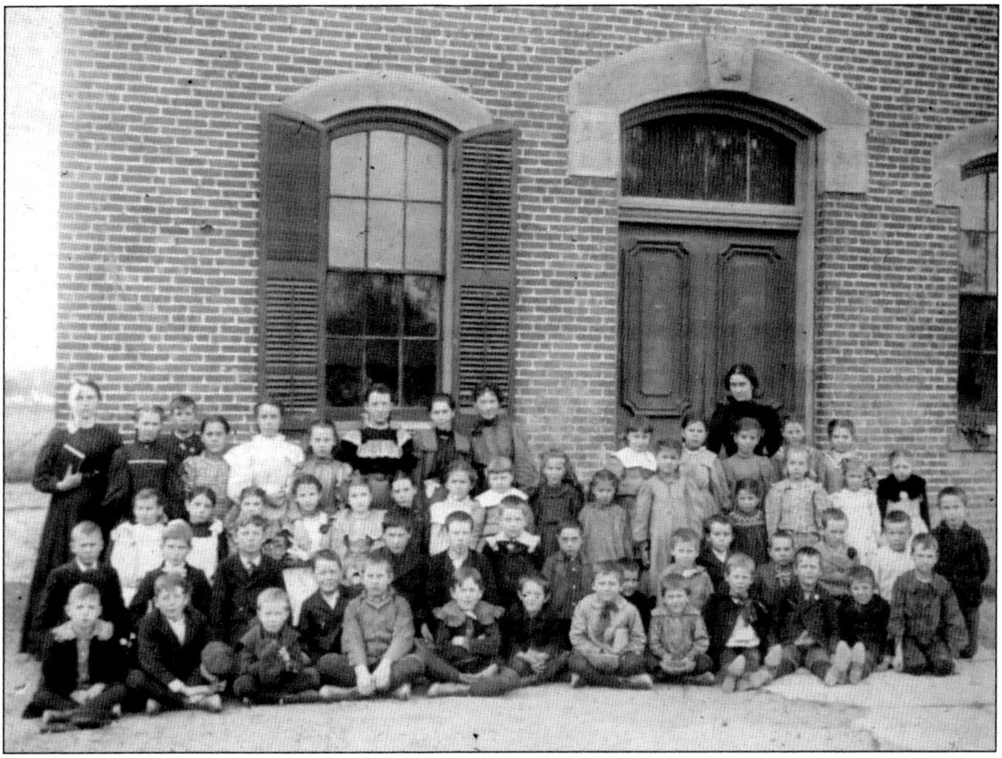

This picture from about 1898 of the Dover Center School classes shows Mary C. Powell (left), the lower grades teacher, and Miss Earle (right), the upper grades teacher. (Courtesy of William Robishaw Collection, Westlake Porter Public Library.)

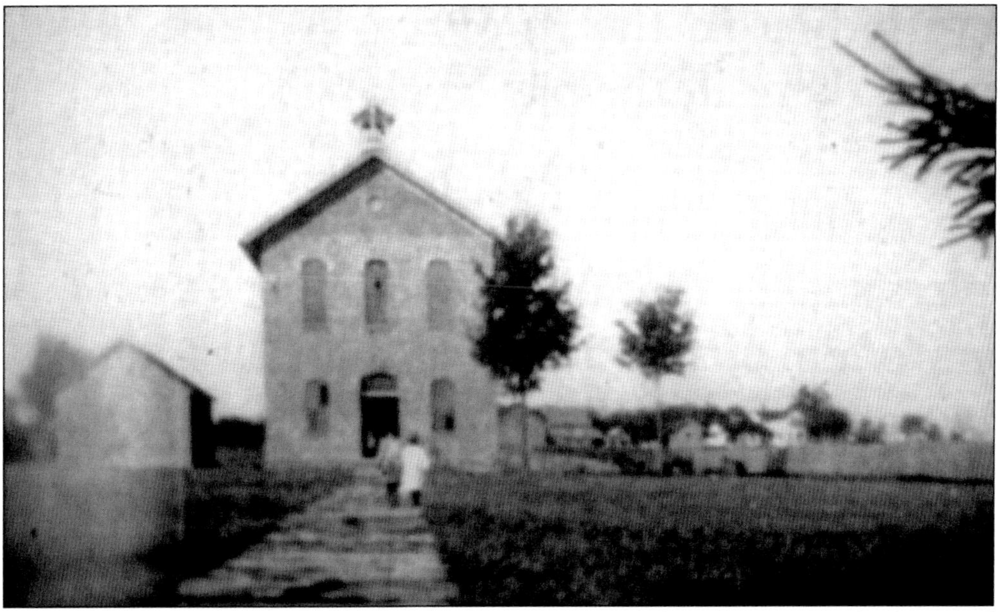

Located on Dover Center Road along the west side of the road, Dover Center School's central location brought students from a radius of two or three miles. A flagstone walk led to the front door. (Courtesy of William Robishaw Collection, Westlake Porter Public Library.)

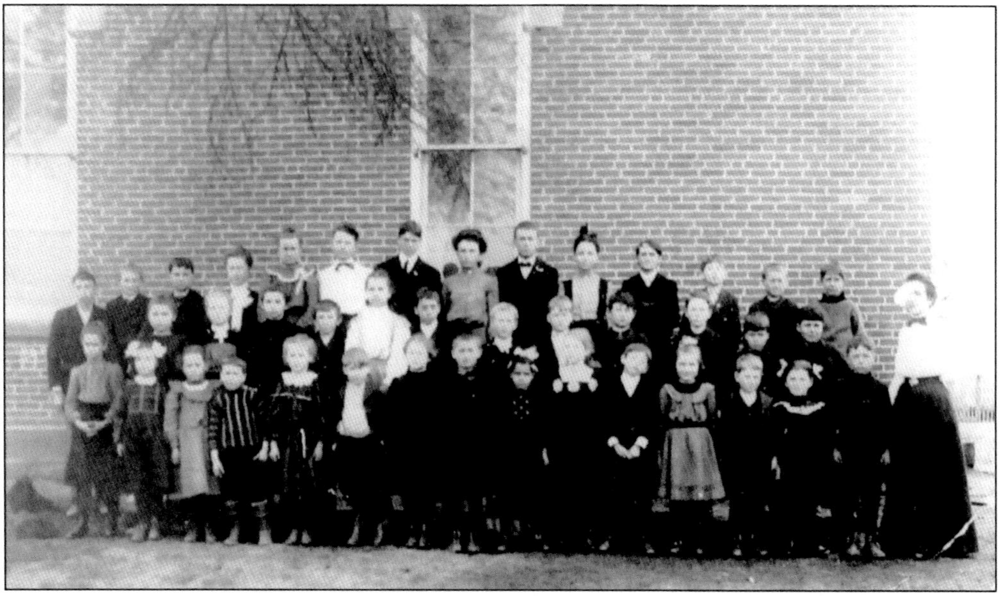

The attendants of Reed School are pictured here around 1904 or 1905 with A. Louise Haas Robinson, their teacher, at far right. Seen here are Lauretta Schwartz, Alfred Glendenning, Ann Dietz, Harvey Orvis, Ruth Biddulph, William Schwartz, Lillian Brazie, Josephine Biddulph, Albert Simonds, Stella Eberling, Newl Ford, Clara Oster, Edgar Terrell, Margaret Eberling, Rose Oster, Adeline Simonds, Sterling Simonds, Florence Haber, Ralph Simonds, Harry Dorer, George Orvis, Edward Oster, Archie Ford, Ralph Terrell, Edward Eberling, Christine Kiesel, Clarence Simonds, Joseph Schwartz, Edward Schneider, Mary Kiesel, Louise Schwartz, Emma Haber, Percy Robinson, Bertha Taft, Andrew Schwartz, Eleanor Terrell, Leland Dorer, Frank Simonds, George Schwartz, Miles Brazie, and Florence Brazie. (Courtesy of Diane Oster.)

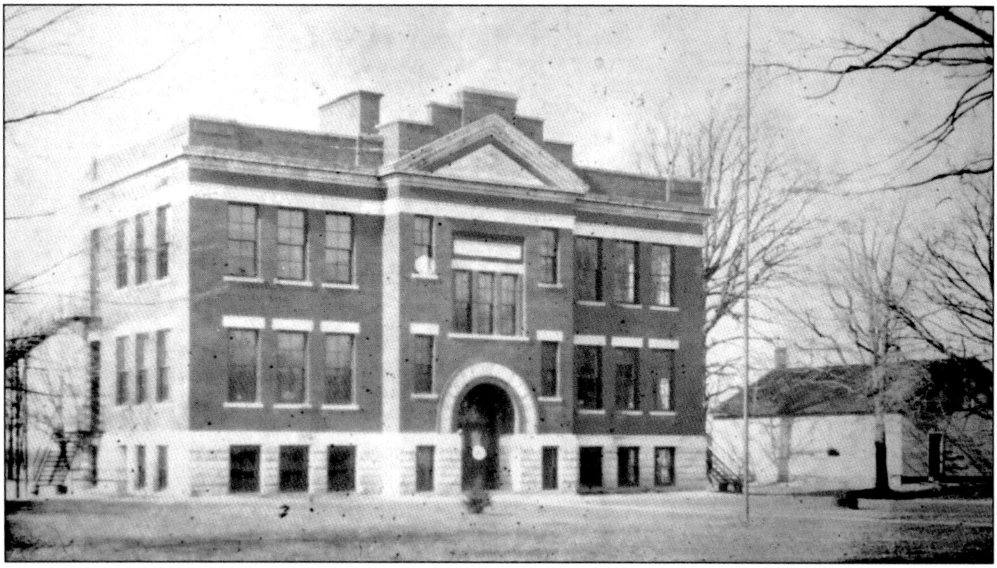

In 1916, Dover became part of the Cuyahoga County School System. The Red Brick School, built in 1909, still stands on Dover Center Road north of Center Ridge Road. (Courtesy of William Robishaw Collection, Westlake Porter Public Library.)

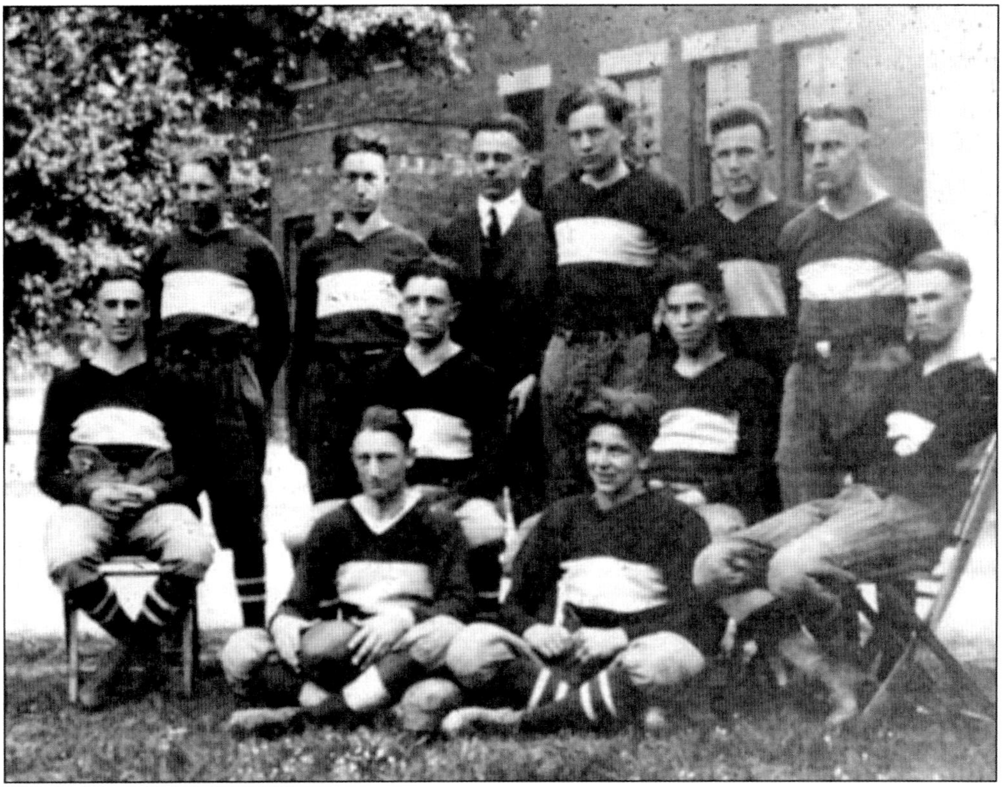

Dover's 1921 high school football team is shown here in uniform. (Courtesy of William Robishaw Collection, Westlake Porter Public Library.)

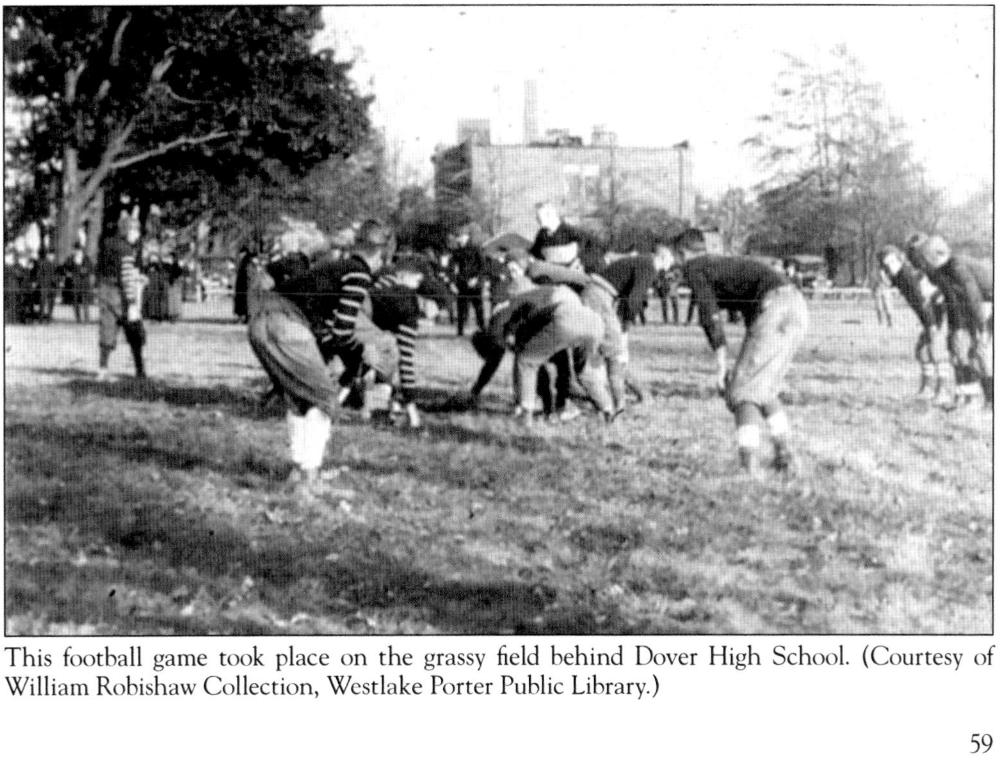

This football game took place on the grassy field behind Dover High School. (Courtesy of William Robishaw Collection, Westlake Porter Public Library.)

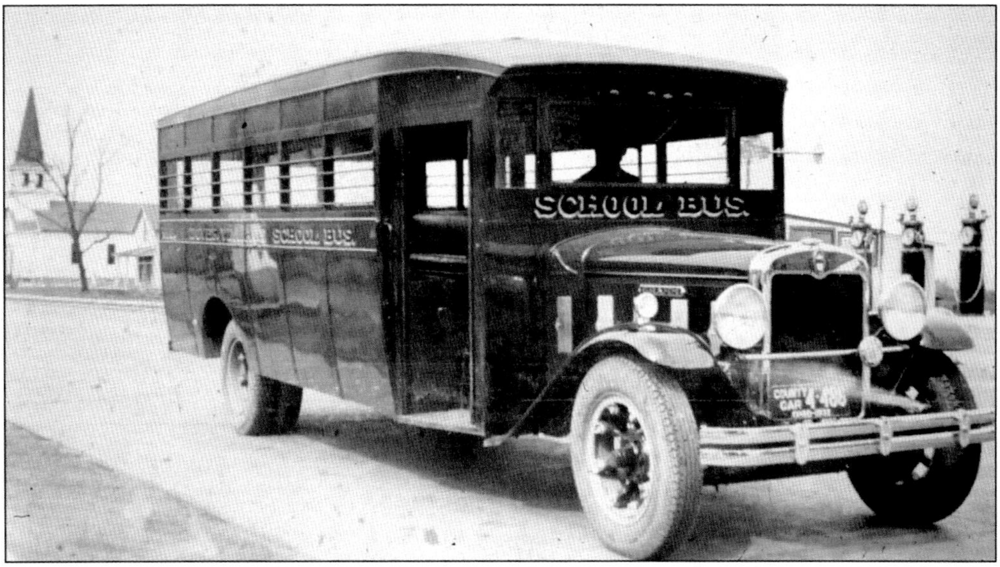

This school bus was driven by George Weston. Weston gave up his job as a North Olmsted, Dover, and Bay Village mail carrier to become the Westlake school's first bus driver, beginning in 1922. He made four trips in the morning and four at night, carrying from 40 to 60 students on each trip. The old Mack bus he drove had a maximum speed of 16 miles per hour. Weston continued farming 10 acres of fruits and vegetables and worked as custodian of the Dover Congregational Church while bus driving. (Courtesy of William Robishaw Collection, Westlake Porter Public Library.)

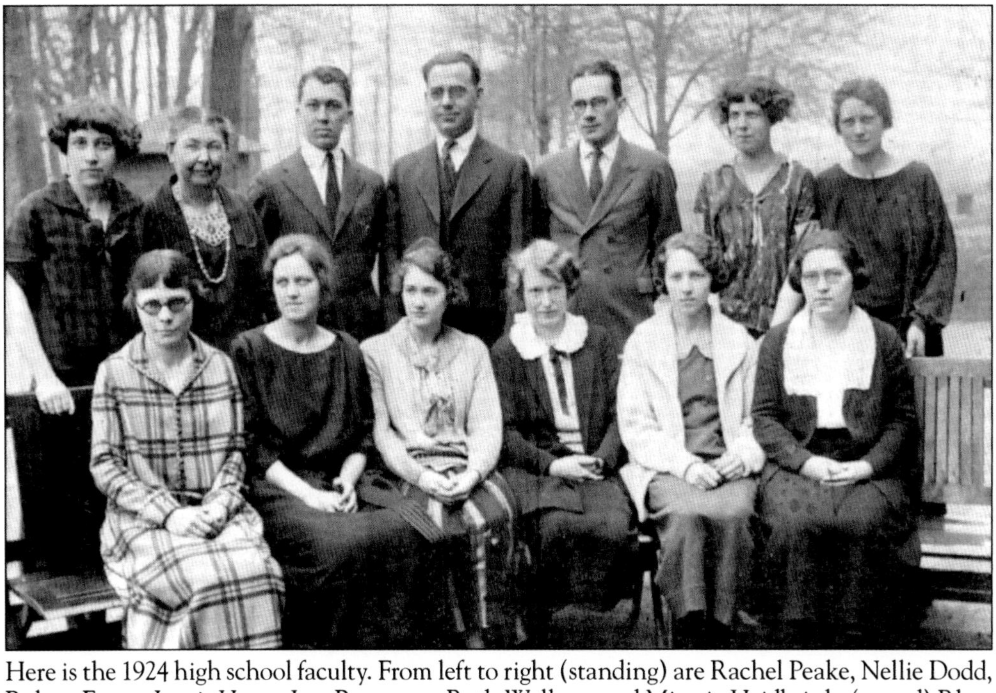

Here is the 1924 high school faculty. From left to right (standing) are Rachel Peake, Nellie Dodd, Robert Foster, Lewis Hayes, Lee Burneson, Ruth Wallace, and Minnie Heidbrink; (seated) Rhea Benedict, Ida Heidbrink, Lucille Martin, Esther Avery, Oleta Shover, and Gladine Shields. (Courtesy of William Robishaw Collection, Westlake Porter Public Library.)

Roger Williams shows his rabbit to classmates at Dover Elementary School in 1953. (Courtesy of Cleveland State University, Cleveland Memory Project, Cleveland Press Collection, Joseph E. Cole, donor.)

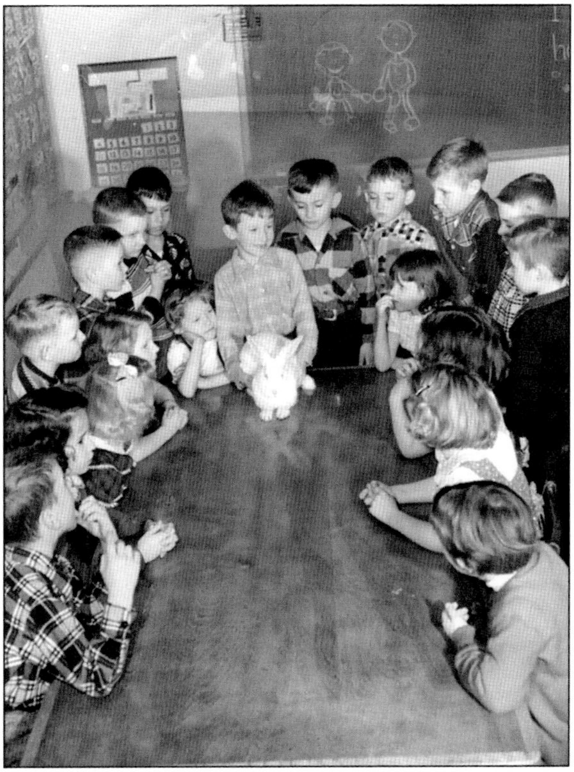

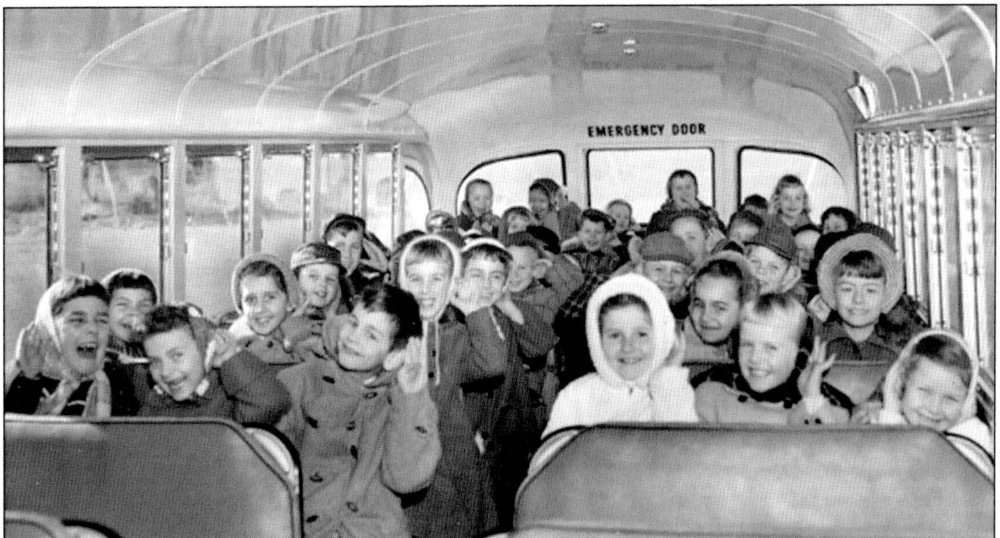

Dover Elementary School's kindergarten and second-grade students listened to soothing music on an experimental bus radio in 1957. Whether due to the music or the photographer's attention, the children wore bright smiles. (Courtesy of Cleveland State University, Cleveland Memory Project, Cleveland Press Collection, Joseph E. Cole, donor.)

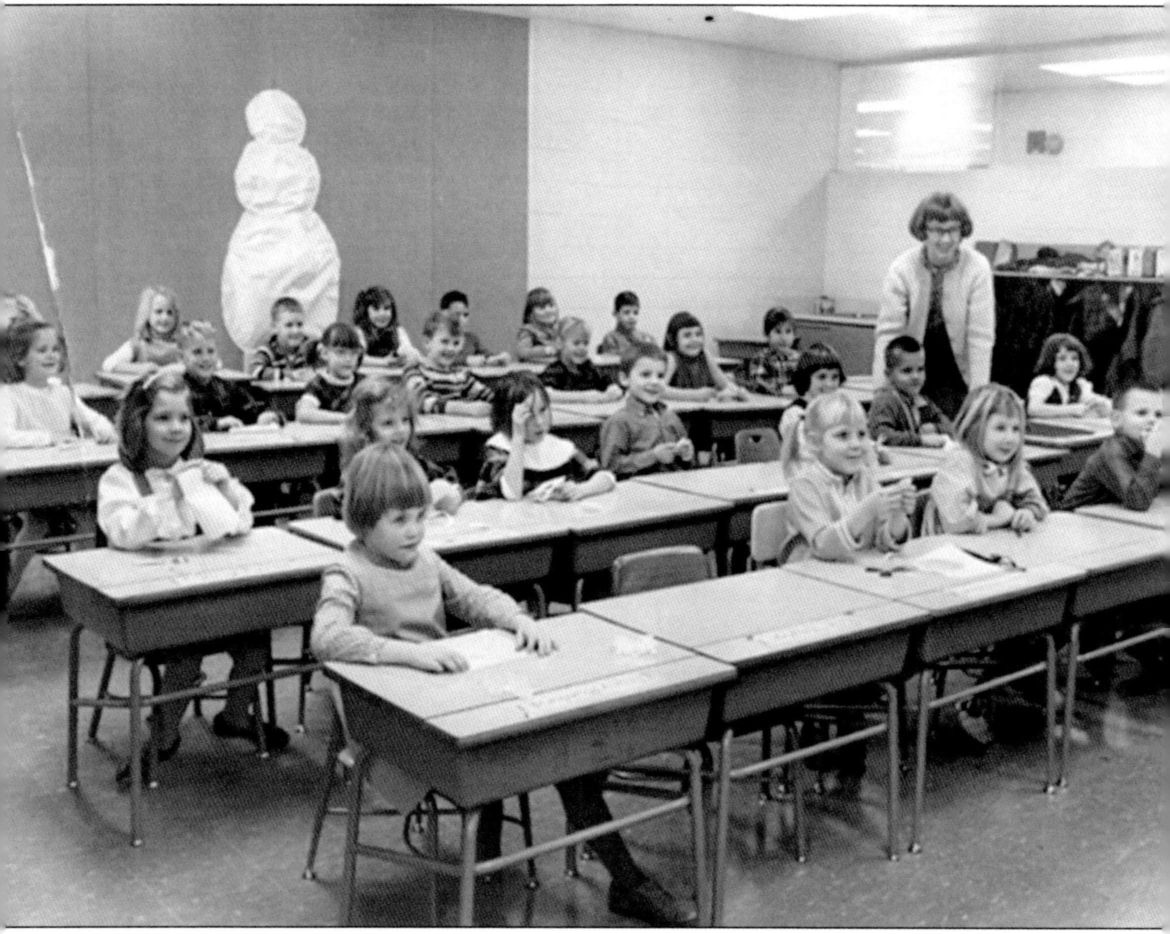

This photograph shows the first day of school at the new Bassett Elementary School in Westlake on January 4, 1968. This is the first-grade room of Virginia Royer. The building had seven teaching stations but had been designed so that future additions would triple its size and potential enrollment. Construction costs were the last funds from a 1963 bond issue. (Courtesy of Cleveland State University, Cleveland Memory Project, Cleveland Press Collection, Joseph E. Cole, donor.)

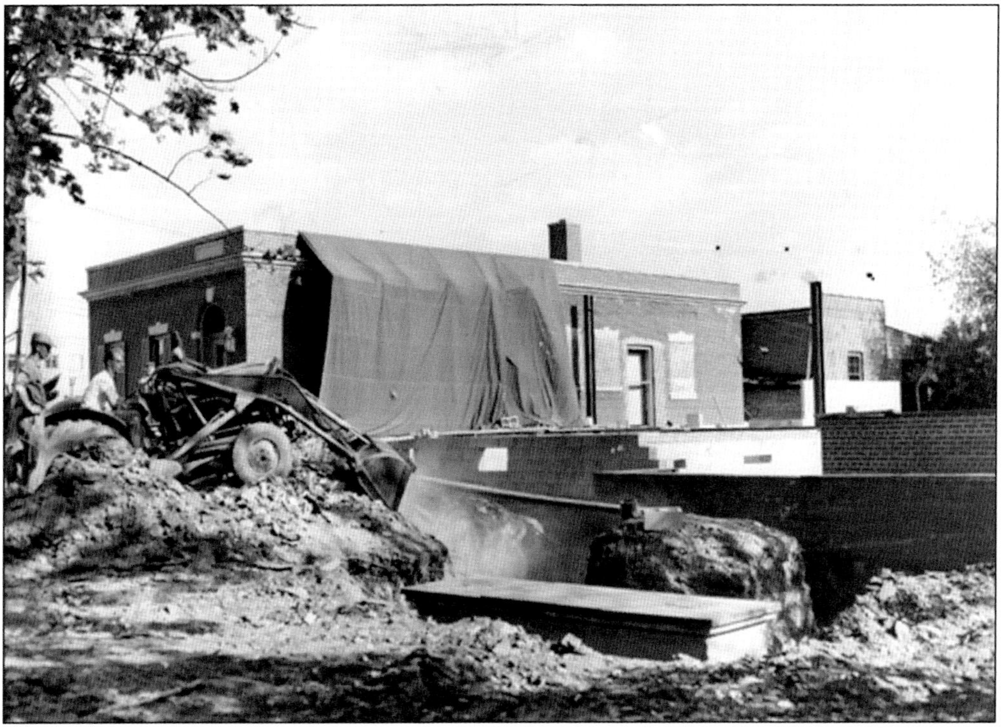

The Westlake Porter Public Library is pictured here in 1958. The photograph shows the building renovation's progress. (Courtesy of Cleveland State University, Cleveland Memory Project, Cleveland Press Collection, Joseph E. Cole, donor.)

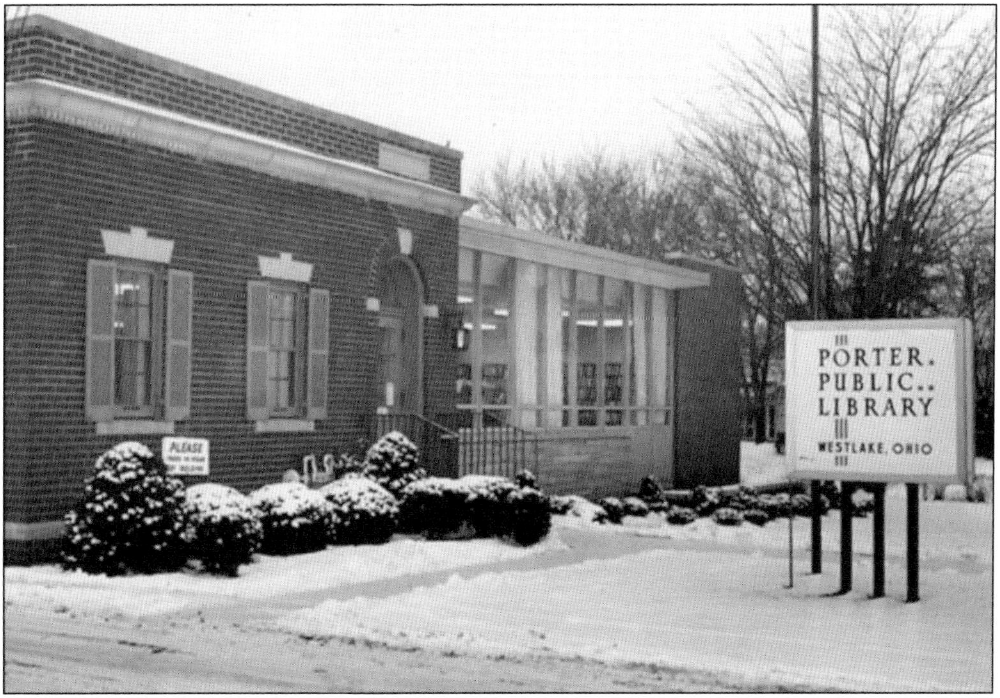

In 1961, the building project was complete. (Courtesy of Westlake Porter Public Library.)

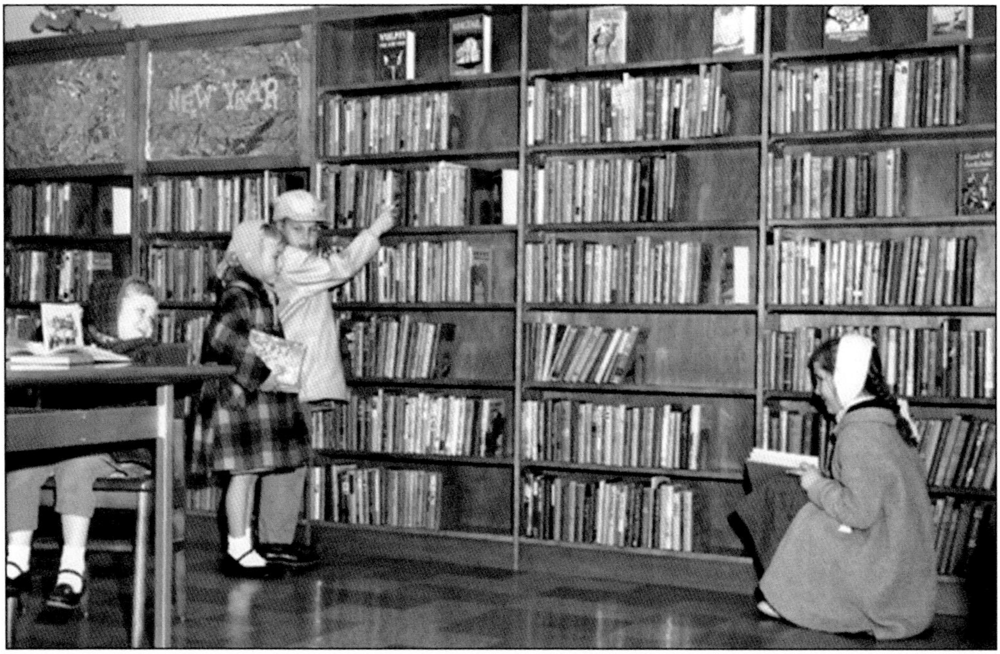

This picture shows the inside of the children's area at Westlake Porter Public Library in 1961. Shown from left to right are Debra Aldrich, Jill Dix, Ann Dix, and Catherine Aldrich. (Courtesy of Cleveland State University, Cleveland Memory Project, Cleveland Press Collection, Joseph E. Cole, donor.)

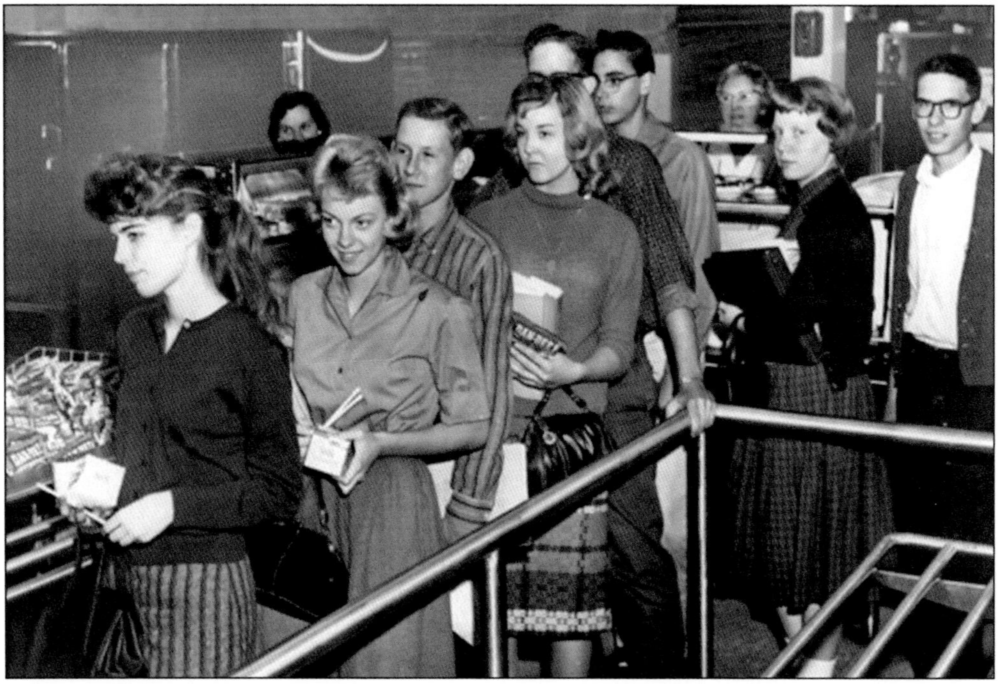

Students are waiting in the lunch line in the Westlake High School cafeteria on November 15, 1961. (Courtesy of Cleveland State University, Cleveland Memory Project, Cleveland Press Collection, Joseph E. Cole, donor.)

Can-can dancers perform for the high school musical in 1961. From left to right are Sharon Brown, Charlotte Wilford, and Pamela Saunders. (Courtesy of Cleveland State University, Cleveland Memory Project, Cleveland Press Collection, Joseph E. Cole, donor.)

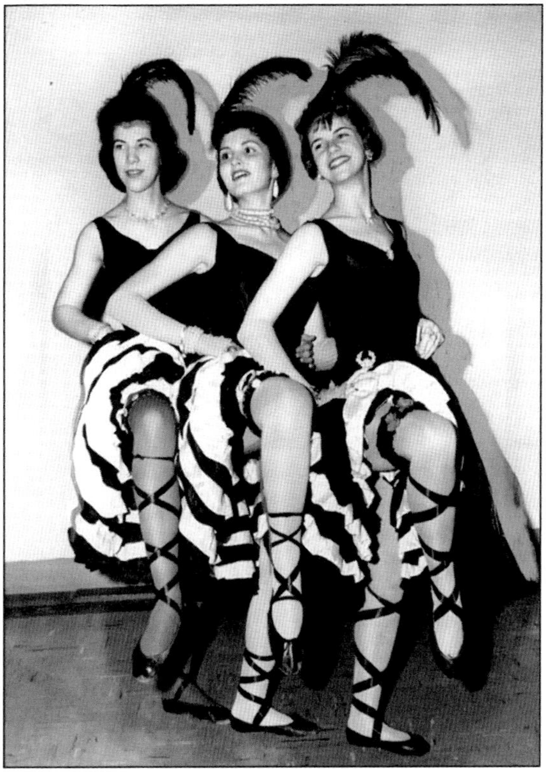

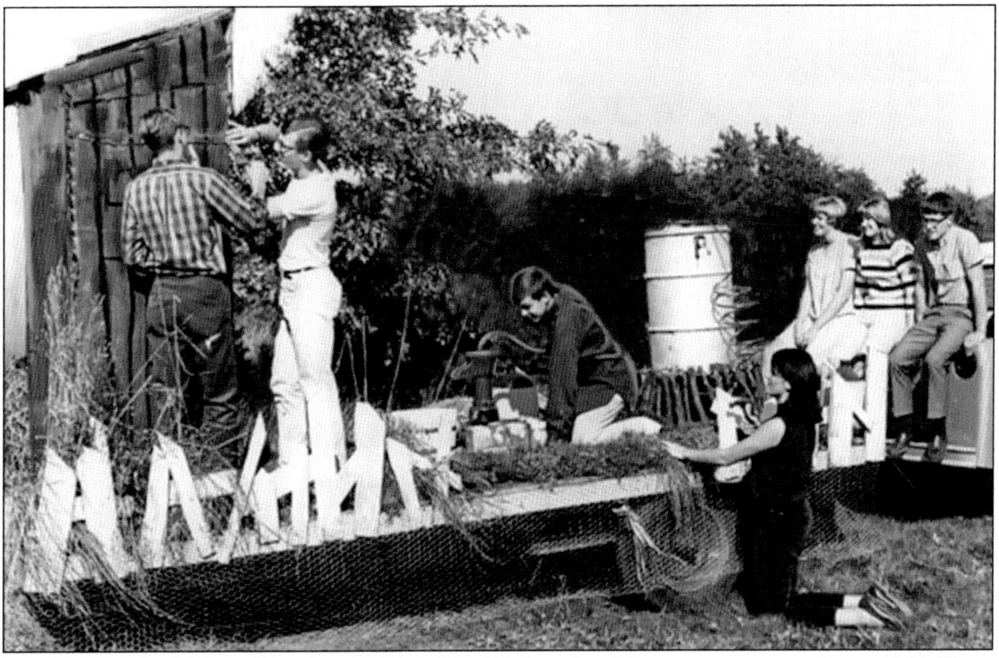

Students are building a float for the Westlake High School homecoming parade in 1966. From left to right are Larry Hiller, Eric Demerling, Rick Nelsen, Dede Ward, Linda Marvin, Vicki Reynolds, and Dave Thomas. (Courtesy of Cleveland State University, Cleveland Memory Project, Cleveland Press Collection, Joseph E. Cole, donor.)

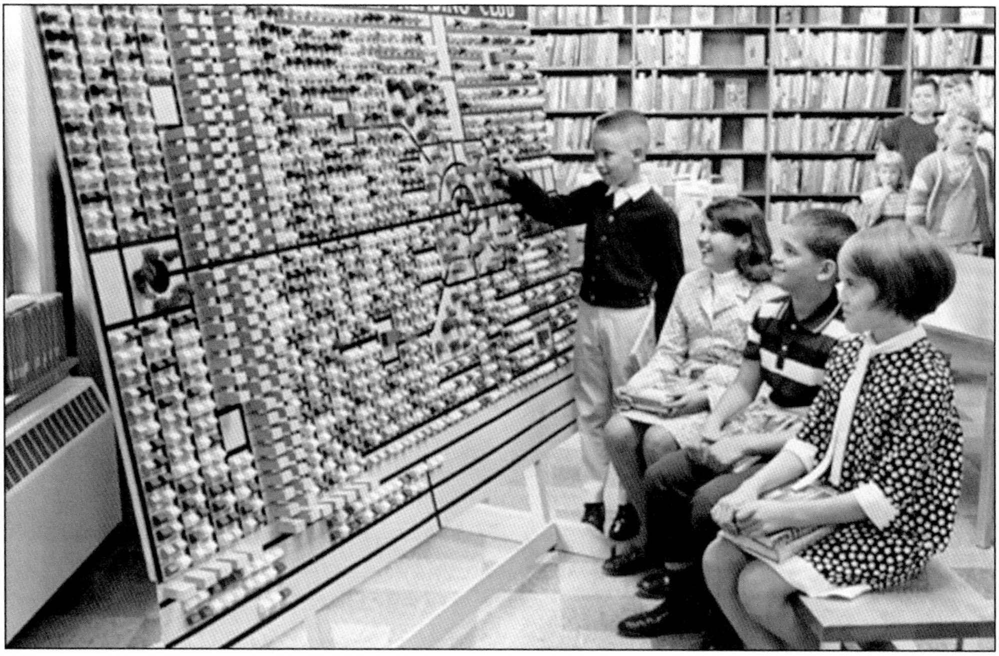

This picture shows Westlake Porter Public Library's Build a City summer reading program in 1967. Pictured from left to right are Jeffrey Holter, Annette Baluk, Paul Stanca, and Laura Swann. (Courtesy of Cleveland State University, Cleveland Memory Project, Cleveland Press Collection, Joseph E. Cole, donor.)

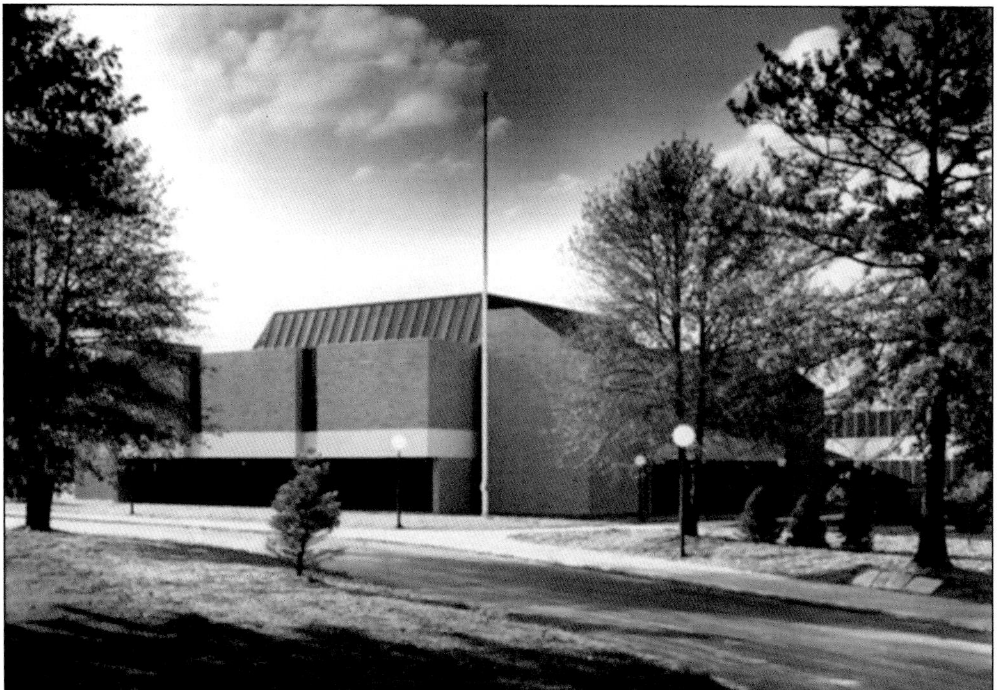

Westlake High School is shown here in 1970. (Courtesy of Cleveland State University, Cleveland Memory Project, Cleveland Press Collection, Joseph E. Cole, donor.)

Five

THE CITY'S FINEST

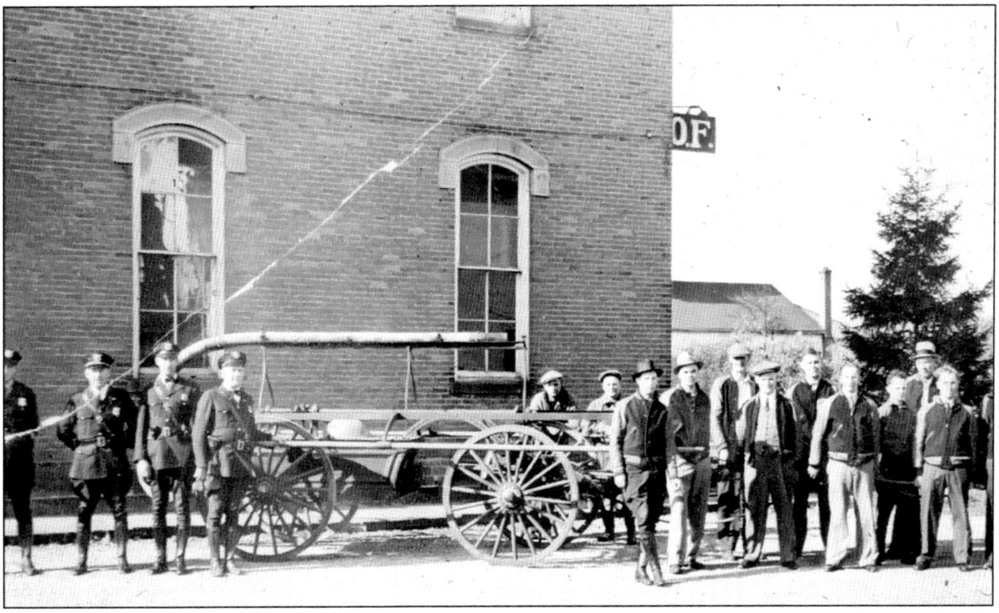

The hand-pump brigade is shown here in front of the old town hall. (Courtesy of William Robishaw Collection, Westlake Porter Public Library.)

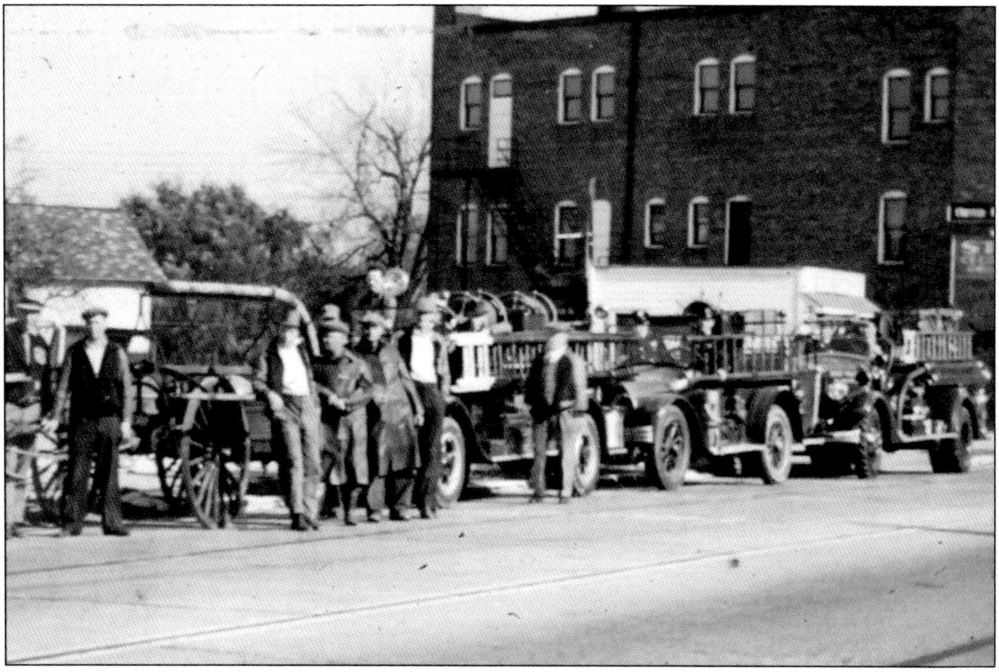

Early fire brigade volunteers participate in a parade on Center Ridge Road. (Courtesy of William Robishaw Collection, Westlake Porter Public Library.)

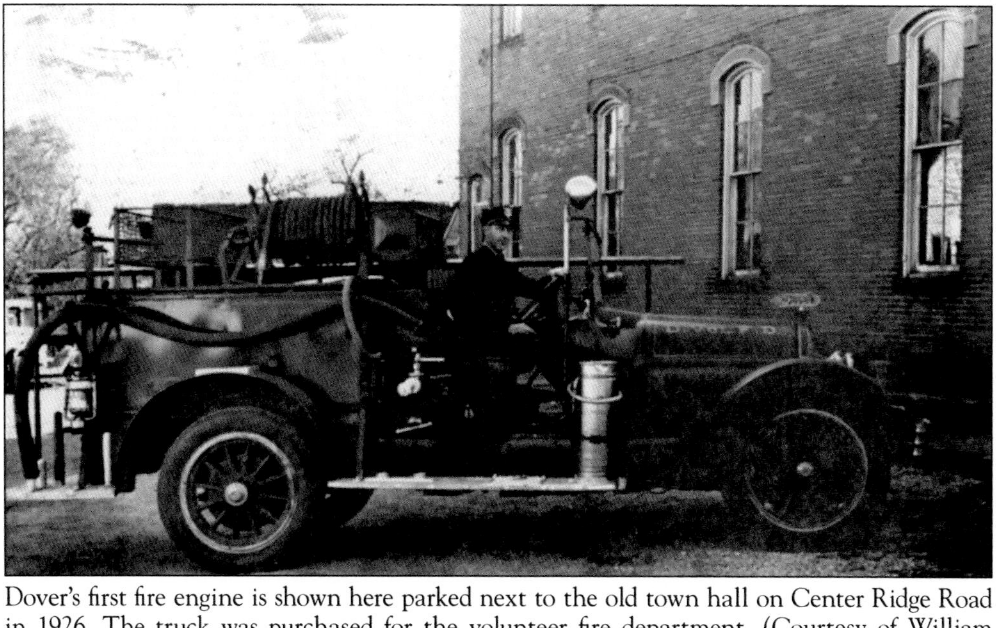

Dover's first fire engine is shown here parked next to the old town hall on Center Ridge Road in 1926. The truck was purchased for the volunteer fire department. (Courtesy of William Robishaw Collection, Westlake Porter Public Library.)

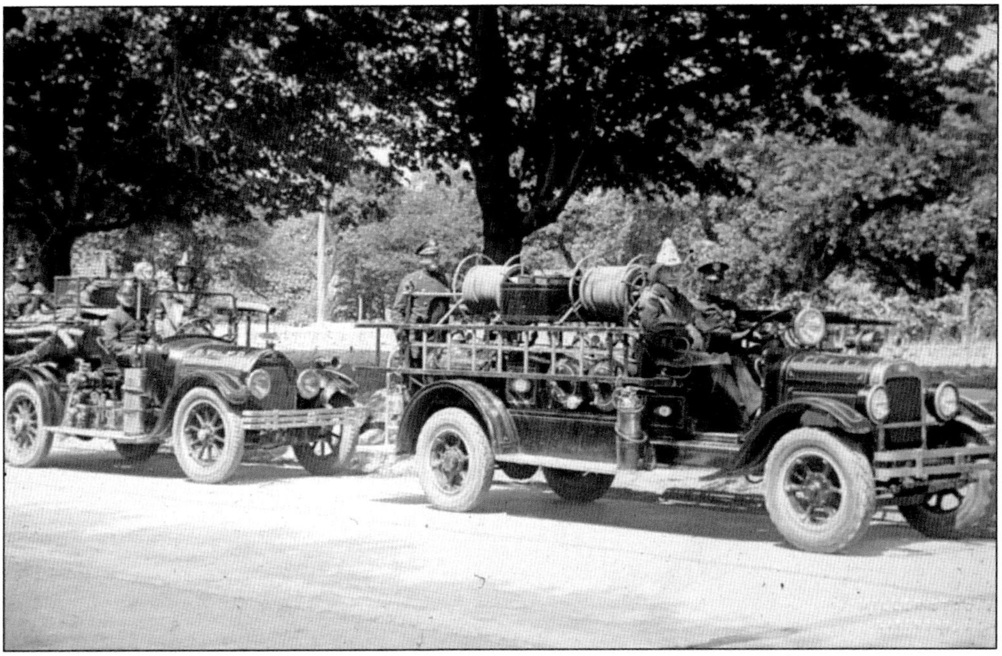

This photograph of the Dover Village Fire Department equipment was taken in 1929. Dover's first fire truck was purchased in 1926. The second fire truck was purchased in 1927. (Courtesy of William Robishaw Collection, Westlake Porter Public Library.)

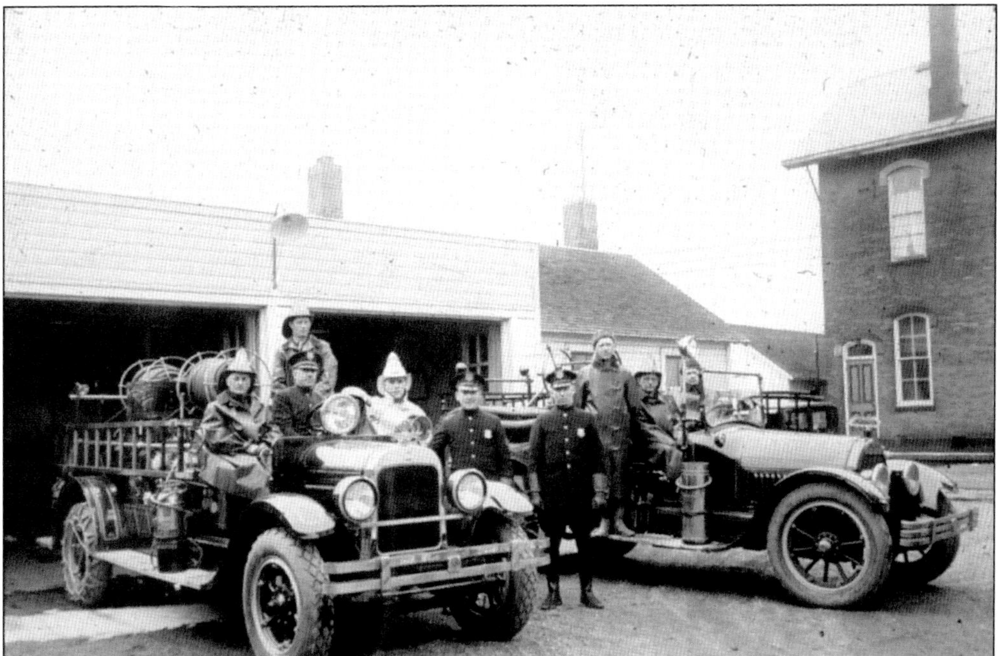

The fire trucks were prepared for action and equipped with ready volunteers. (Courtesy of William Robishaw Collection, Westlake Porter Public Library.)

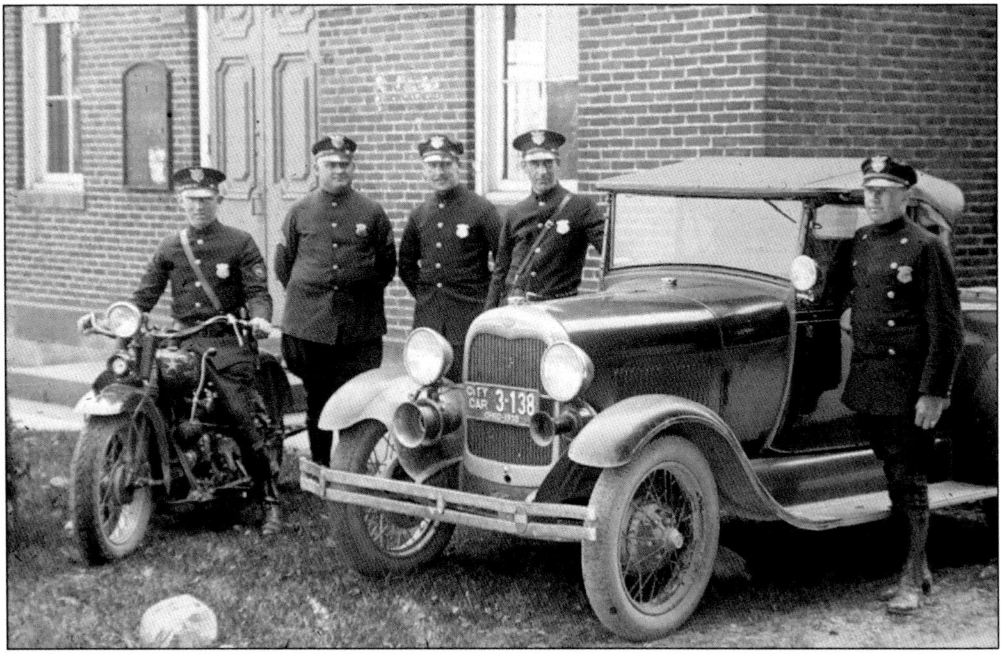

The Dover Village police car of preference was a Model A Ford coupe. Pictured around 1929, the police officers from left to right are Norm Hunger, Eugene Albers, Clarence Grube, Dewey Bailey, and Edwin Hille. (Courtesy of William Robishaw Collection, Westlake Porter Public Library.)

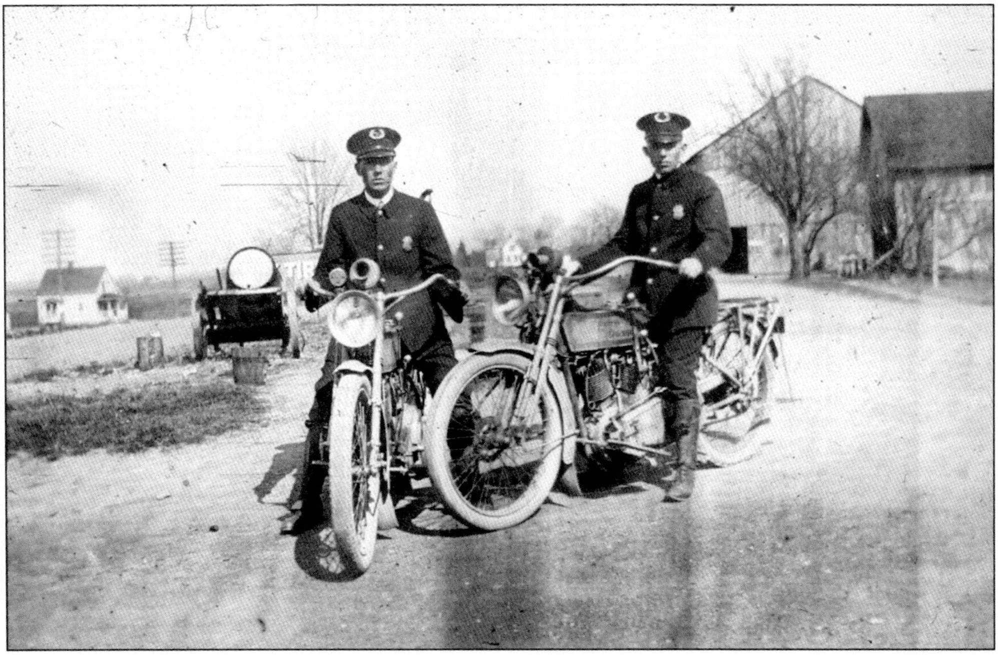

The two motorcycle policemen in this photograph are unidentified. (Courtesy of William Robishaw Collection, Westlake Porter Public Library.)

Edwin Hille served with Chief George Jackson. He was a police officer and a sergeant and then became chief of police before retiring in 1954. He died in 1986 and is buried in Lakewood Park Cemetery in Rocky River. (Courtesy of William Robishaw Collection, Westlake Porter Public Library.)

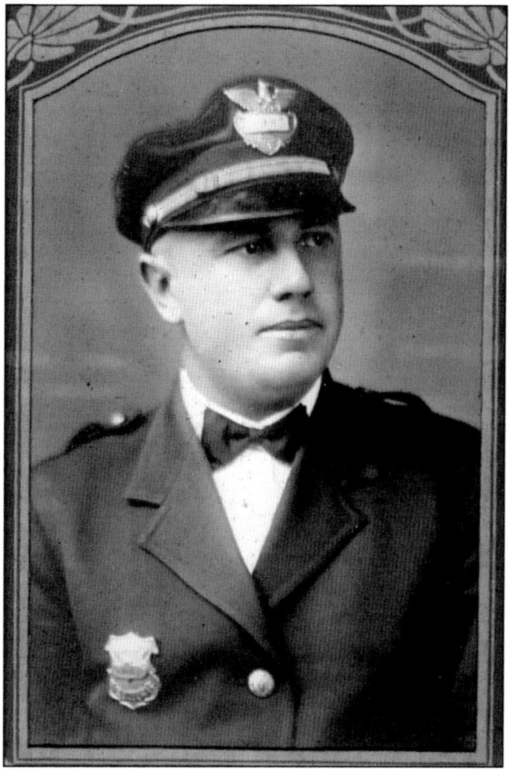

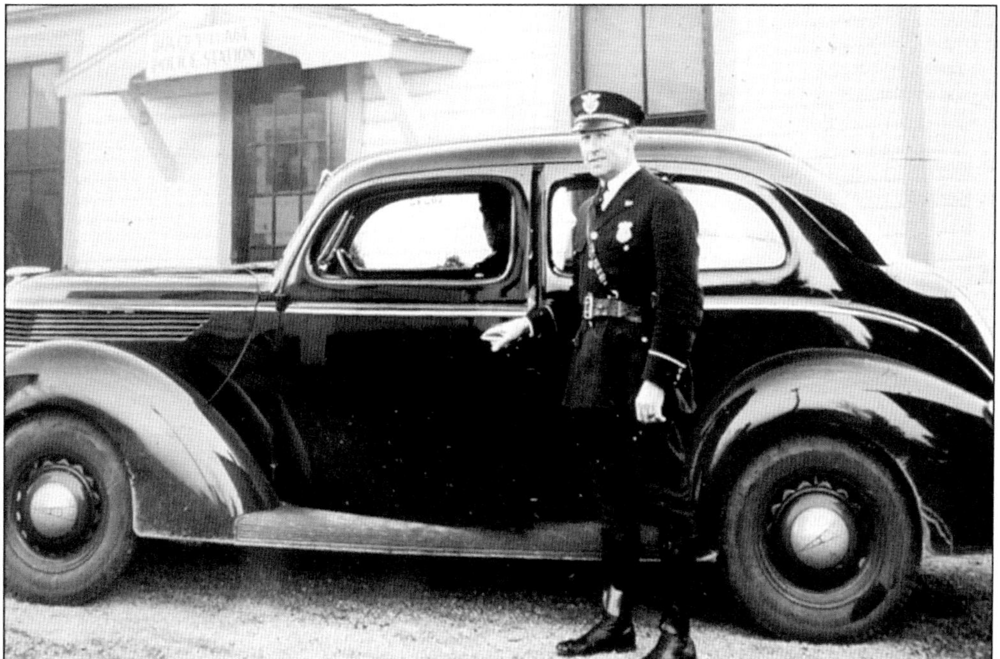

Sgt. Edwin Hille poses in front of the police car at the Dover Police Station. (Courtesy of William Robishaw Collection, Westlake Porter Public Library.)

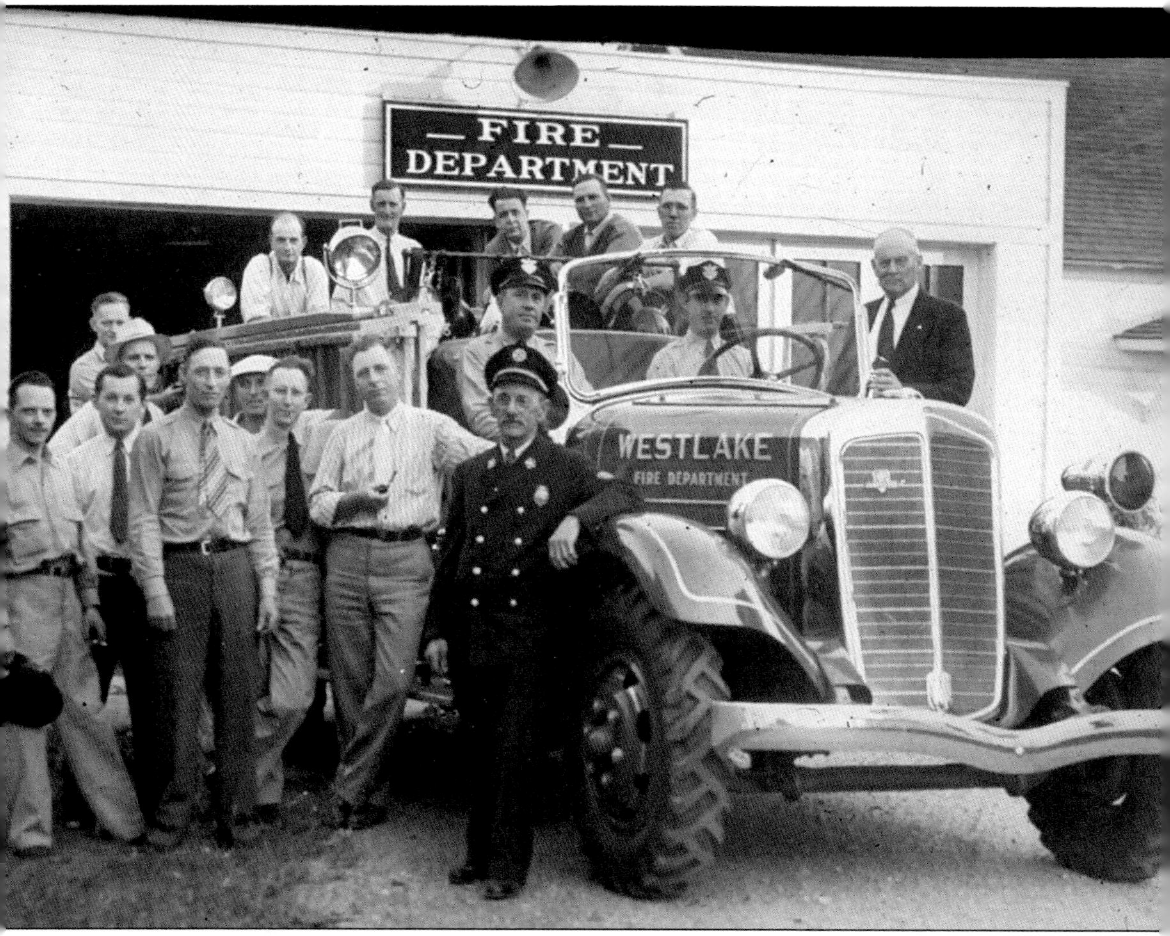

The fire engine, an Ahrens-Fox, was the first real pumper in Westlake. It was purchased for $7,000 and was capable of pumping 980 gallons of water per minute. Members of the Dover Village Fire Department gathered in 1938 for this picture. From left to right are (first row) Bill Ulmer, Gil Burkey, George Jackson, Pete Gorski, Harry Bailey, Sylvanus Phinney, Herb Aring, Howard Tanner, and Fire Chief Frank Sauer; (second row) Bert Phinney, John Ingersoll, Mike Cornish, Nelson Bailey, Melvin Jenkins, and Mayor Edward E. Campbell. Dewey Bailey is behind the wheel, and Edwin Hille is seated beside him. (Courtesy of William Robishaw Collection, Westlake Porter Public Library.)

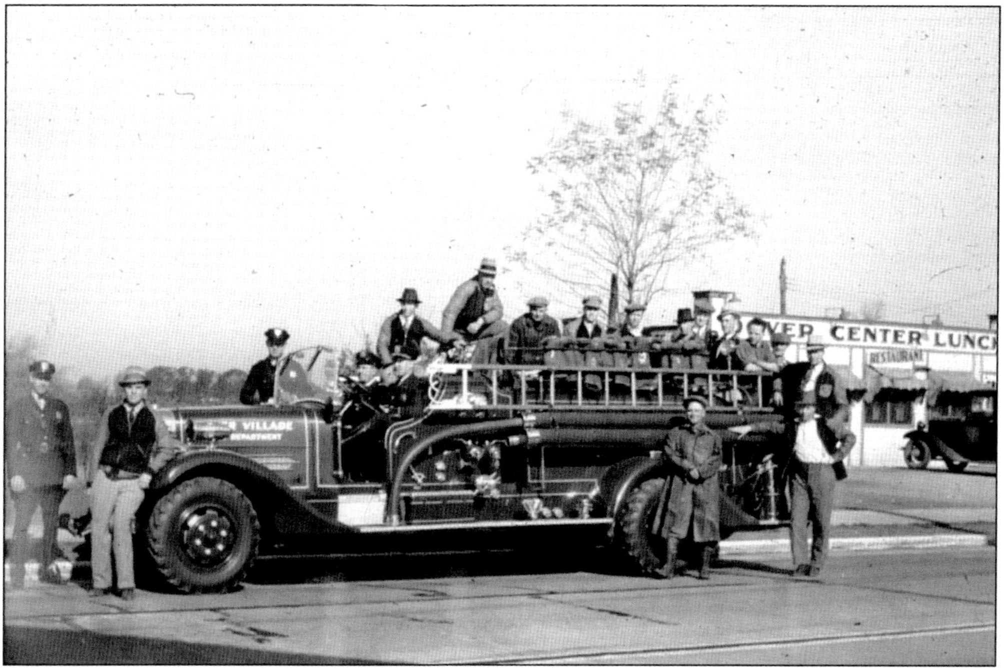

Another view of the new Dover Village fire truck is shown here. The photograph participants are unidentified. (Courtesy of William Robishaw Collection, Westlake Porter Public Library.)

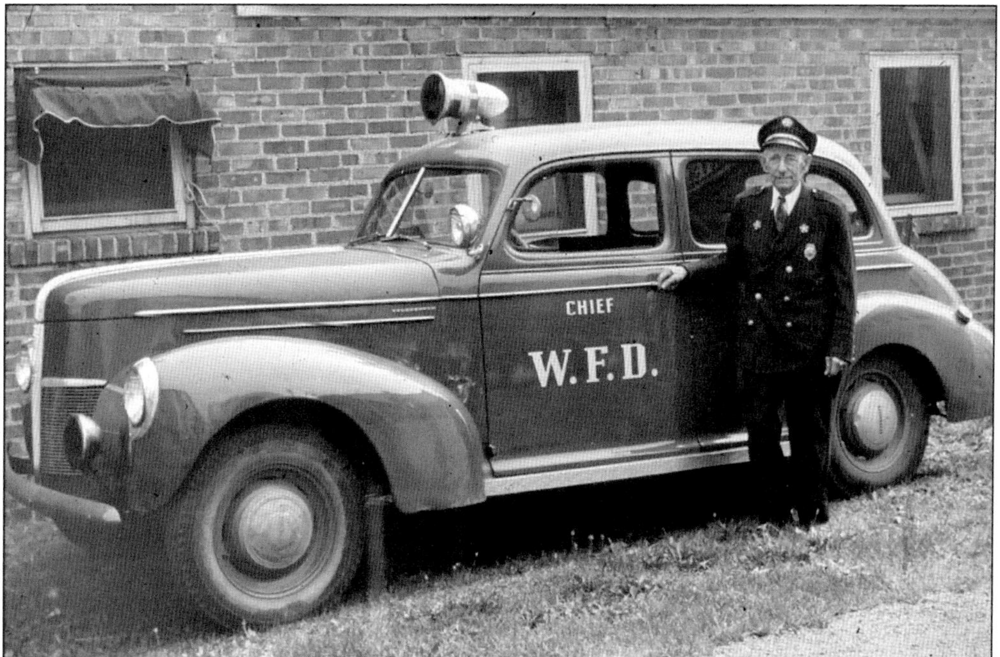

Sauer poses in front of this Studebaker, the official vehicle of the Westlake Fire Department, in 1935. (Courtesy of William Robishaw Collection, Westlake Porter Public Library.)

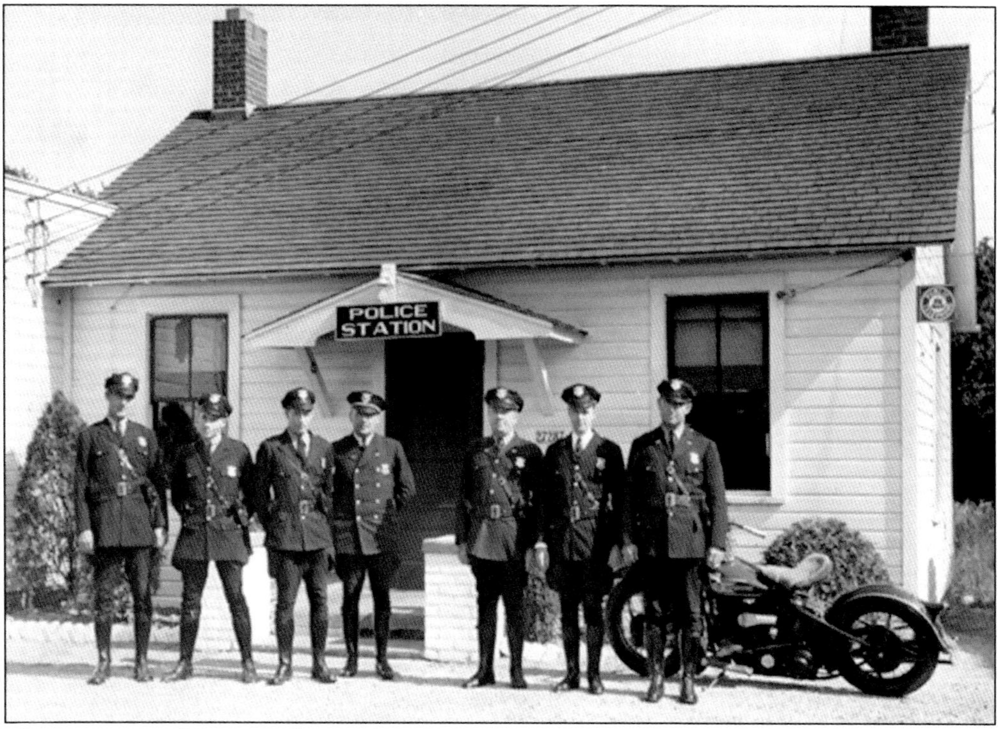

These pictures of Dover Village policemen were taken in 1941. Pictured from left to right are Dewey Bailey, Ralph Sinzinger, Harry Bailey, Chief Clarence Grube, Edwin Hille, Maurice Heston, and Robert Prechtel. The address of 27287 on the station locates the building just behind the Porter Library. (Courtesy of William Robishaw Collection, Westlake Porter Public Library.)

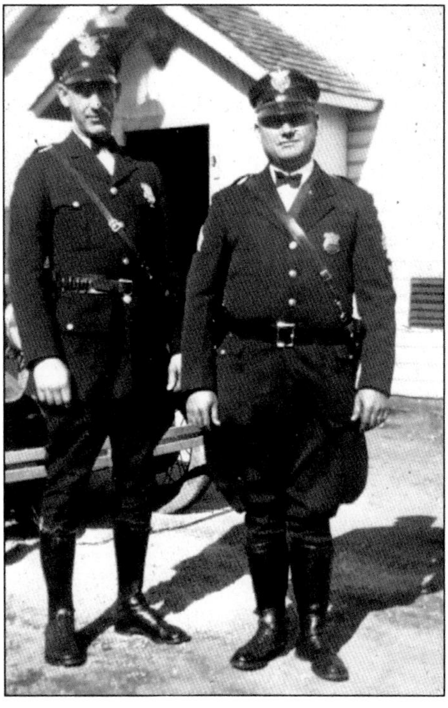

Two of Dover's finest policemen pose in front of the police station. (Courtesy of William Robishaw Collection, Westlake Porter Public Library.)

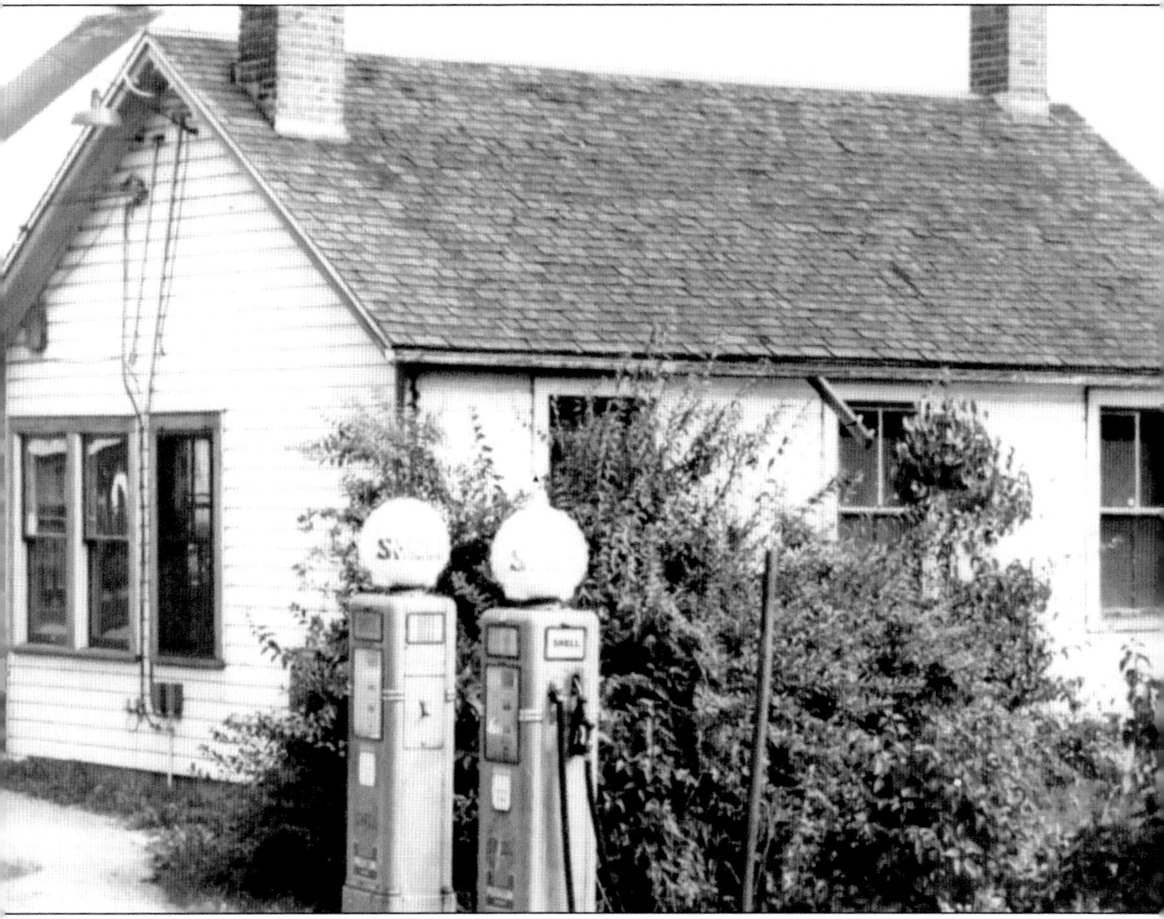

A back view of the Westlake Police Department is shown here. The gasoline pumps were used to service police and fire city vehicles. (Courtesy of George Jindra.)

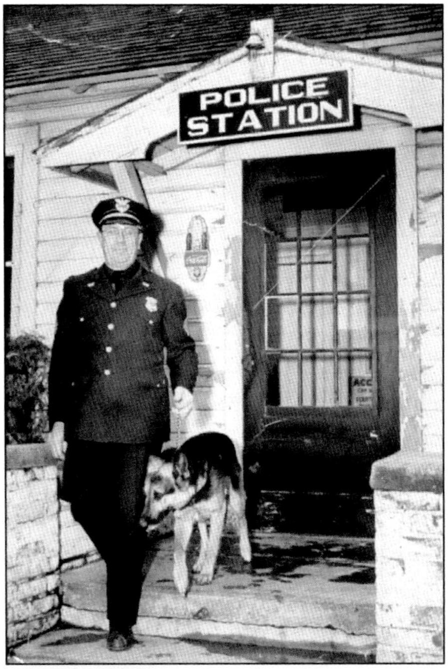

Police officer Edwin Hille starts his rounds with one of Westlake's canine corps used during the World War II era. (Courtesy of William Robishaw Collection, Westlake Porter Public Library.)

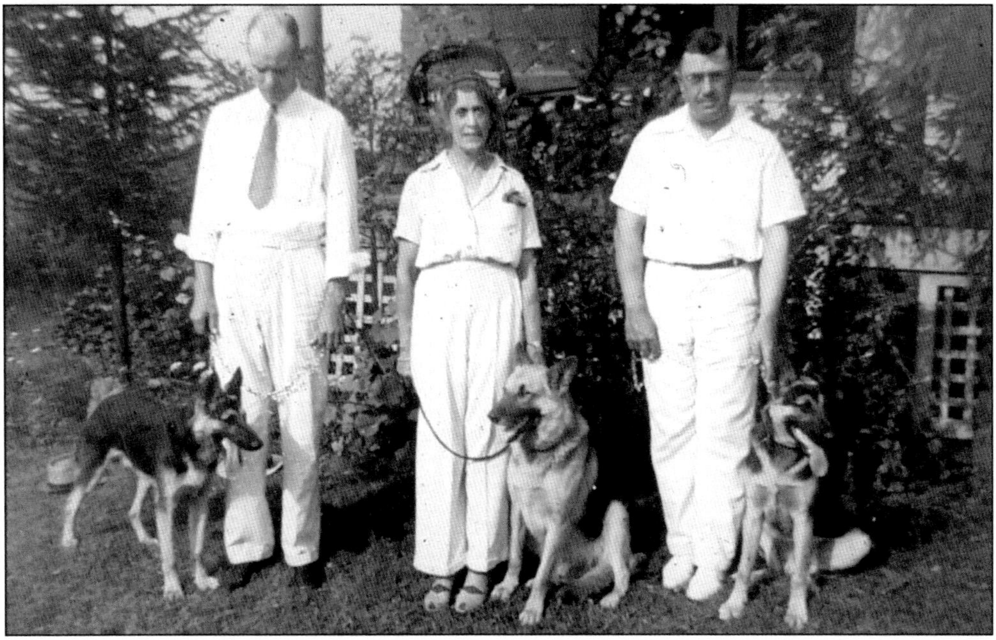

The owner of the Beach Cliff Kennels, Irma Werner, donated three German shepherd puppies to the police department. They were trained as the Westlake Police Canine Corps. While the dogs were officially owned by the city of Westlake, the individual policemen to whom they were given cared for them. Chief George Jackson's dog was named Victory. Officer Robert Prechtel cared for Defense. Officer Ralph Sinzinger cared for Liberty, all fitting names for the war era. The puppies were sired by Champion Schatz and Beach Cliff Kennels' Trudi. Like the Germans who used dogs in their armed forces, the Westlake Police Force intended to teach the dogs to work for the policemen who cared for them. (Courtesy of William Robishaw Collection, Westlake Porter Public Library.)

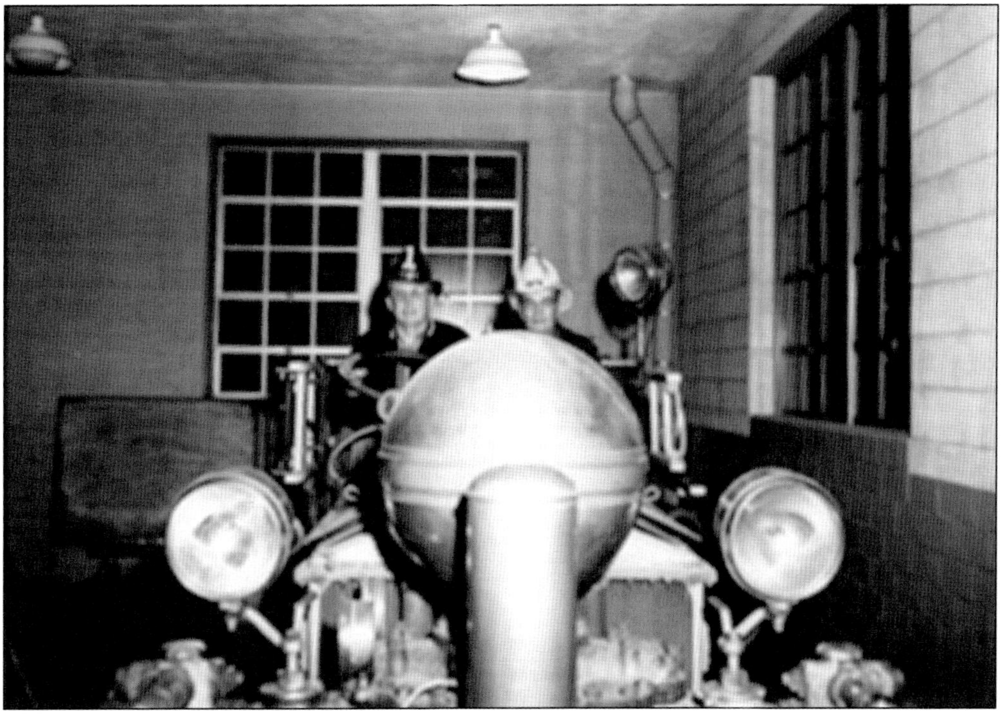

Ollie Dietz (left), a Westlake firefighter, is seated in the fire engine. The other firefighter is unidentified. (Courtesy of Bill Dietz.)

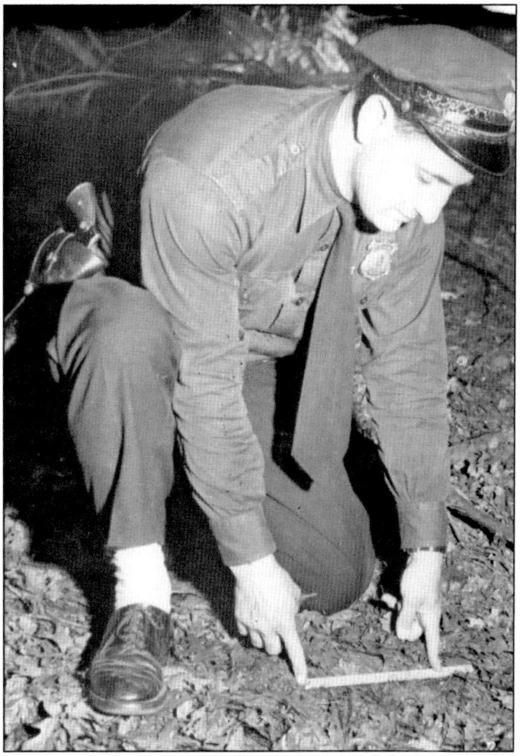

Officer Tony Bisceglia is at the scene of a crime measuring footprints. (Courtesy of George Jindra.)

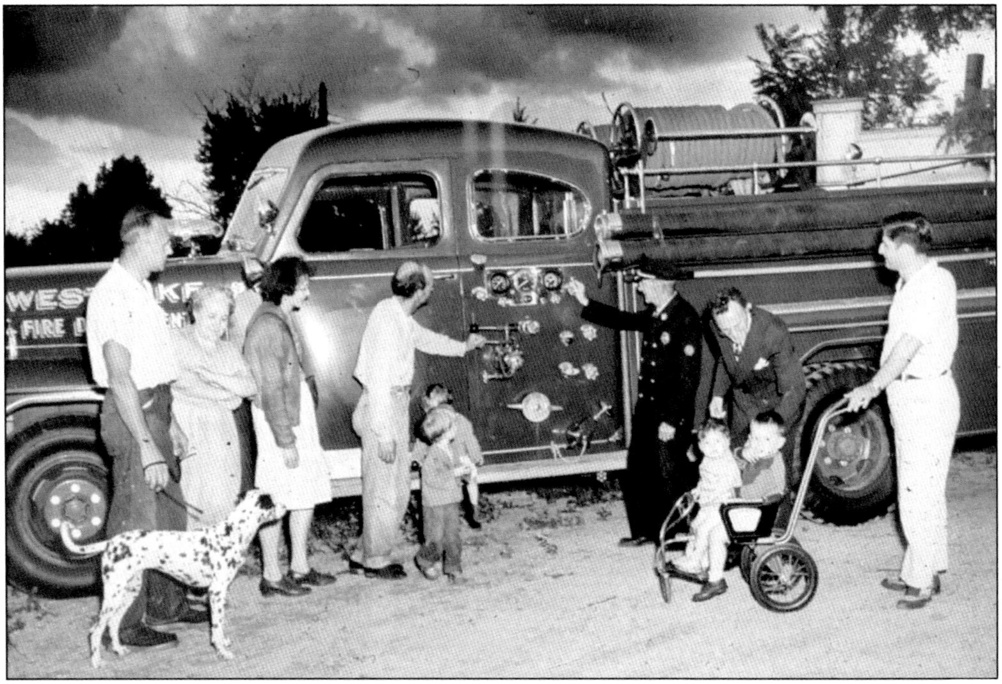

This 1945 picture shows Fire Chief Frank Sauer standing in front of a Dover fire truck. The hose was available from the top of the truck. Additional equipment was accessed from the driver's side. (Courtesy of William Robishaw Collection, Westlake Porter Public Library.)

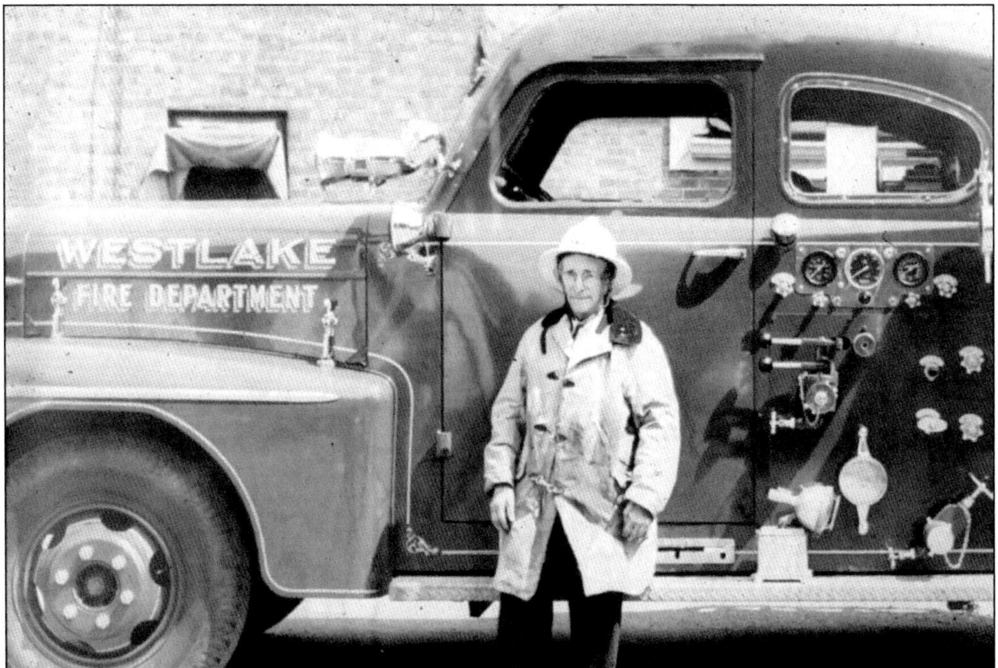

Chief Sauer is dressed in firemen's gear, including a protective helmet. (Courtesy of William Robishaw Collection, Westlake Porter Public Library.)

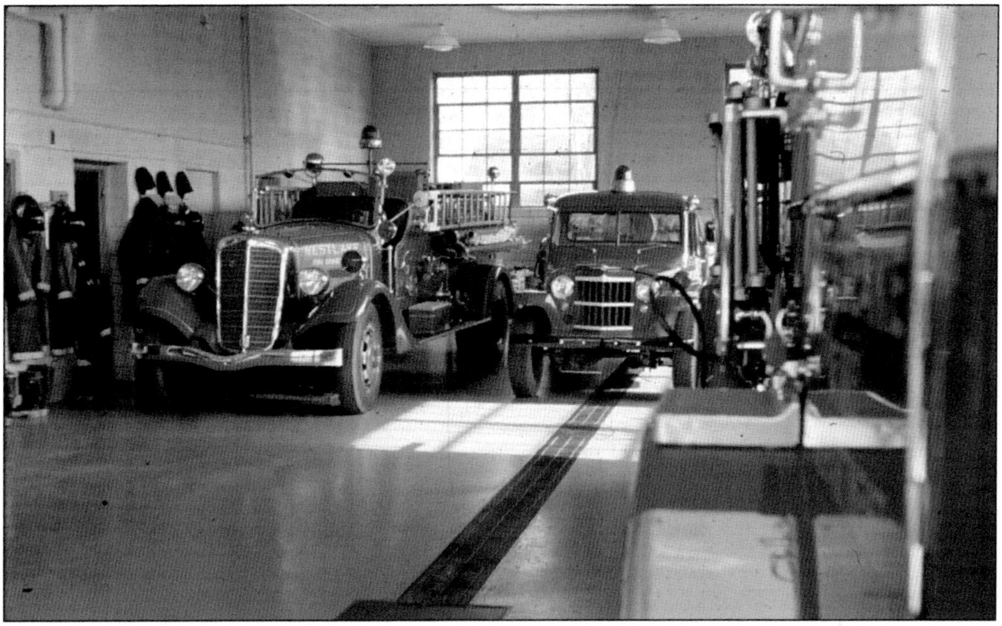

Here is an inside view of the fire station. In 1955, the fire department moved into the new municipal building at Dover and Hilliard Roads. Three full-time firemen worked with the fire chief, and by 1959, there were 11 full-time and 13 part-time firemen on the staff. Edmund Geiger followed Frank Sauer as chief in 1959. (Courtesy of William Robishaw Collection, Westlake Porter Public Library.)

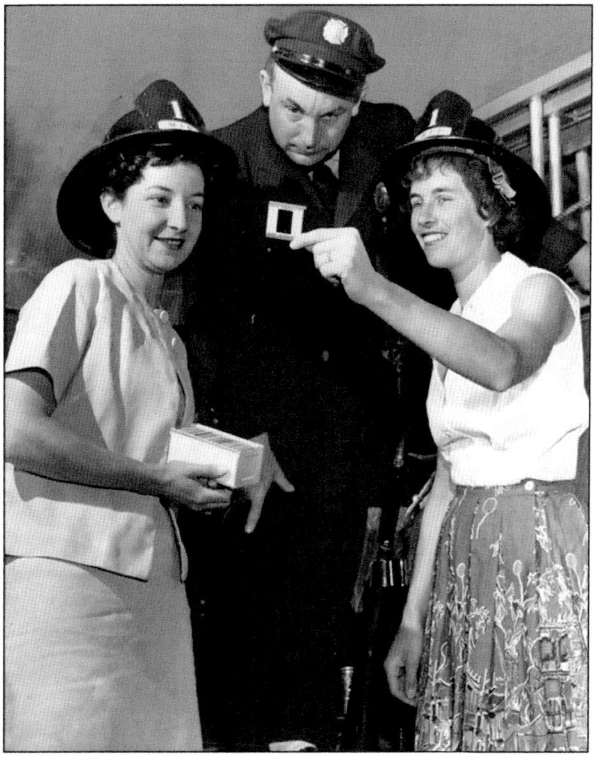

In 1959, the Westlake Fire Safety Program was sponsored by the Westlake Junior Women's Club. Here they discuss what to do in case of fires in the home. Ann Hansen (left), Chief Geiger, and Jean Fromm are pictured. (Courtesy of Cleveland State University, Cleveland Memory Project, Cleveland Press Collection, Joseph E. Cole, donor.)

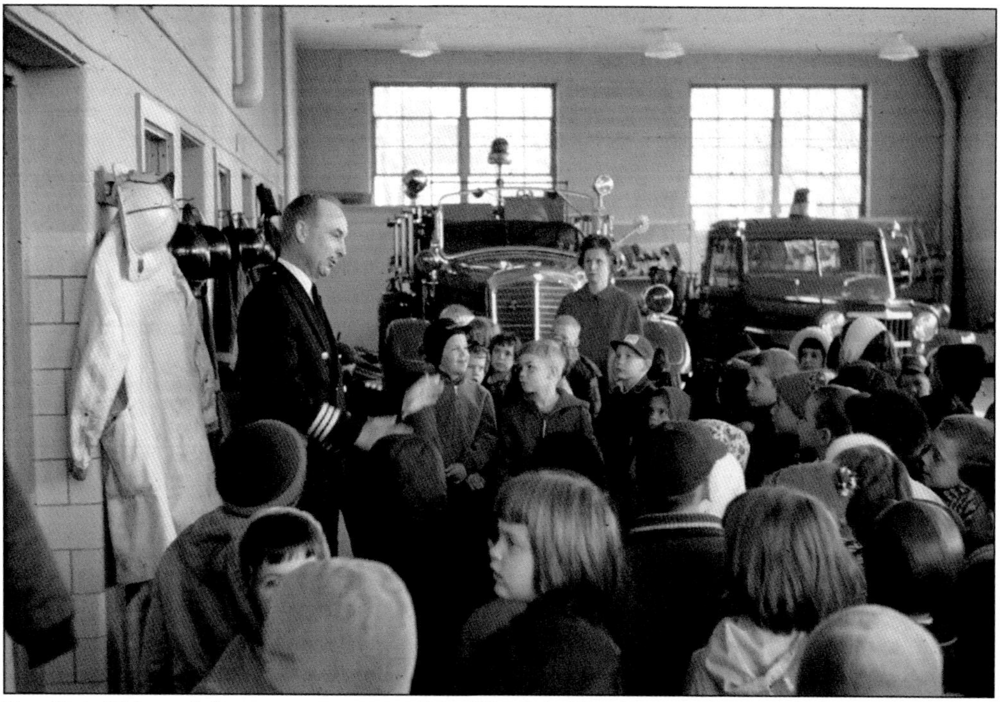

Fire Chief Edmund Geiger gives a tour of the Westlake Fire Department, and elementary school students learn about fire safety. (Courtesy of Westlake Fire Department.)

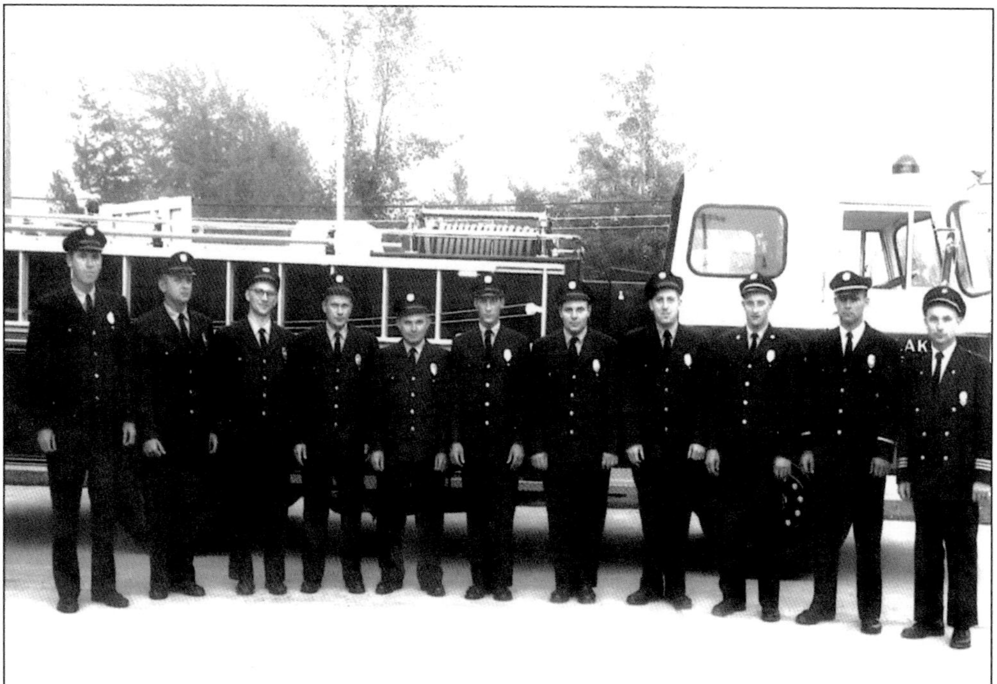

Chief Geiger (far right) and his men are pictured. Geiger retired in 1980, and Robert Patton succeeded him. (Courtesy of William Robishaw Collection, Westlake Porter Public Library.)

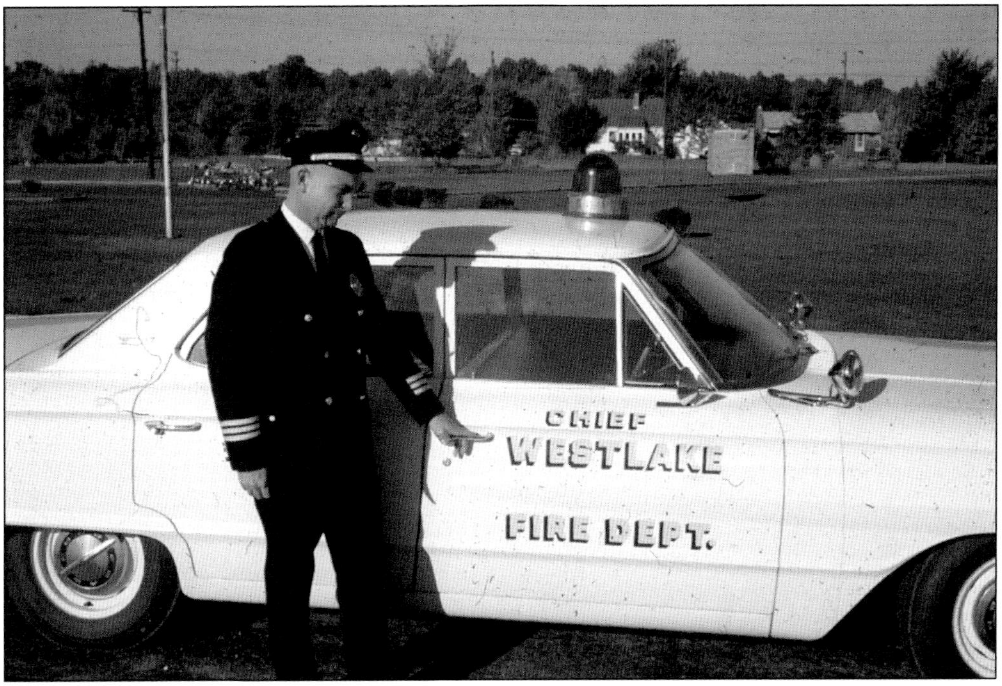

Chief Edmund Geiger stands in front of the official fire chief vehicle in 1960. (Courtesy of John Kish, Westlake Fire Department.)

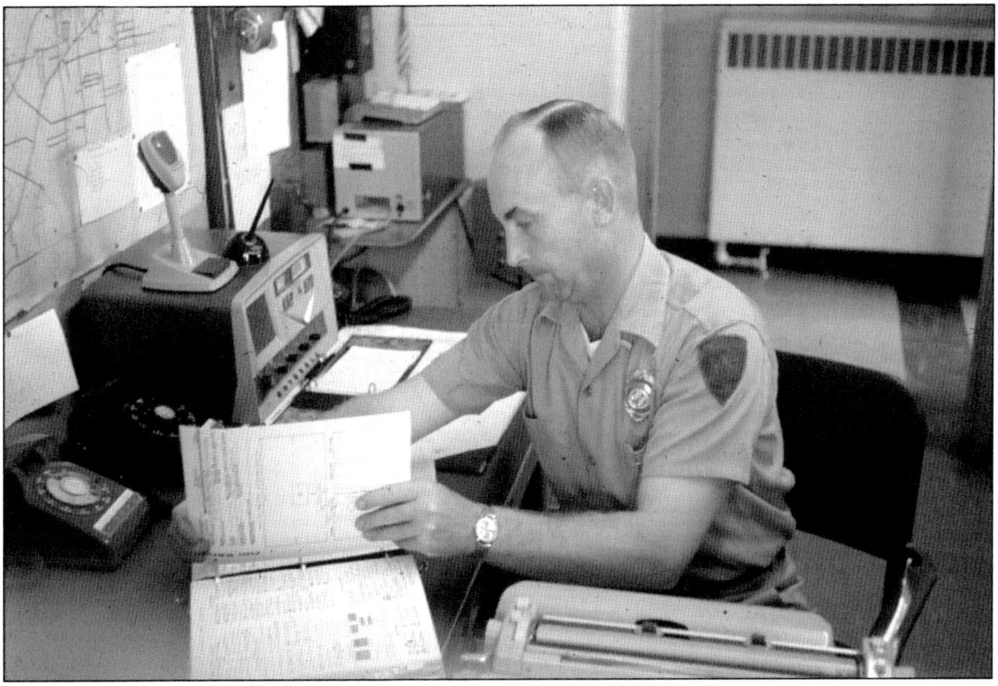
Chief Geiger is pictured here in the police radio room. (Courtesy of John Kish, Westlake Fire Department.)

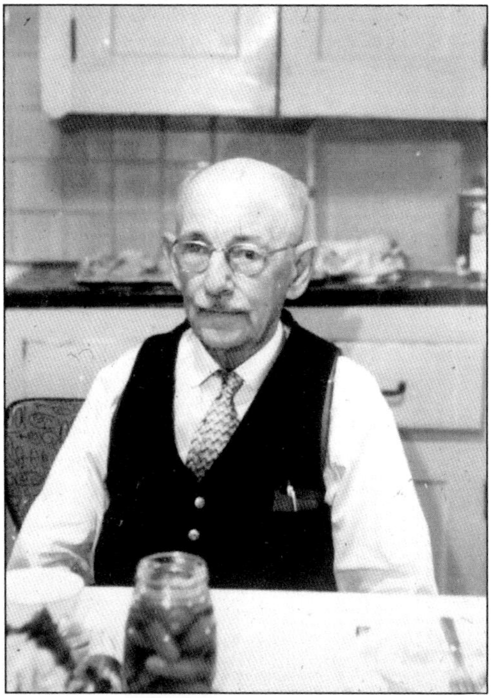

Frank Sauer is seated at the fire station kitchen table at left. Sauer remained fire chief from 1937 to 1966, when he retired at the age of 83. (Courtesy of William Robishaw Collection, Westlake Porter Public Library.)

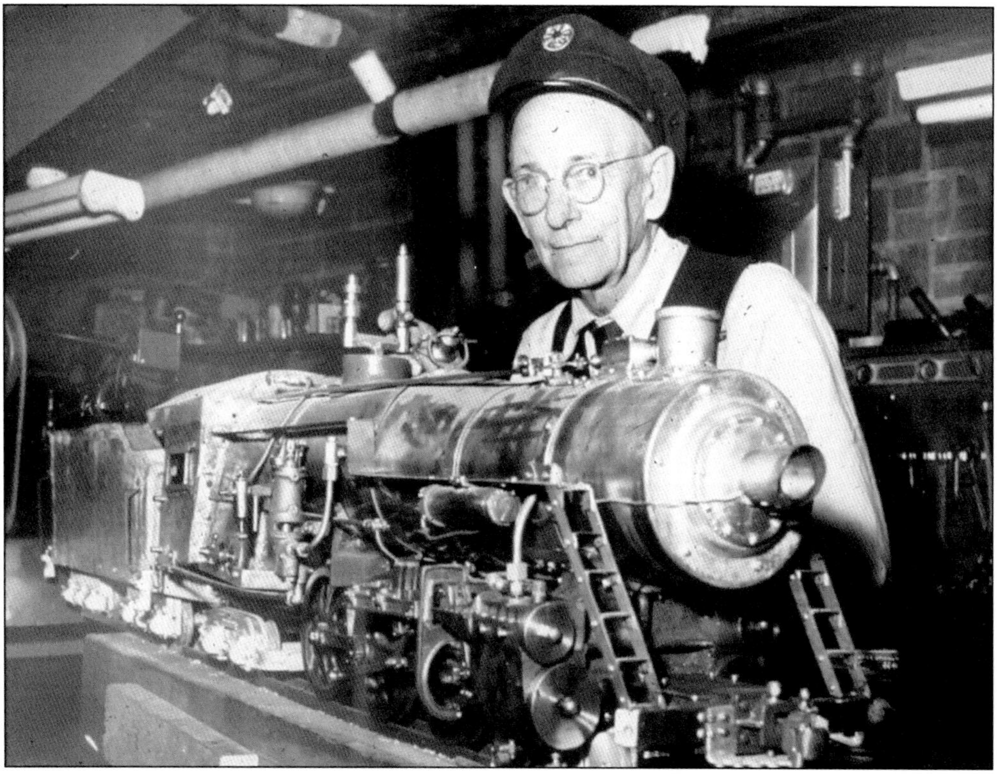

Sauer is shown here with the model train he built. (Courtesy of William Robishaw Collection, Westlake Porter Public Library.)

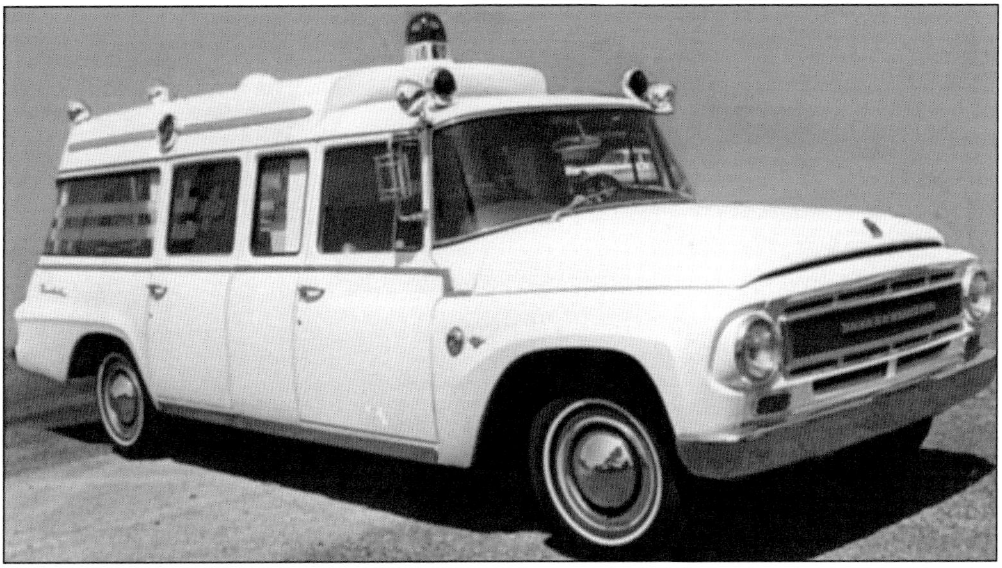

Westlake's first city-owned ambulance is shown here in 1967. The picture's caption from the *Cleveland Press* stated, "Westlake will soon begin the first city-operated ambulance runs in this new International. Purchase of the $9500 vehicle from Northwest International Inc. was authorized last week by Council and it now is being fitted with special equipment. Supplementing the city service by the fire department will be the Jenkins Funeral Chapel wagons." (Courtesy of Cleveland State University, Cleveland Memory Project, Cleveland Press Collection, Joseph E. Cole, donor.)

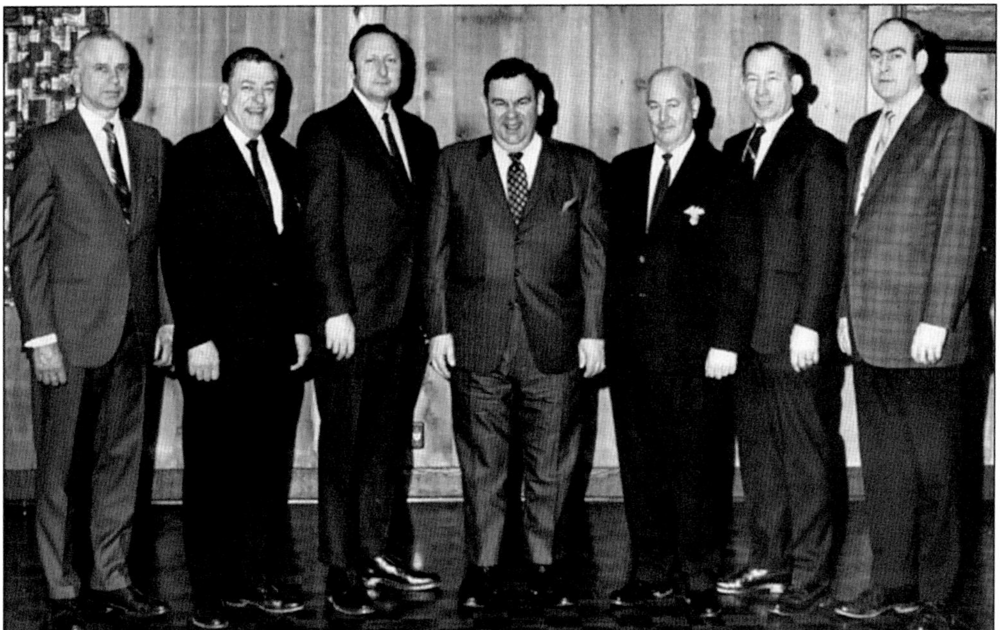

The Westlake auxiliary police are shown in 1970. Pictured from left to right are 1st Sgt. William Sauernheimer, 2nd Sgt. Raymond Jerkofsky, police chief John Fleischer, Mayor Alex Roman, Capt. Ed Scott, Lt. Casey Kalman, and 3rd Sgt. Robert Borcher. (Courtesy of Cleveland State University, Cleveland Memory Project, Cleveland Press Collection, Joseph E. Cole, donor.)

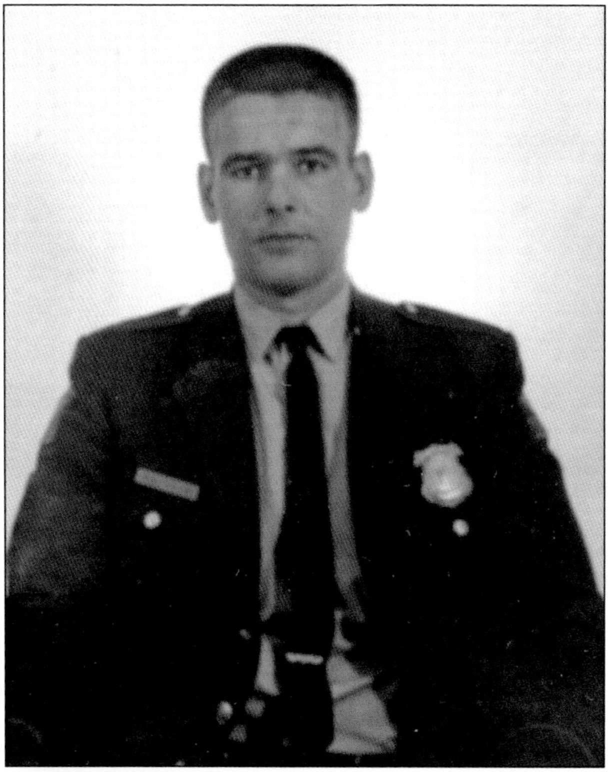

Waldemar Schilkowski was a member of the four-man pistol team that won the west side competition in 1968. (Courtesy of Waldemar Schilkowski, Westlake Police Department.)

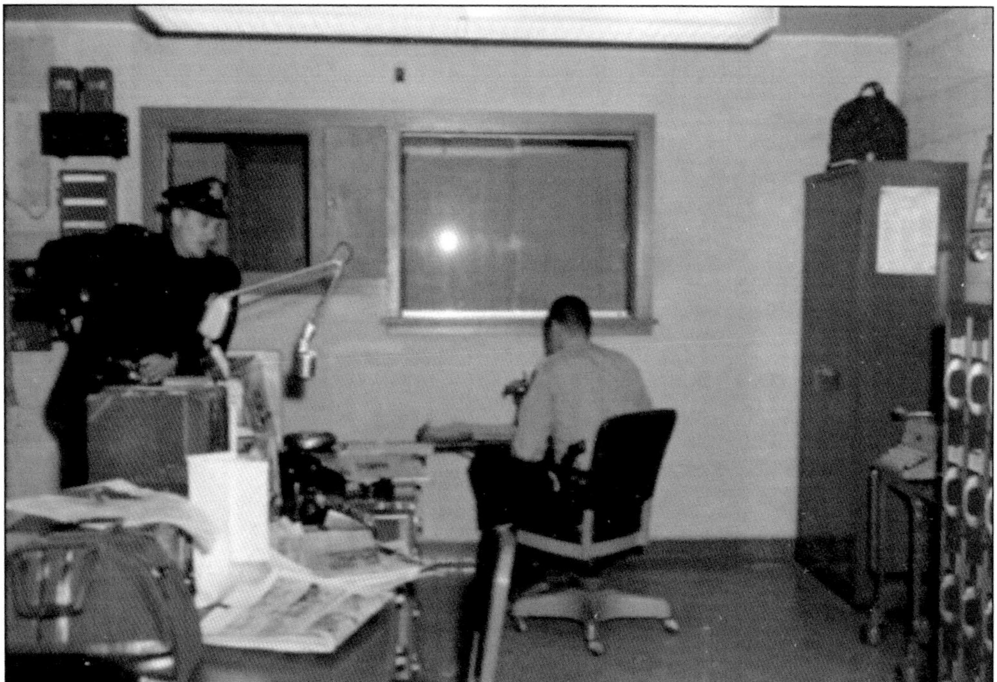

The police radio room is shown here in 1980. (Courtesy of Waldermar Schilkowski, Westlake Police Department.)

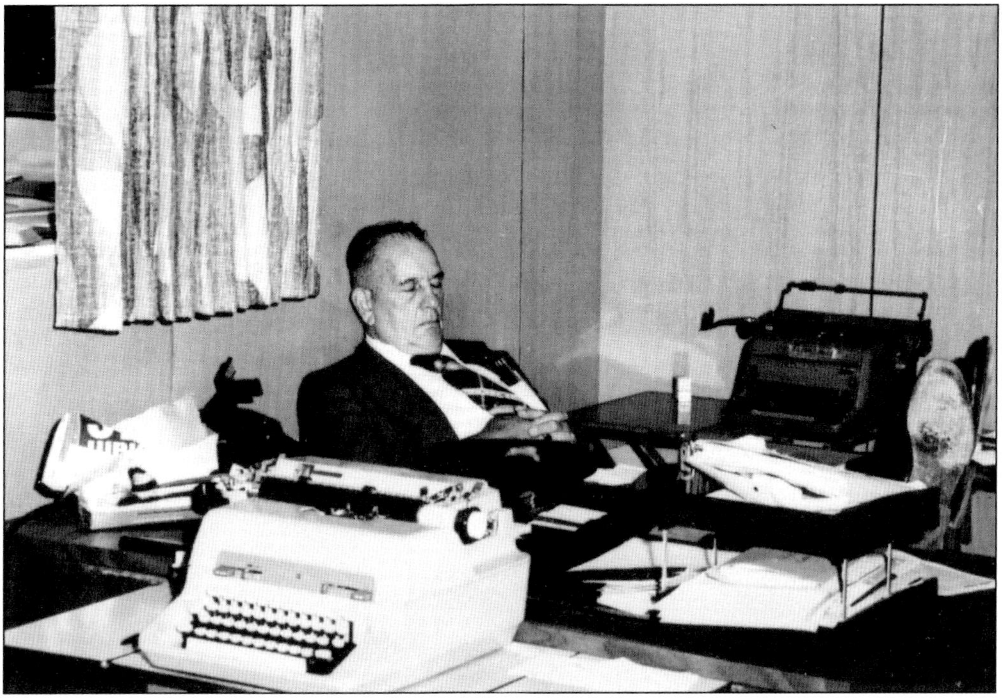

Capt. Harold Wilbert is caught with his feet up. Wilbert was a detective on the Westlake police force. He and George Jindra arrested Richard Eberling, a window washer in the area, after finding stolen items from Marilyn Sheppard's home in Bay Village. (Courtesy of George Jindra.)

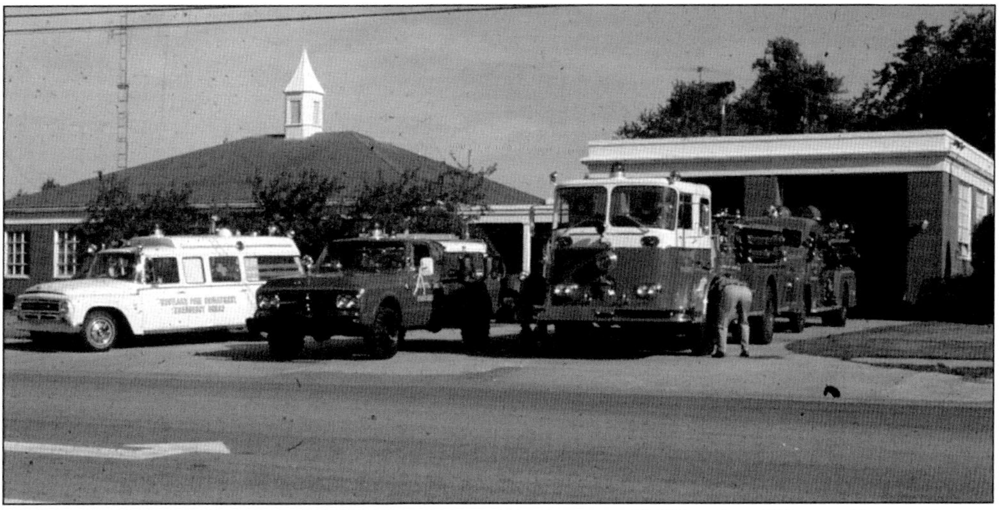

This picture shows the Westlake fire station at the corner of Hilliard and Dover Center Roads. (Courtesy of William Robishaw Collection, Westlake Porter Public Library.)

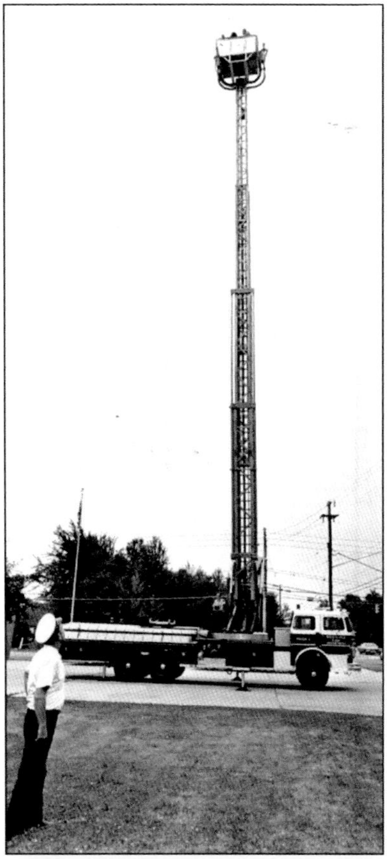

These photographs show the Westlake Fire Department ladder truck in 1974. (Courtesy of Cleveland State University, Cleveland Memory Project, Cleveland Press Collection, Joseph E. Cole, donor.)

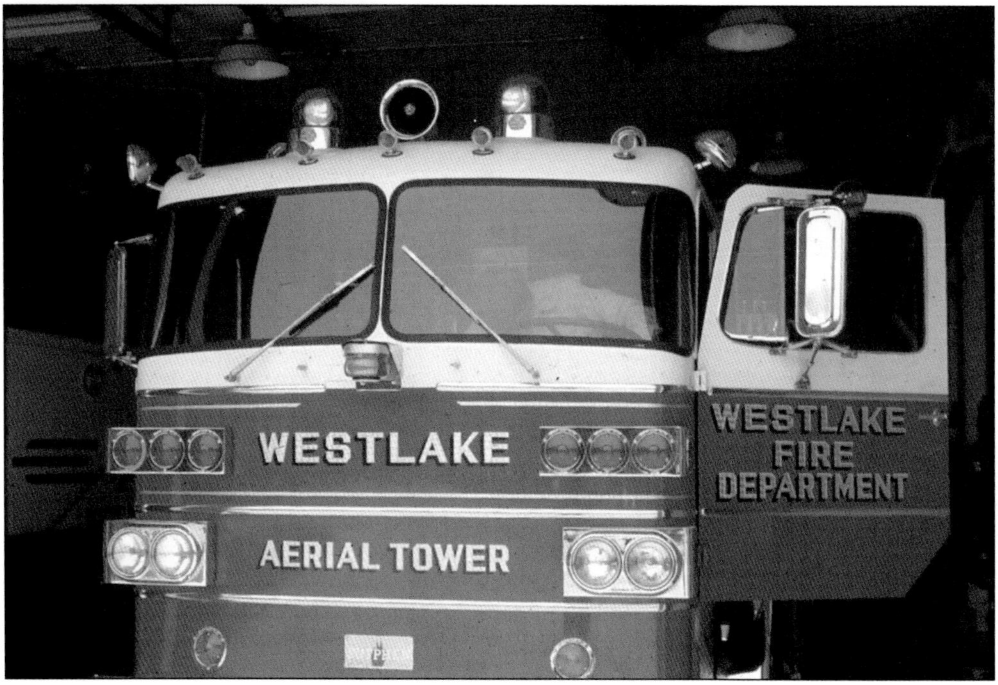

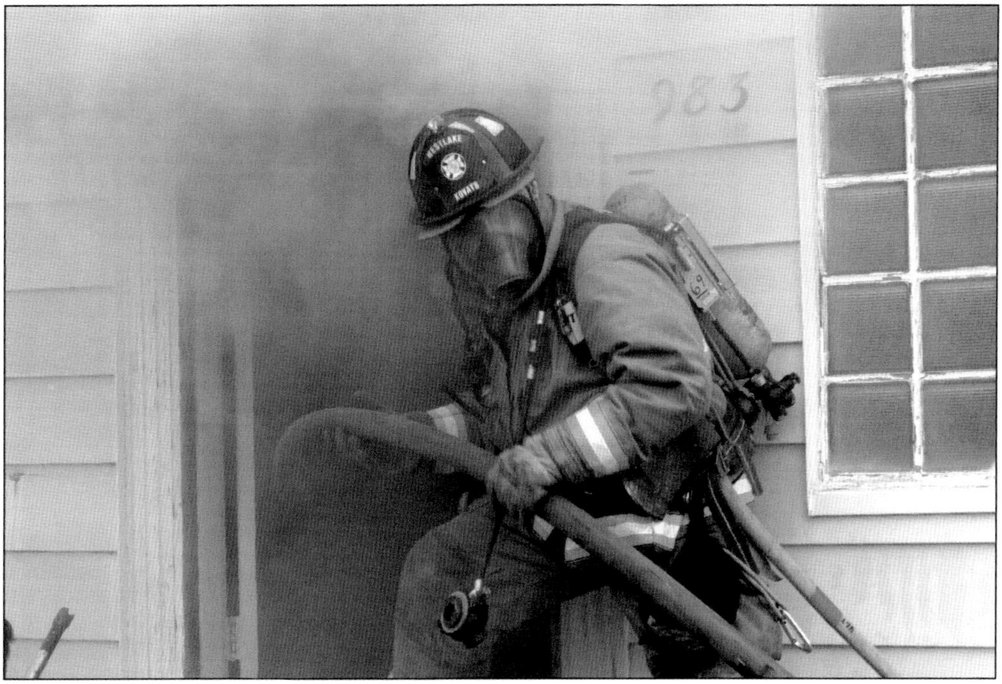

One of the city's finest is caught in action. (Courtesy of John Kish, Westlake Fire Department.)

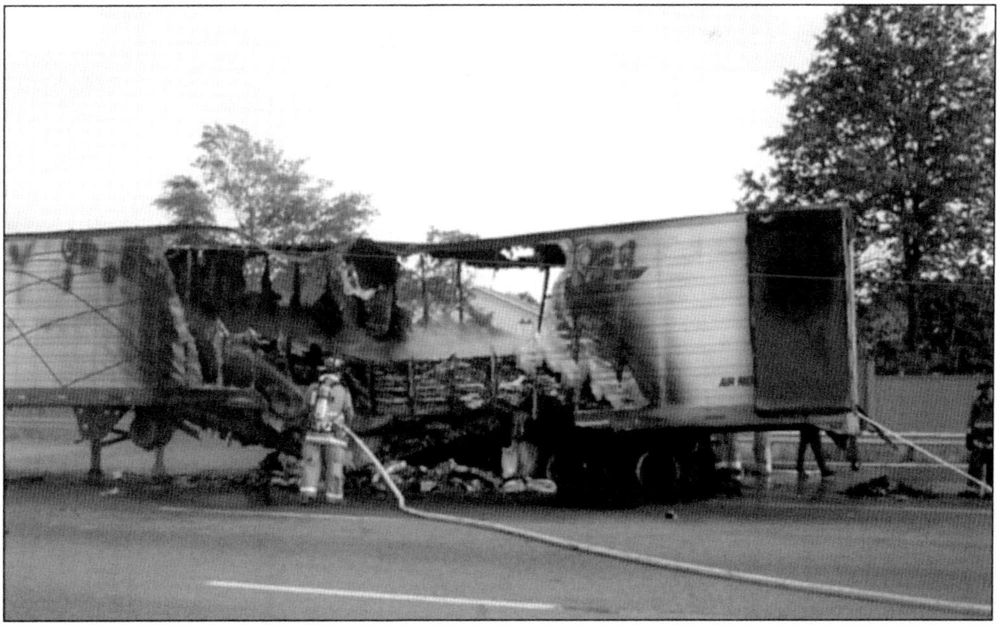

A truck is pictured after it caught fire on Interstate 90. (Courtesy of John Kish, Westlake Fire Department.)

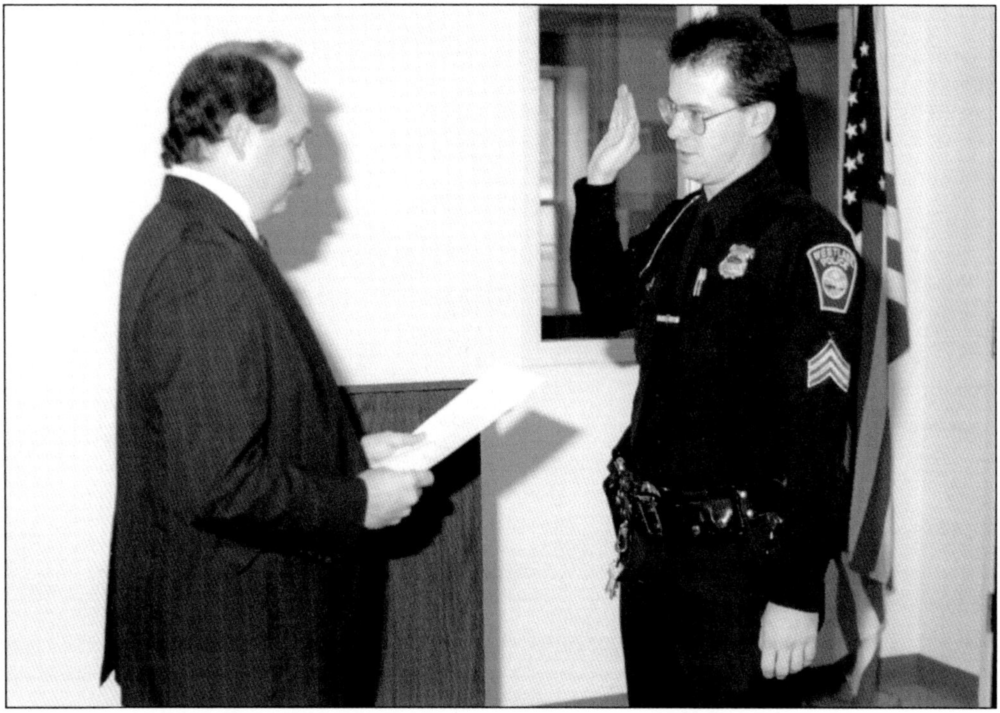

Mayor Dennis Clough and Guy Turner are pictured here in October 1992 when Turner was sworn in as a lieutenant. (Courtesy of Capt. Guy Turner, Westlake Police Department.)

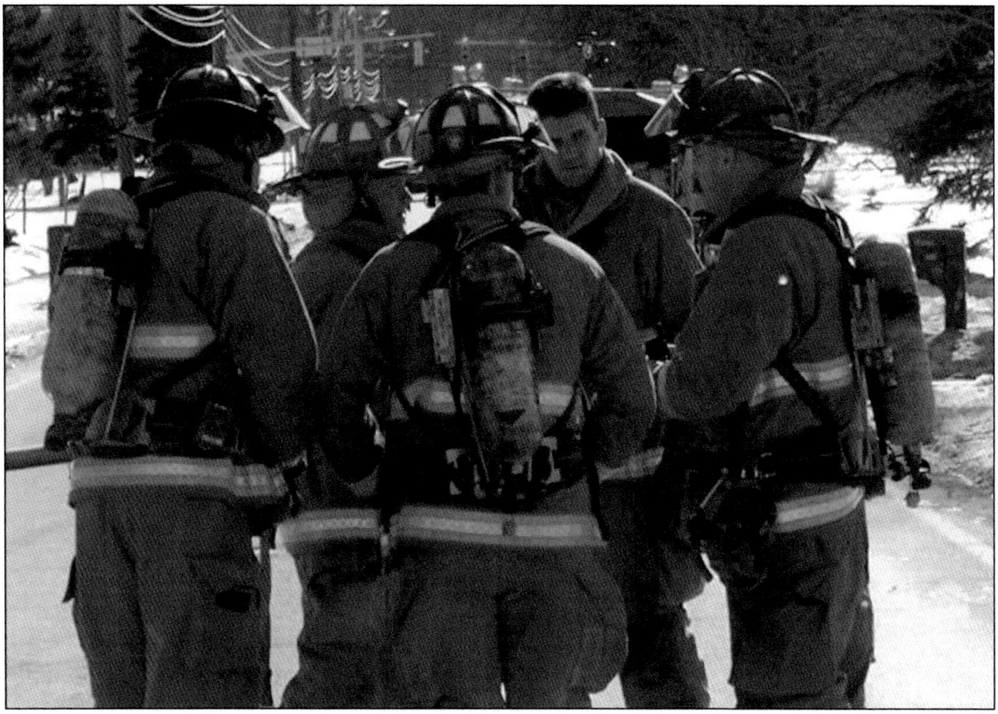

Westlake firemen planned a course of action when a power line fell on a house and electrically charged the entire structure. (Courtesy of John Kish, Westlake Fire Department.)

Six

Farms and Barns

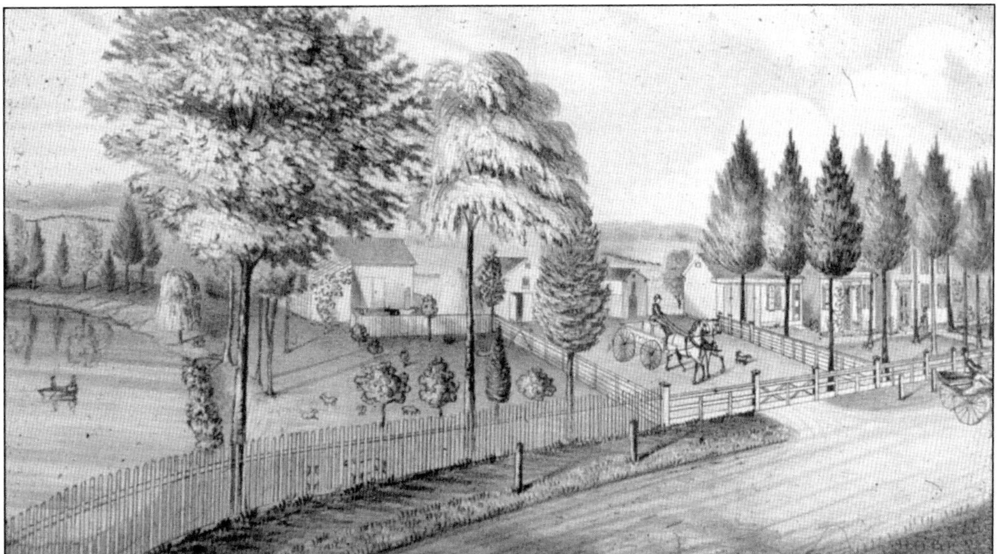

This image depicts the home and farm of J. N. Hurst on Detroit Road, west of Bradley Road. The house was built in 1872. (Courtesy of William Robishaw Collection, Westlake Porter Public Library.)

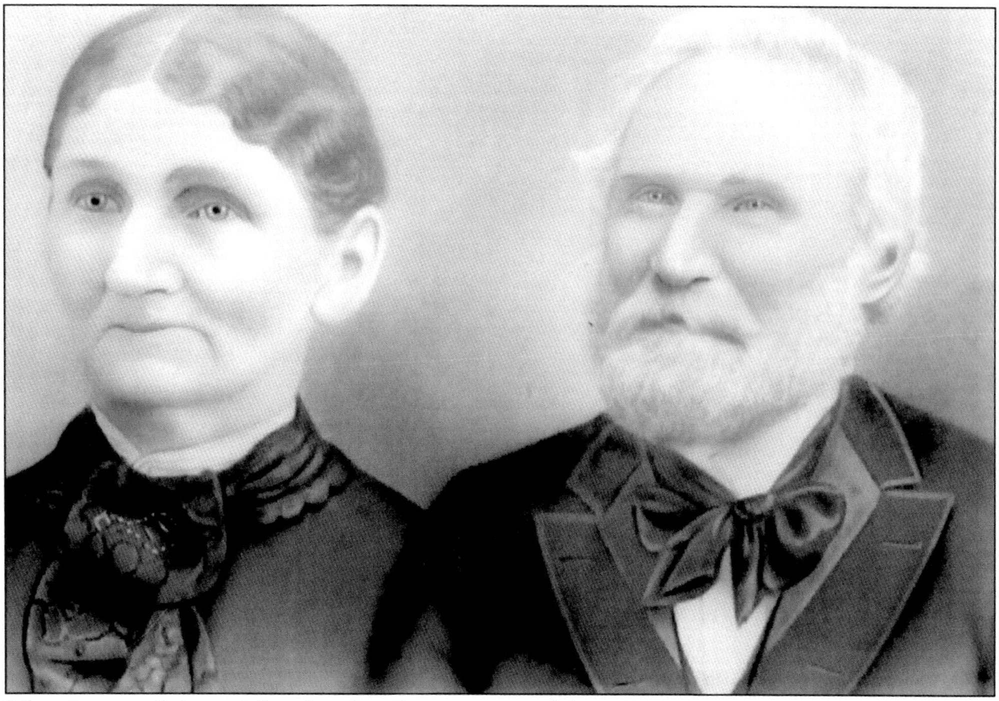

John Oster and Anna Mary Junglas Oster emigrated from Germany on a sailing ship in 1852. They met on the boat, married in 1856, and settled in the Prospect Avenue and Ninth Street area of Cleveland. In 1872, the Osters bought property on Bradley Road. They lived in a log cabin while they built their home and farm. (Courtesy of Diane Oster.)

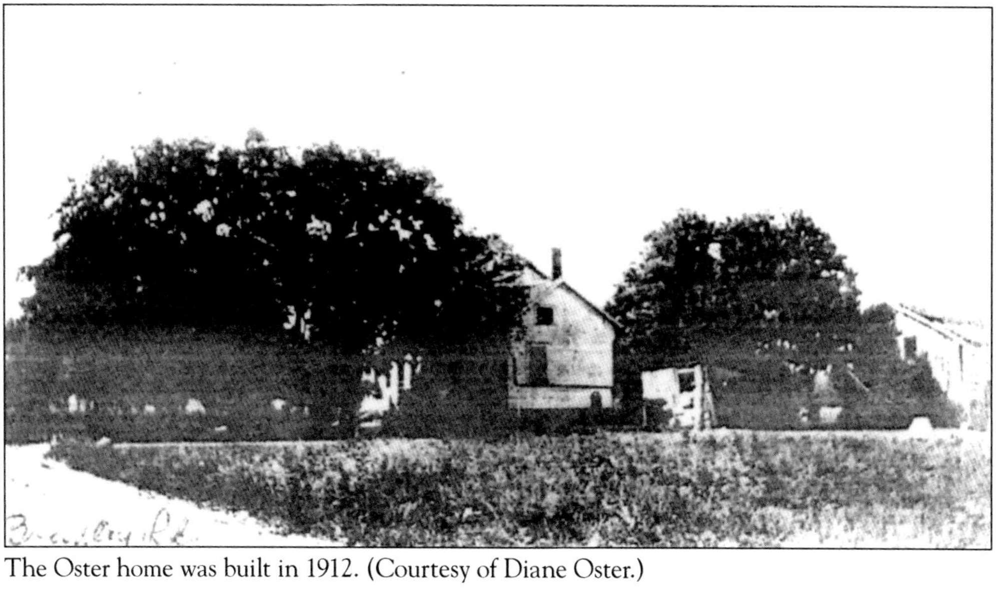

The Oster home was built in 1912. (Courtesy of Diane Oster.)

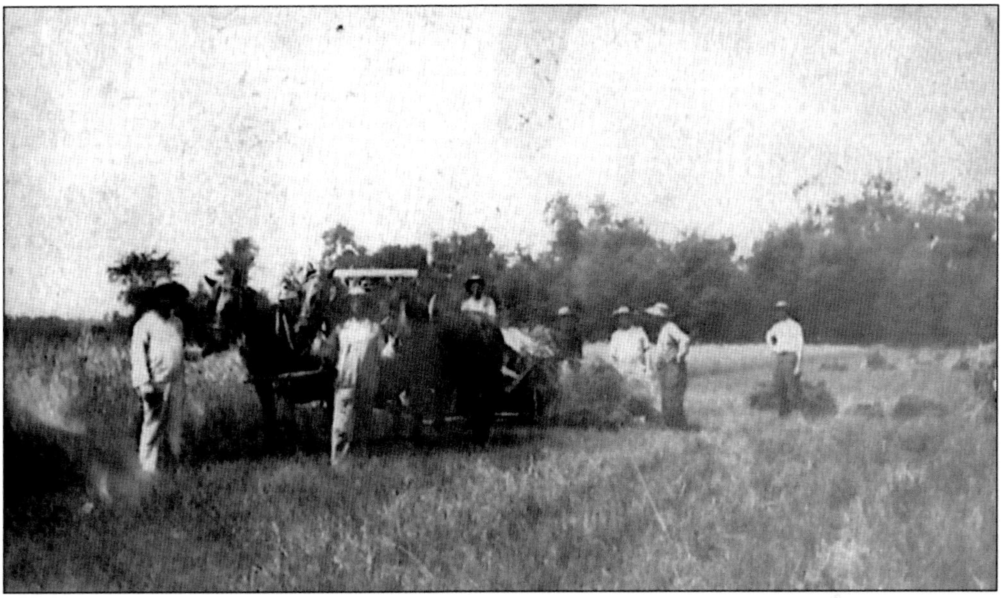

The Oster farm had a gas well on the property. The family cultivated grapes, beans, corn, onions, tomatoes, potatoes, and hay. They raised pigs and chickens and sold produce at a roadside stand. This picture shows haying on the Oster farm. (Courtesy of Diane Oster.)

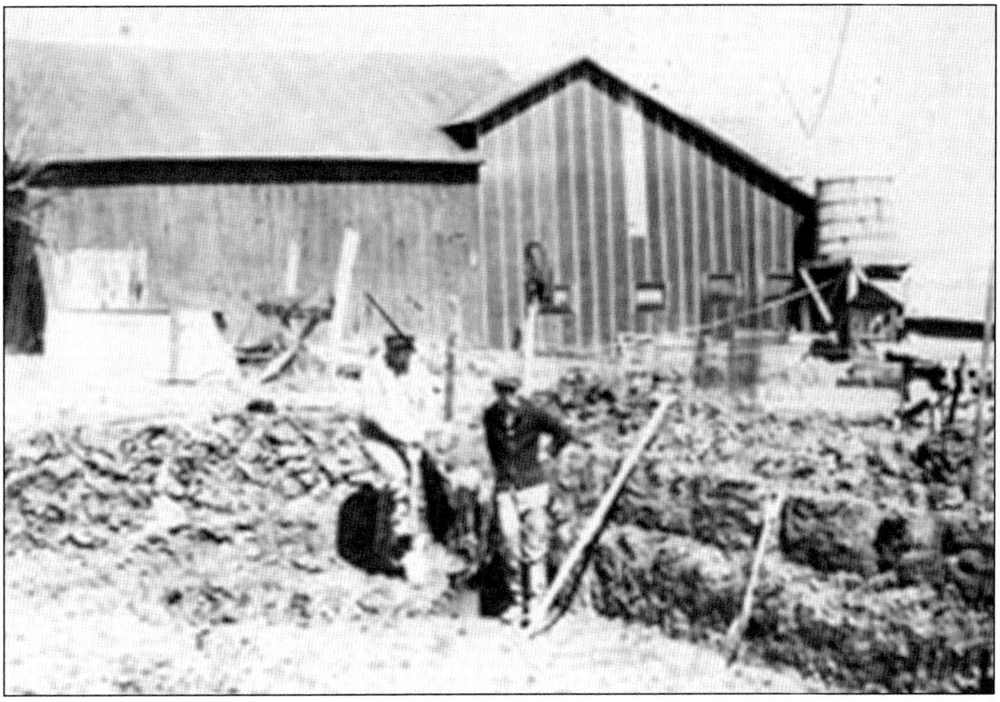

Alva Tanner moved to Dover in 1884 and worked on Amos Sperry's farm. Tanner purchased land in 1895 to build a frame home and barn at 2365 Clague Road in what is now the Quail Hollow development. He installed the first irrigation system in the area, which pumped water from Sperry Creek. The Tanner family cultivated fields of apples, corn, spinach, cabbages, and other crops. (Courtesy of William Robishaw Collection, Westlake Porter Public Library.)

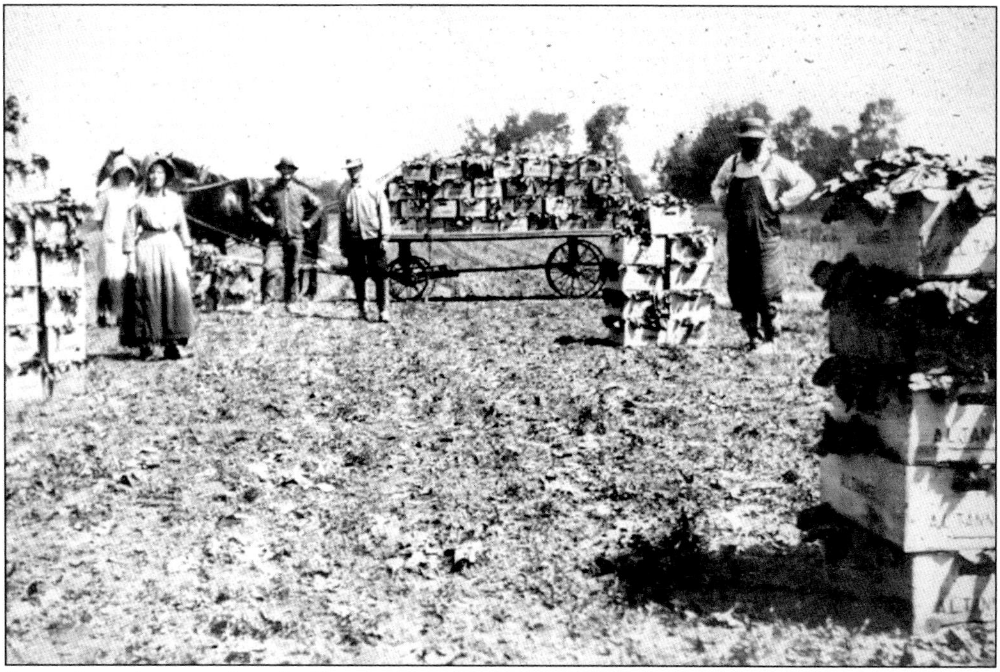

Spinach was harvested on the Tanner farm. (Courtesy of William Robishaw Collection, Westlake Porter Public Library.)

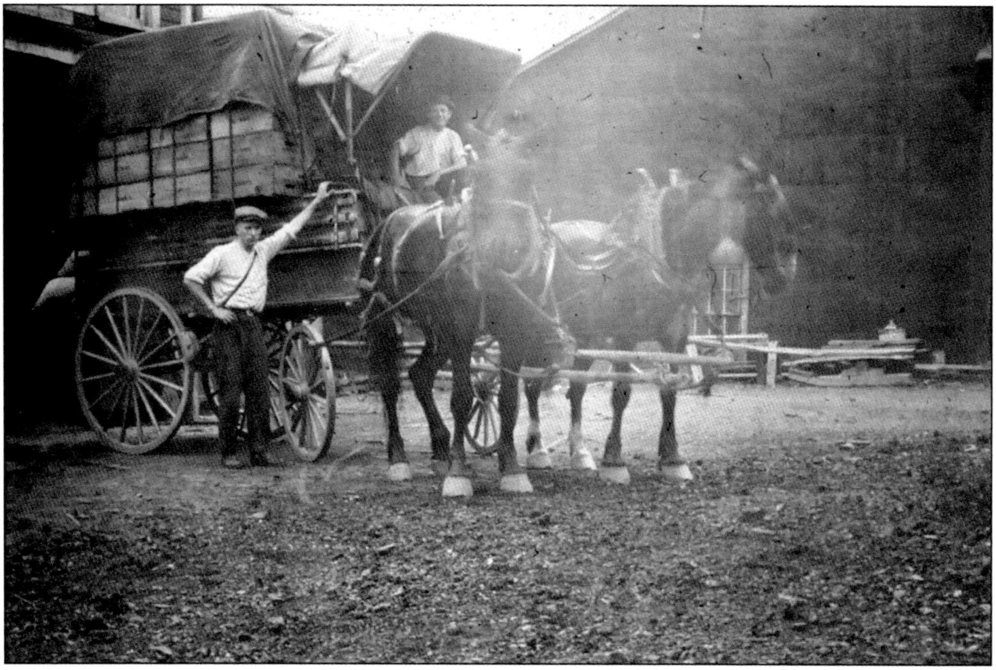

Alva Tanner and Frank Nekle return from a market trip, pausing to pose for this picture. Nekle was a hired hand on the Tanner farm. (Courtesy of William Robishaw Collection, Westlake Porter Public Library.)

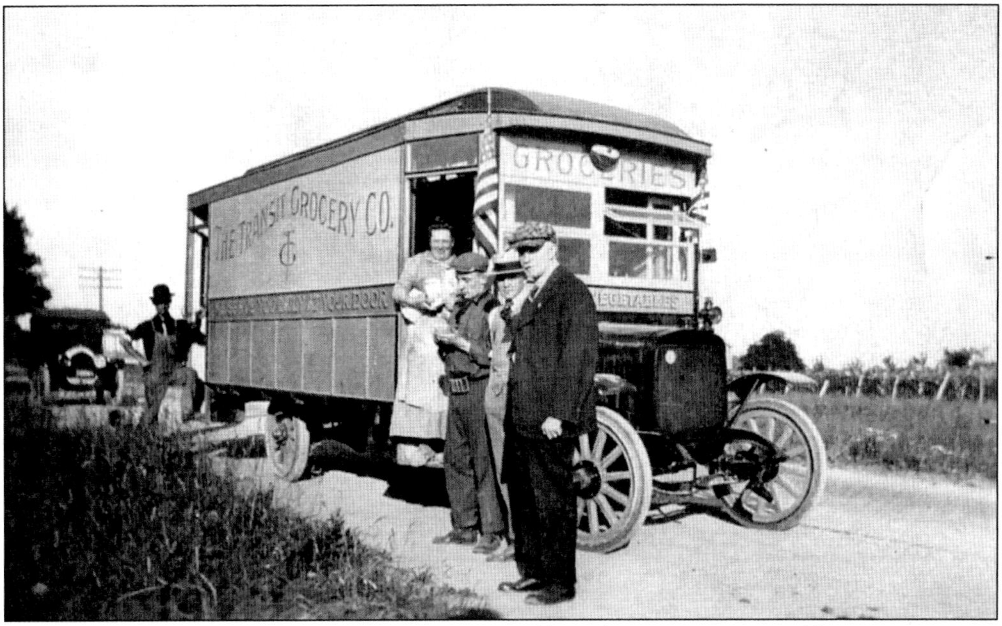

Around the dawn of the 20th century in Dover Village, farmers were visited by a grocery store on wheels. This picture of the Transit Grocery Company was taken in front of the Dorow farm at 26396 Detroit Road. Houlda Dorow smiles as she carries her purchases off the truck. (Courtesy of Ken Given.)

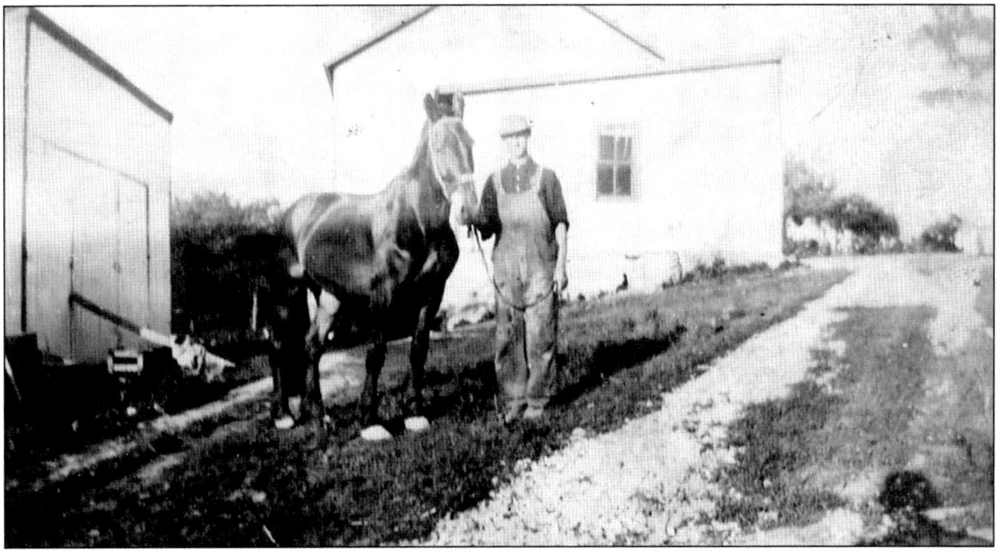

Elmer Dorow poses with his horse on the Dorow farm on Detroit Road. The barn and garage are still standing. (Courtesy of Ken Given.)

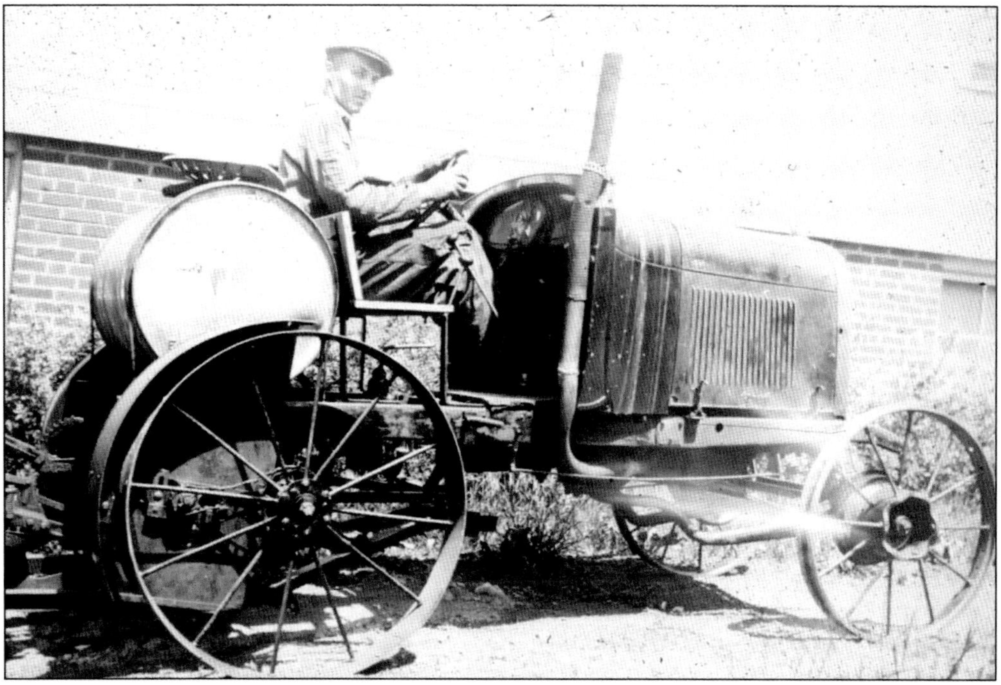

A gasoline-powered tractor with steel wheels is shown here from the Sauer's Corner photograph collection. (Courtesy of William Robishaw Collection, Westlake Porter Public Library.)

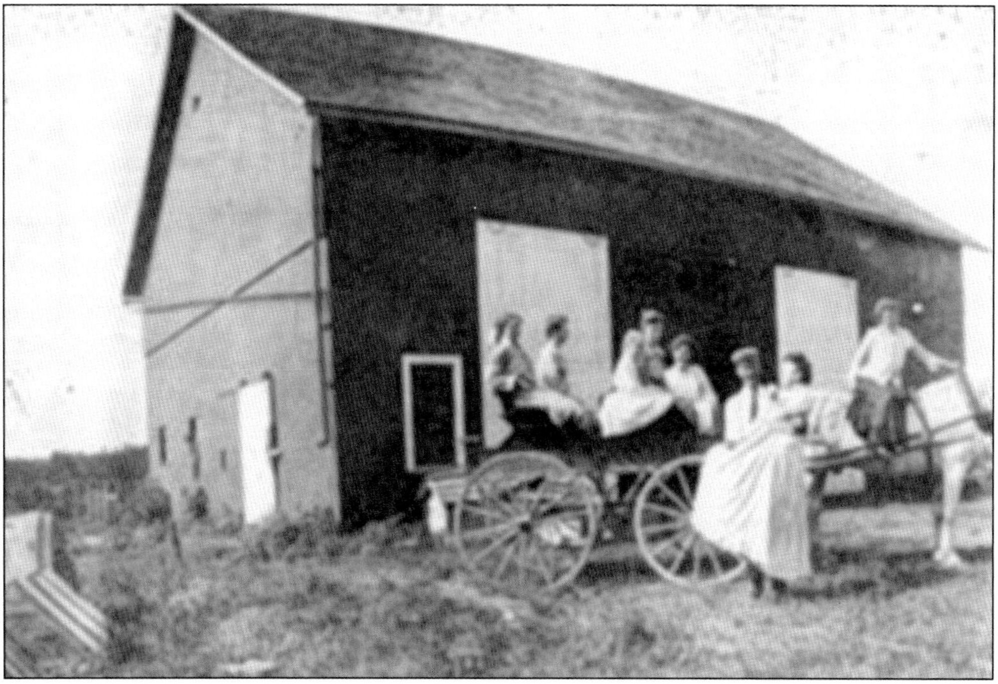

This 1906 photograph shows the Lewis farm, which was located at 24629 Detroit Road, midway between Columbia and Clague Roads. (Courtesy of William Robishaw Collection, Westlake Porter Public Library.)

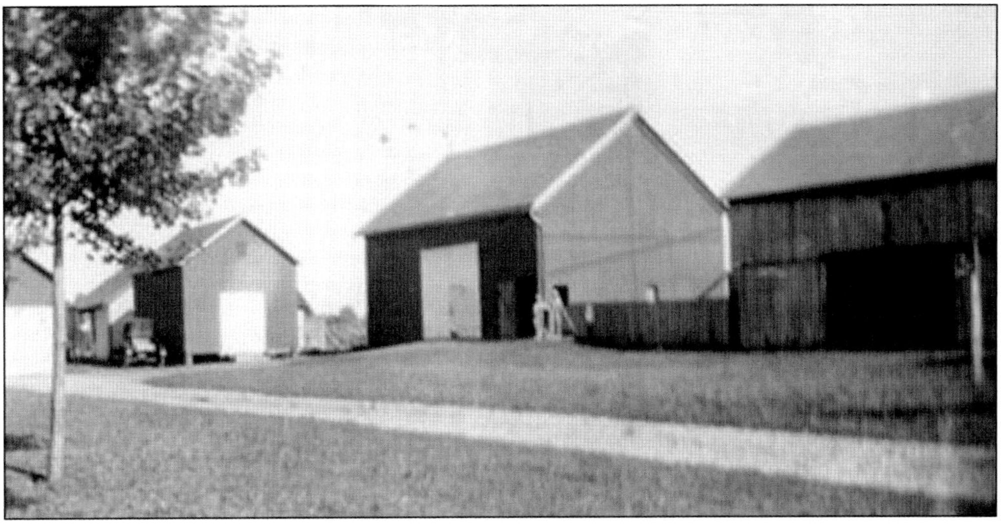

Leonard Albers's barn and vineyards were located at 2105 Bassett Road, just north of Bassett Elementary School. Albers was an active member of the farm bureau council. At the dawn of the 20th century, Dover was the second-largest grape producer in the United States. At that time, the grapes were harvested by hand. In 1930, there were 1,200 acres of Dover fields devoted to grape vineyards, which made grape juice and wine. Concord grapes were the most common variety, with a sugar content of about 22 percent. In the 1950s, local farmers purchased the Welsh Grape Juice Company. In 1970, Albers joined with other farmers to purchase a $27,000 grape-picking machine. (Courtesy of William Robishaw Collection, Westlake Porter Public Library.)

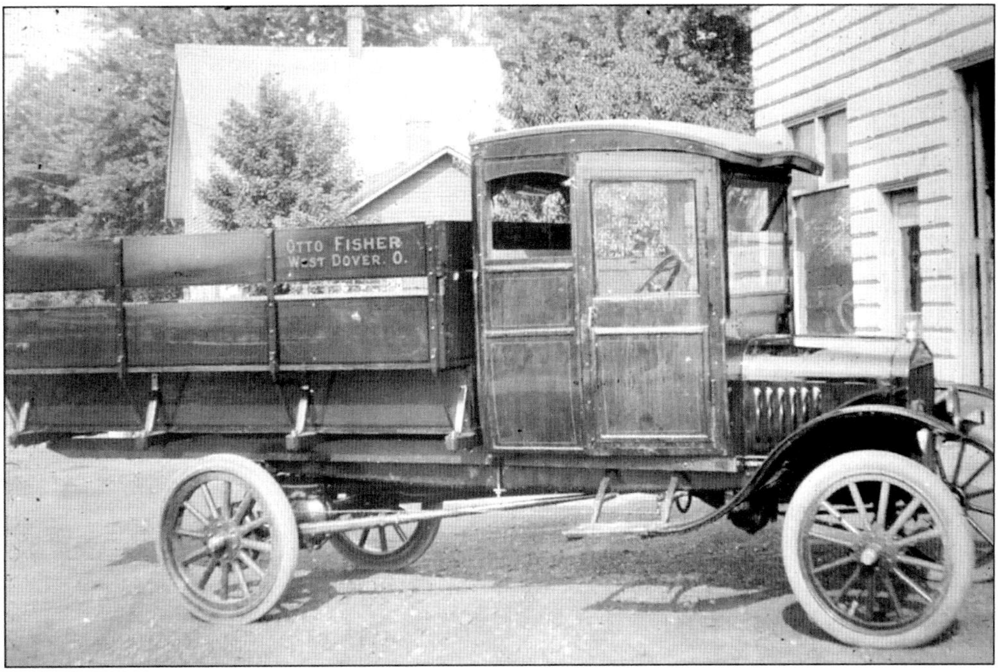

Around 1920, Otto Fisher's truck had a wooden cab and sides. (Courtesy of William Robishaw Collection, Westlake Porter Public Library.)

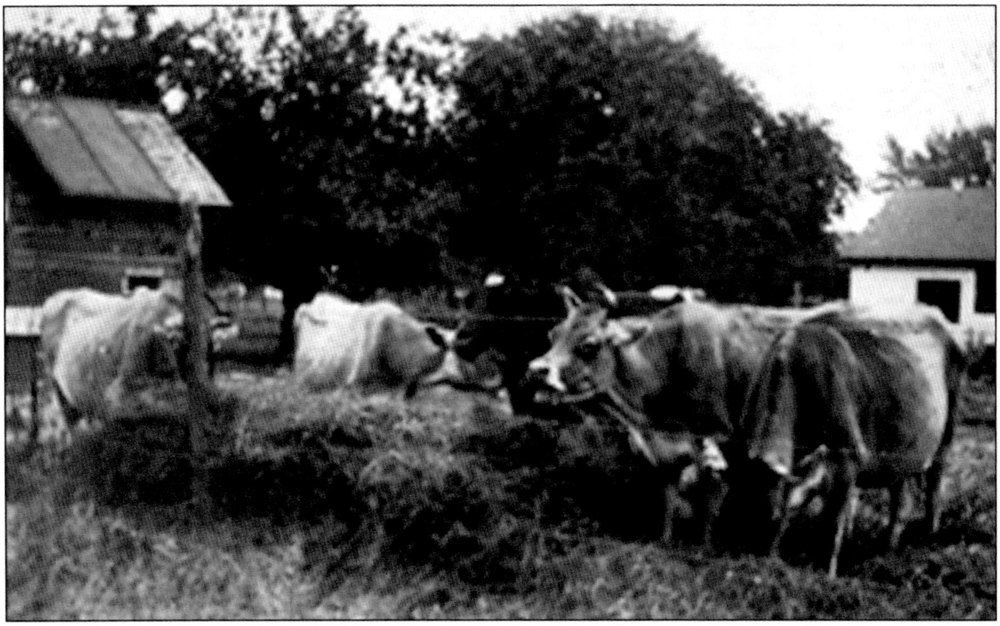

Dairy cattle were raised on the Cooley farm. Asher Cooley arrived in Dover Township on October 19, 1818, to settle on 44 acres he purchased from the Connecticut Land Grant. Cooley and his wife, Lydia, had seven sons and three daughters. The Cooley family thrived in the area. His descendants still reside in Westlake today. (Courtesy of William Robishaw Collection, Westlake Porter Public Library.)

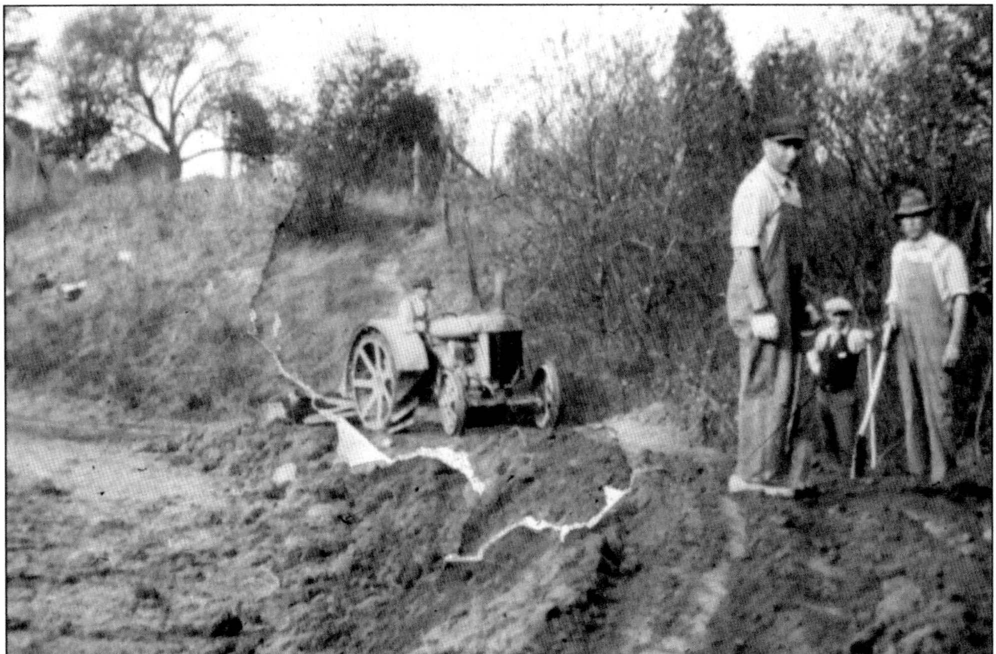

Walter Clague began construction of the Clague pond in the 1920s. Workers dug trenches and built a dam. The area is still enjoyed by the community and is inhabited by ducks and other water birds. (Courtesy of William Robishaw Collection, Westlake Porter Public Library.)

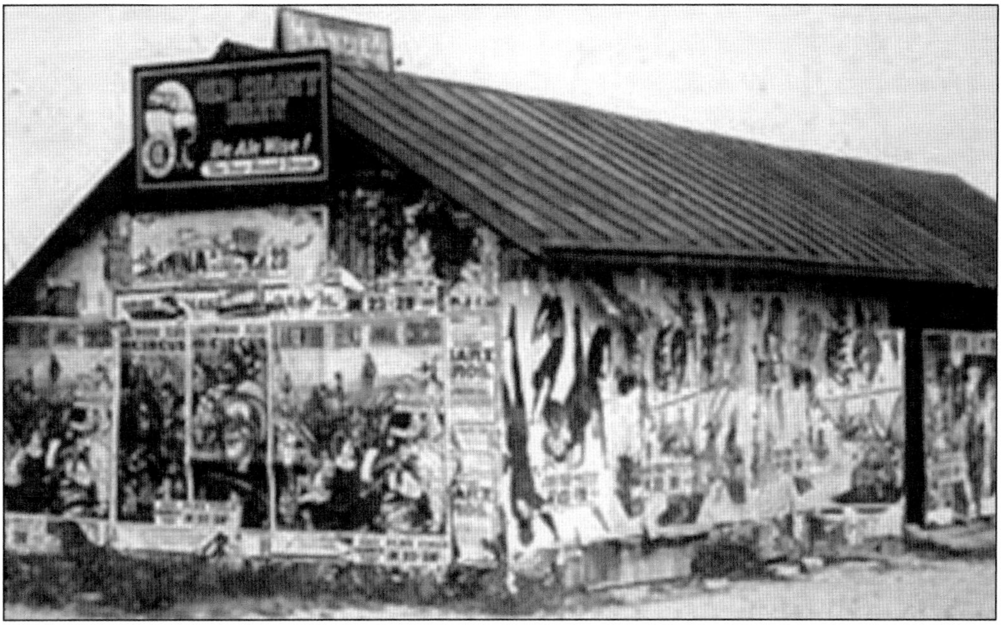

This photograph from about 1930 shows a barn on Center Ridge Road that was covered with advertising flyers before it was torn down. (Courtesy of William Robishaw Collection, Westlake Porter Public Library.)

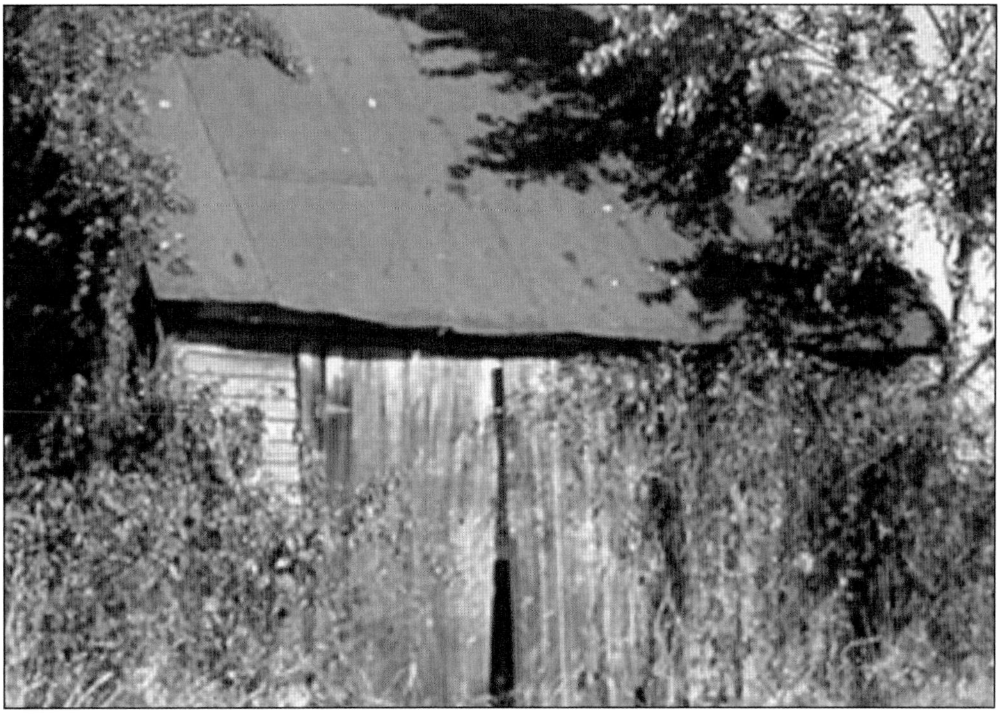

Although most of the barns in the area have been demolished to make way for home construction, there are still several acres of grape fields along Bassett Road to remind residents of the farming heritage of the community. This barn was located at 28161 Bassett Road. (Courtesy of William Robishaw Collection, Westlake Porter Public Library.)

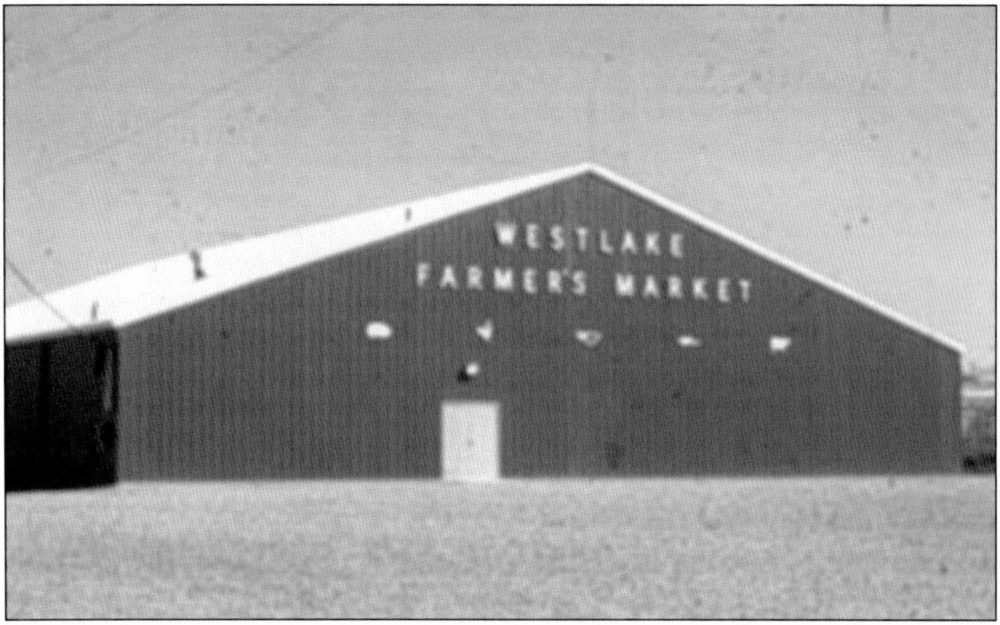

Robert Thibo opened a farmer's market on Center Ridge Road between Porter and Schwartz Roads. He dreamed of a market from an earlier time, much like the West Side Market in Cleveland. Thibo wanted stands for meats, dairy products, and produce. However, a lack of sanitary sewer facilities did not accommodate his plans. The Westlake Farmer's Market was only in operation for a few years, later serving the community as a health promotion center for the Westlake health campus of the present-day St. John West Shore Hospital. (Courtesy of William Robishaw Collection, Westlake Porter Public Library.)

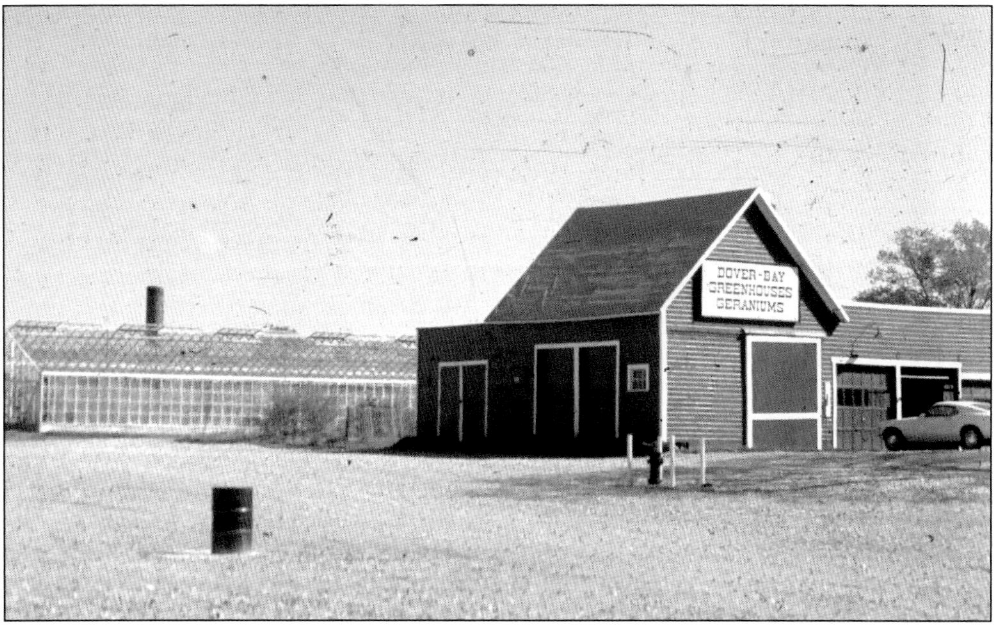

Dover Bay greenhouse was owned by the Thibo family. Robert and Ed Thibo raised glass-grown hothouse tomatoes and flowers. (Courtesy of William Robishaw Collection, Westlake Porter Public Library.)

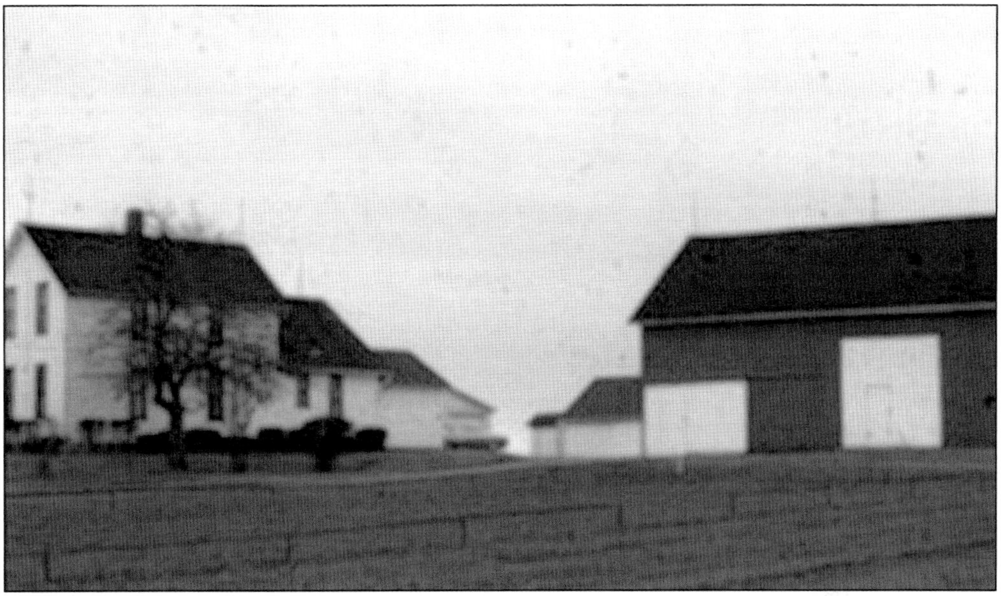

This photograph shows the Juergemeier brothers' farm opposite the Bay West Plaza near the southwest corner of Detroit and Crocker Roads. The property later became the Westlake Promenade and Crocker Park. The Juergemeiers were the last Westlake farmers cultivating table produce. The family emigrated from Germany in the 1860s and settled in the Bassett Road area known as the German settlement. (Courtesy of William Robishaw Collection, Westlake Porter Public Library.)

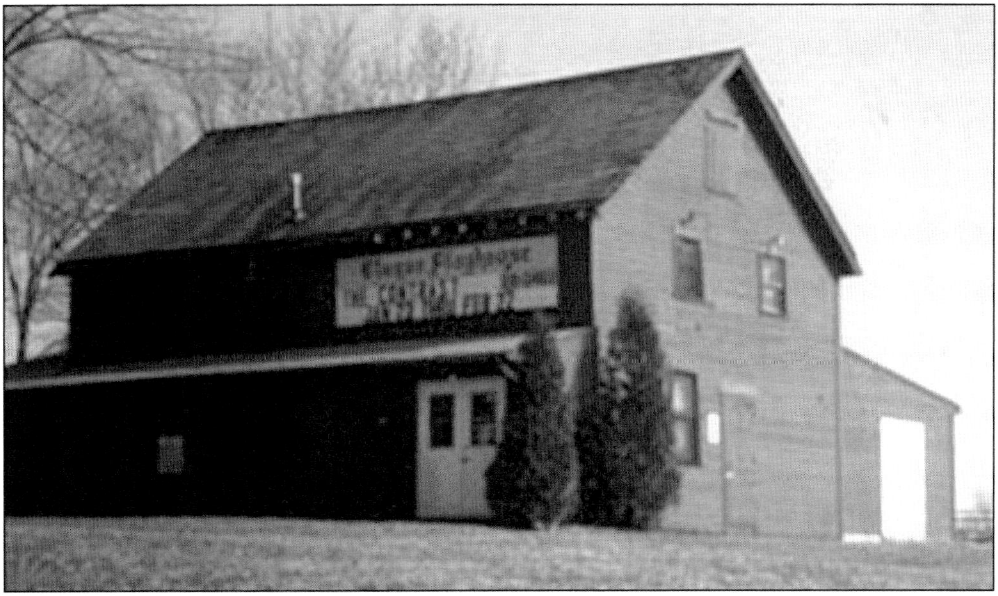

In 1967, the Clague Players converted the Clague barn into an 85-seat theater and opened their first five-show season with *Sunday in New York*. Clague Playhouse, located at 1371 Clague Road, is one of the oldest and most successful community theaters in the country, garnering an excellent reputation with performers, directors, and audiences. The playhouse has three rows of stepped-up seating on three sides. (Courtesy of William Robishaw Collection, Westlake Porter Public Library.)

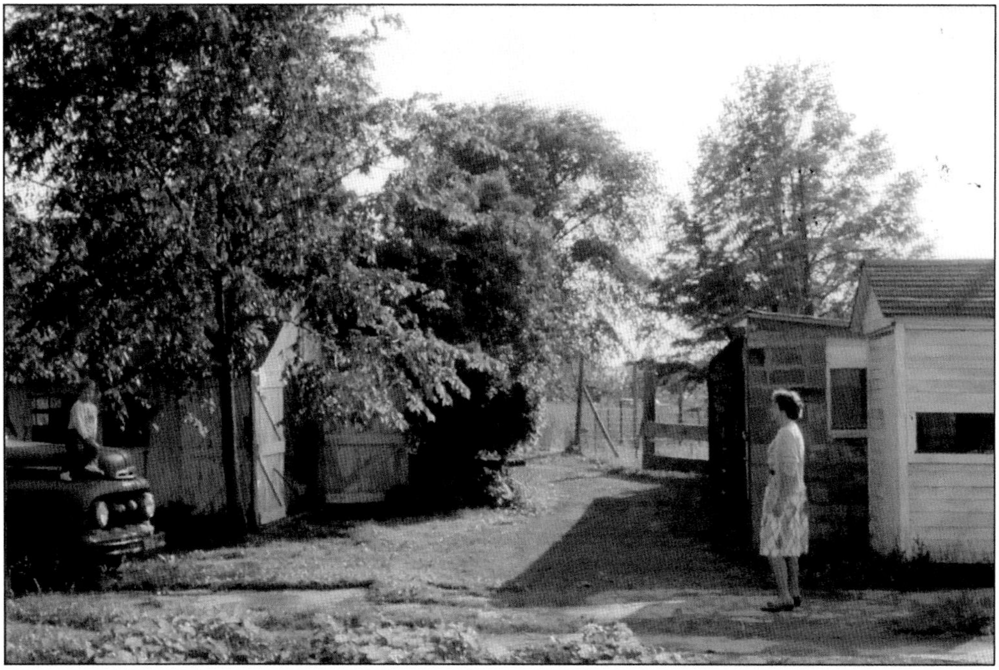

Grace and Tom Essig are pictured here at home on their farm at 31480 Detroit Road. The outbuildings shown here in 1964 are no longer standing. The land is now part of the Burr Oak development. (Courtesy of Barbara Macy.)

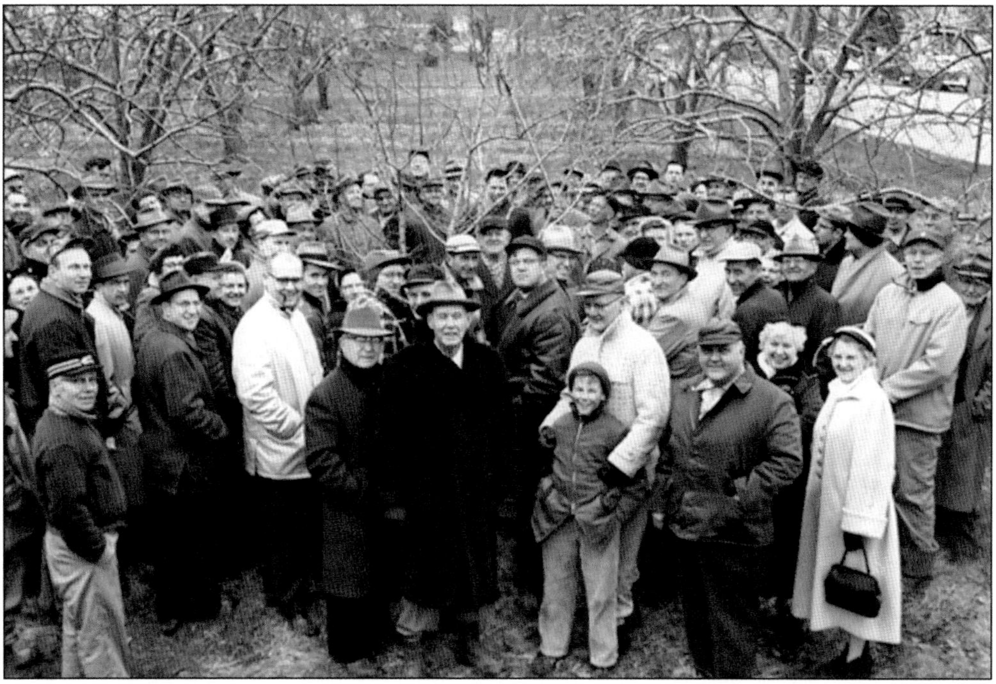

A group from the Greater Cleveland Apple Growers gathered for a grape-trimming demonstration by Norman Lehman of Lehman Orchards at 24961 Detroit Road in 1959. (Courtesy of Cleveland State University, Cleveland Memory Project, Cleveland Press Collection, Joseph E. Cole, donor.)

The Glendenning farm was located at 28989 Center Ridge Road. Alfred Glendenning was an officer in the Ohio Farm Bureau Association in 1963. With the help of neighbor farmer Nick Ripich, Glendenning organized a council to provide suggestions to the farm bureau organization on numerous subjects that affected the quality of life in the area. (Courtesy of William Robishaw Collection, Westlake Porter Public Library.)

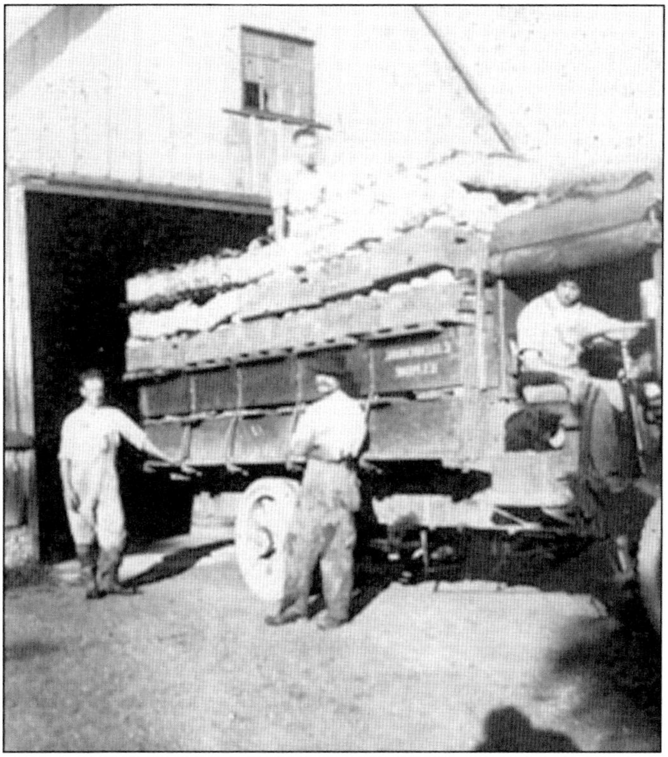

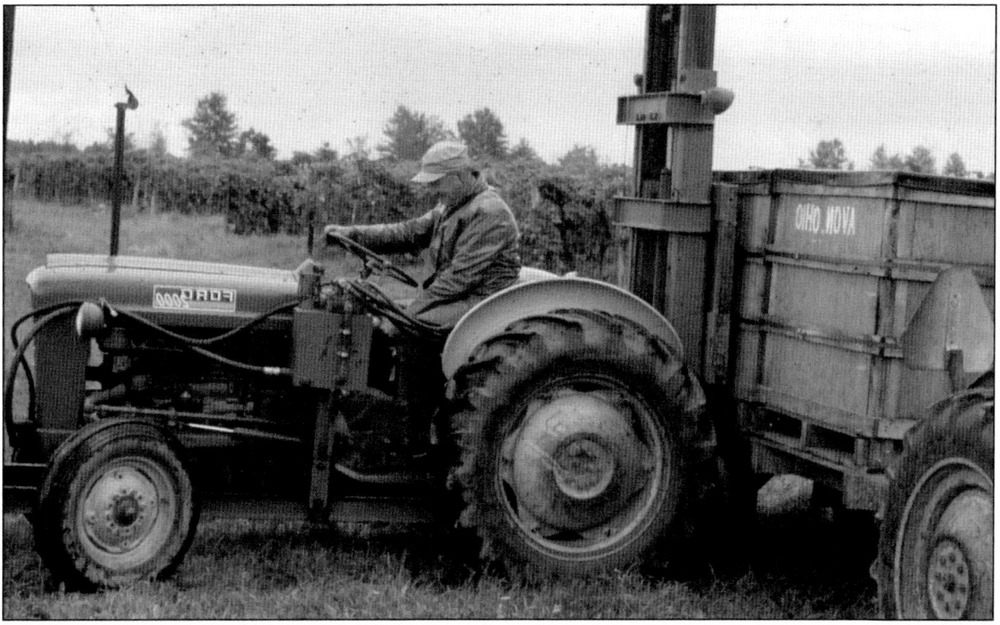

This tractor is ready to harvest the grapes. Growing grapes was a year-round job in Dover, concluding with picking the fully ripe fruit. Since grapes do not become sweeter on the vine, accurately determining ripeness and maturity was essential. The fruit is vulnerable to temperature, handling, decay, and moisture. Farmers in the area were knowledgeable and successful grape producers. (Courtesy of William Robishaw Collection, Westlake Porter Public Library.)

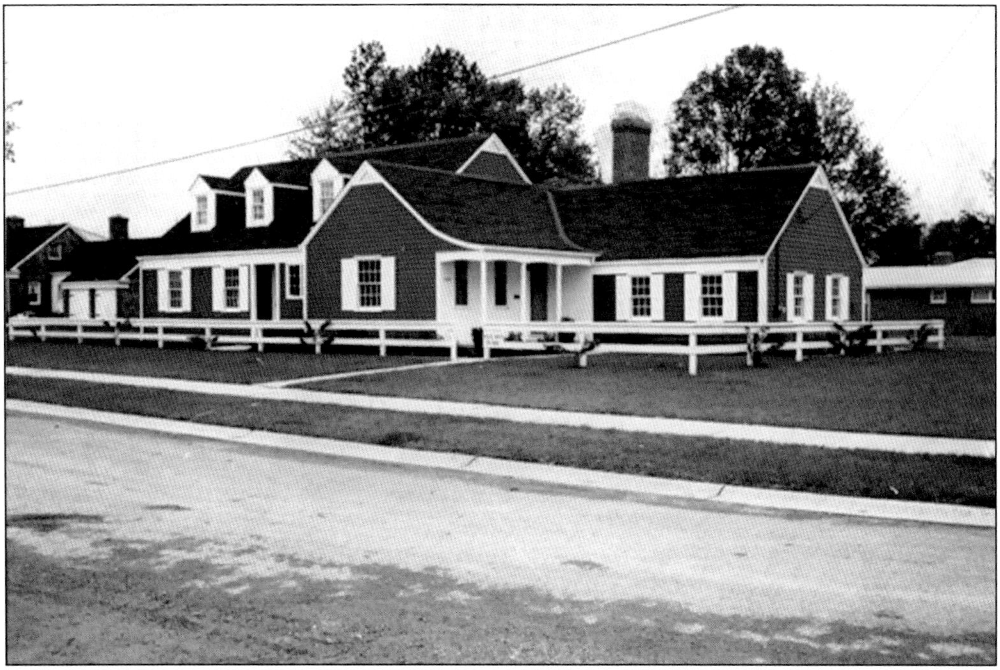

This 1959 photograph shows the Mayer farm, which was located at 1224 Dellwood Drive. (Courtesy of Cleveland State University, Cleveland Memory Project, Cleveland Press Collection, Joseph E. Cole, donor.)

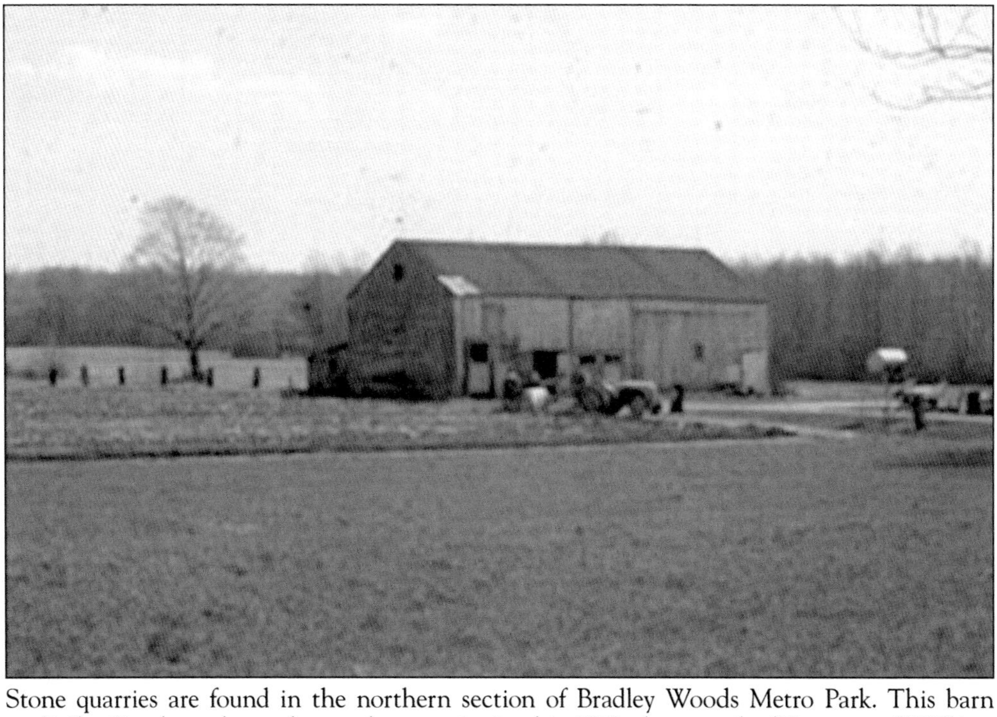

Stone quarries are found in the northern section of Bradley Woods Metro Park. This barn on Bailus Road was located near the quarries in this 1977 photograph. (Courtesy of William Robishaw Collection, Westlake Porter Public Library.)

Seven

THERE IS NO PLACE LIKE HOME

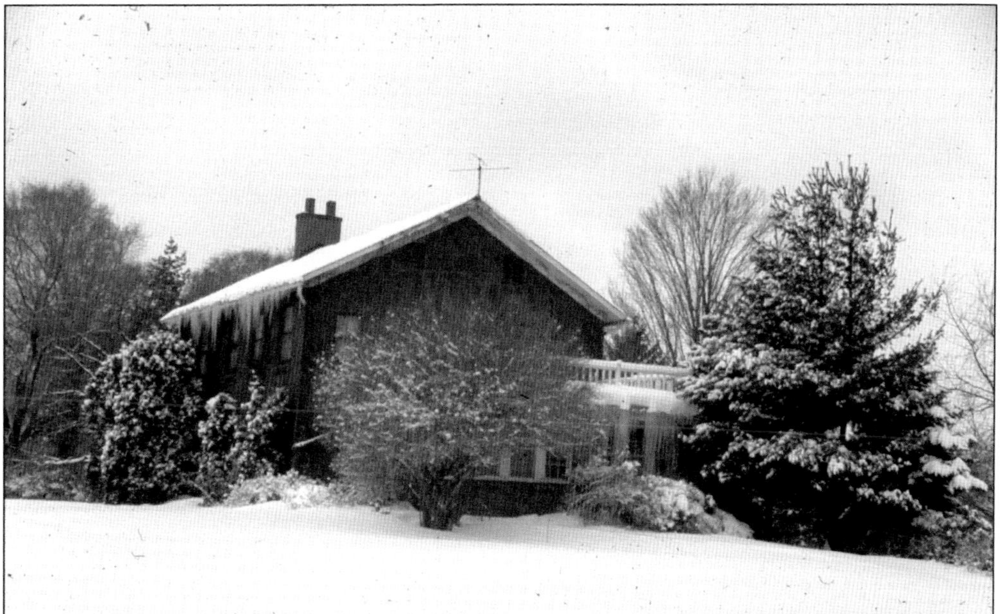

The Abner and Rebecca Smith house, built around 1820, is an example of early-19th-century architecture. Abner Smith was born in 1759. He served in the American Revolution in 1775 and died in 1825. The foundation and basement walls of the house are made of fieldstone. Skinned logs serve as joists for the first floor. Hewed beams provide support, and wood pegs tie the structure together. Large beams on each side of the attic support the roof in a truss-type structure. In recent years, this home became the 1820 Antique and Gift Shop. Currently it is a dentist's office. The house is a lasting historical landmark. (Courtesy of Westlake Historical Society.)

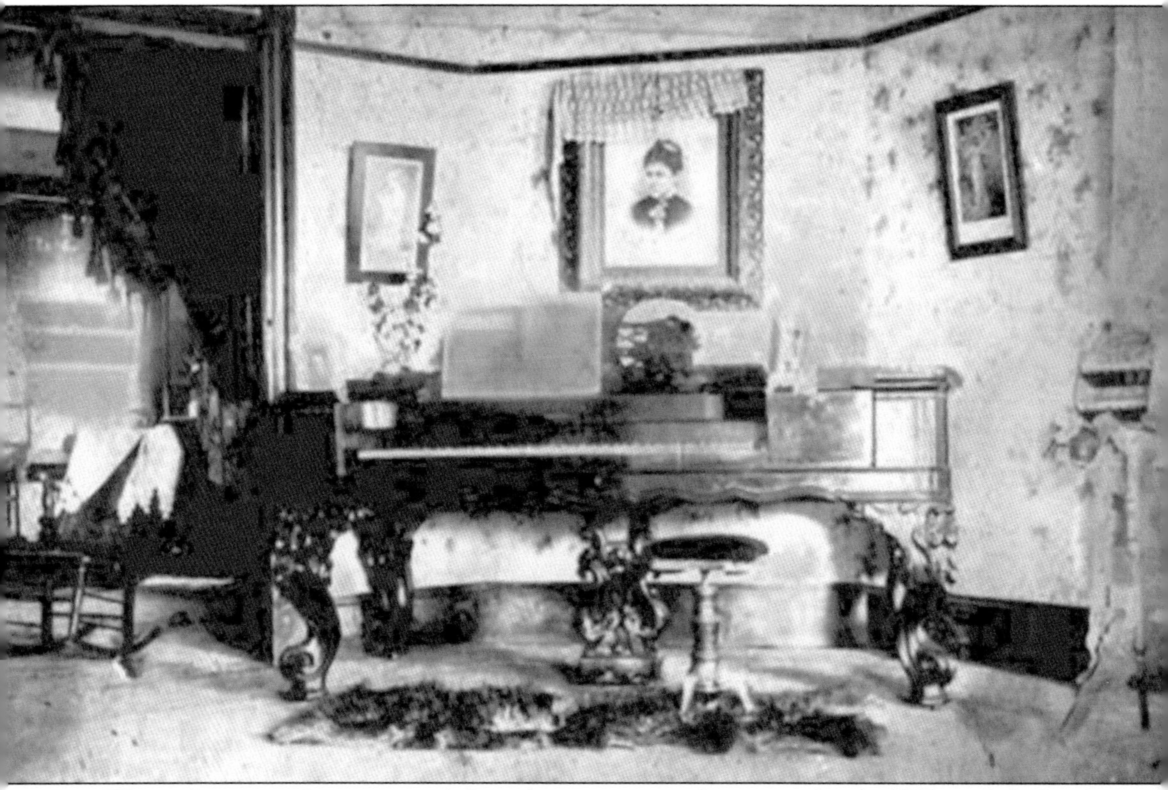

The parlor pictured is an original glass-plate image or ambrotype, taken by William Robishaw's grandfather Otto Balzer between 1861 and 1899. An ambrotype is a collodion glass-plate negative that appears to be a positive when viewed against a dark surface. This transformation is caused with reflected ambient light by the clear areas of the negative appearing dark and the opaque silver areas appearing bright. Balzer lived in Cuyahoga County. Although the exact location of the house in the image is unknown, it is exemplary of parlors of the era. (Courtesy of Robishaw Family Collection, Westlake Historical Society.)

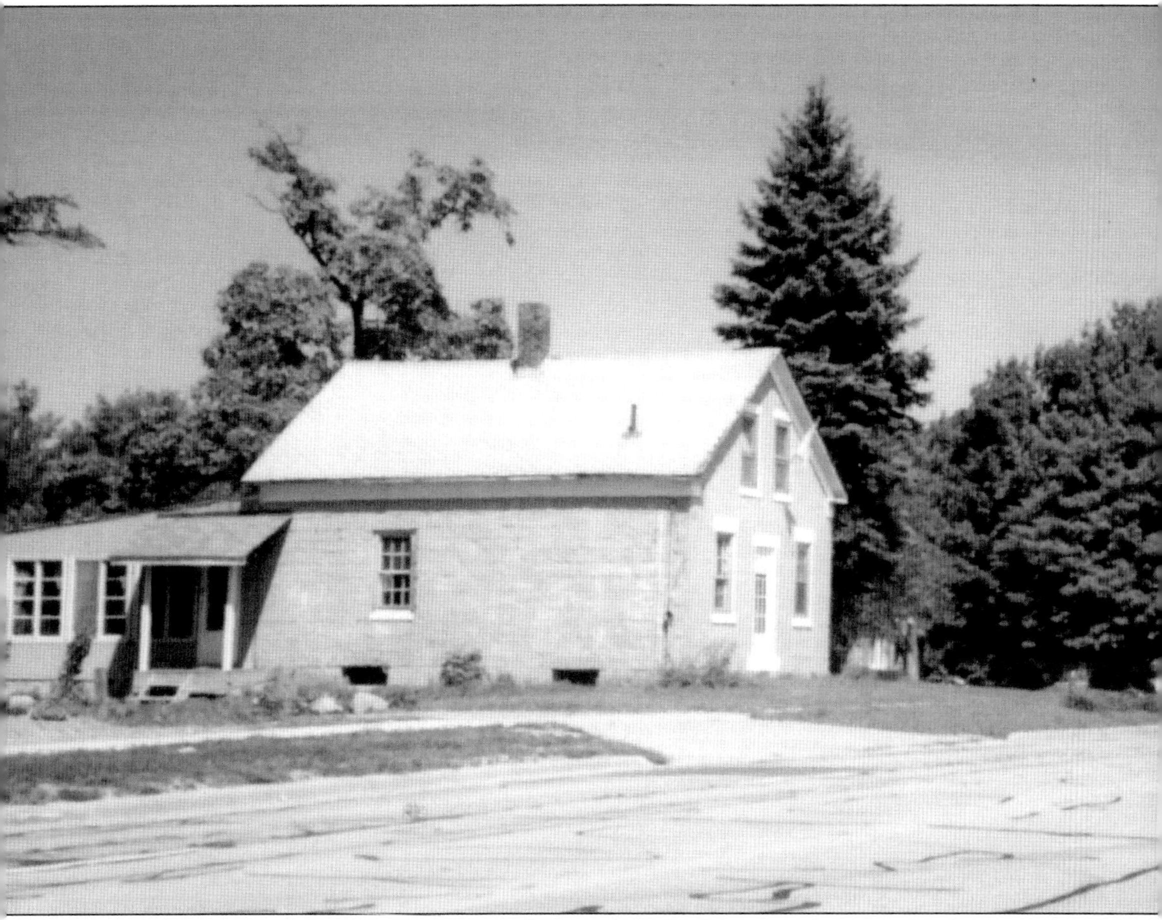

The stone home located at 27946 Center Ridge Road was built in 1844 for Austin and Roxanna Lilly, who arrived in Dover Township in 1832 from Ashfield, Massachusetts. The Smith Weston House, also known as the Lilly house, was nominated by the Ohio Historic Site Preservation Advisory Board as a rare example of 19th-century sandstone construction and Greek Revival style of the 1830s through the 1850s. The property was donated to the City of Westlake by Alice Landanyi, whose great-grandfather and family lived in the home in the 1860s. The house is currently being renovated by the Westlake Historical Society. (Courtesy of Doris Weston Collection, Westlake Porter Public Library.)

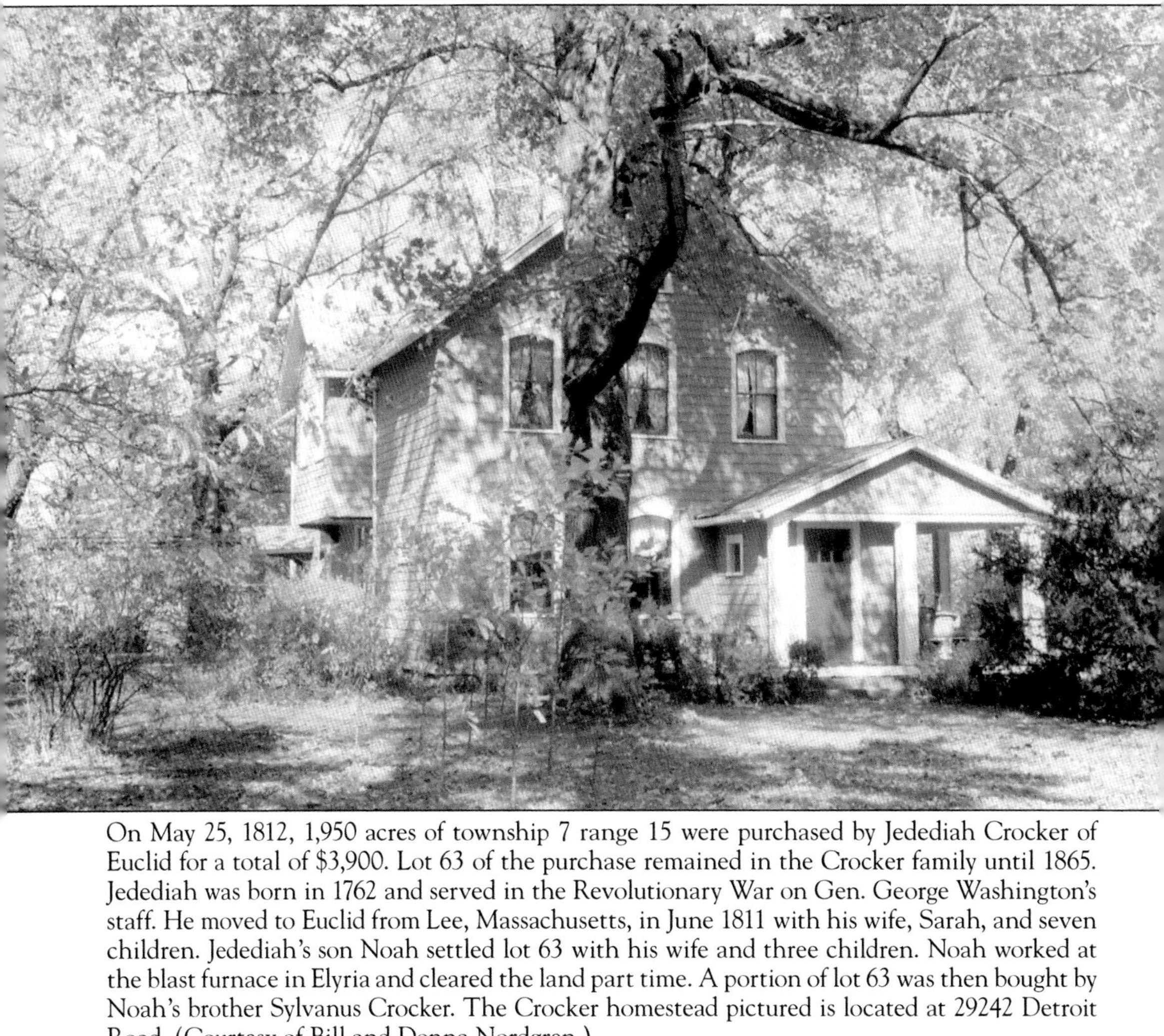

On May 25, 1812, 1,950 acres of township 7 range 15 were purchased by Jedediah Crocker of Euclid for a total of $3,900. Lot 63 of the purchase remained in the Crocker family until 1865. Jedediah was born in 1762 and served in the Revolutionary War on Gen. George Washington's staff. He moved to Euclid from Lee, Massachusetts, in June 1811 with his wife, Sarah, and seven children. Jedediah's son Noah settled lot 63 with his wife and three children. Noah worked at the blast furnace in Elyria and cleared the land part time. A portion of lot 63 was then bought by Noah's brother Sylvanus Crocker. The Crocker homestead pictured is located at 29242 Detroit Road. (Courtesy of Bill and Donna Nordgren.)

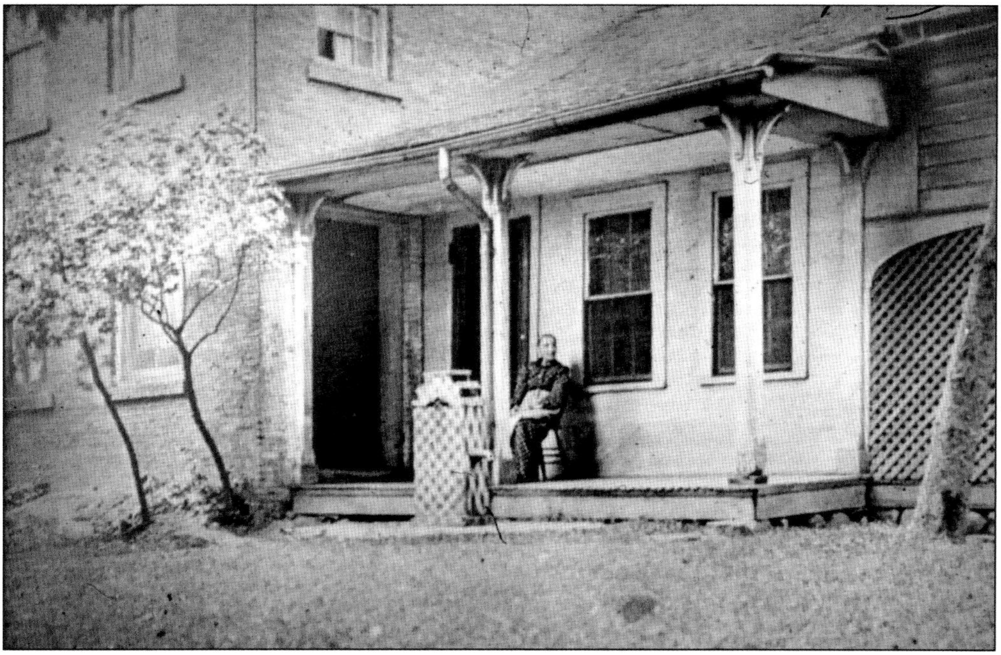

The Trudel family's redbrick home was located on the northwest corner of Glenmore and Center Ridge Roads. (Courtesy of William Robishaw Collection, Westlake Porter Public Library.)

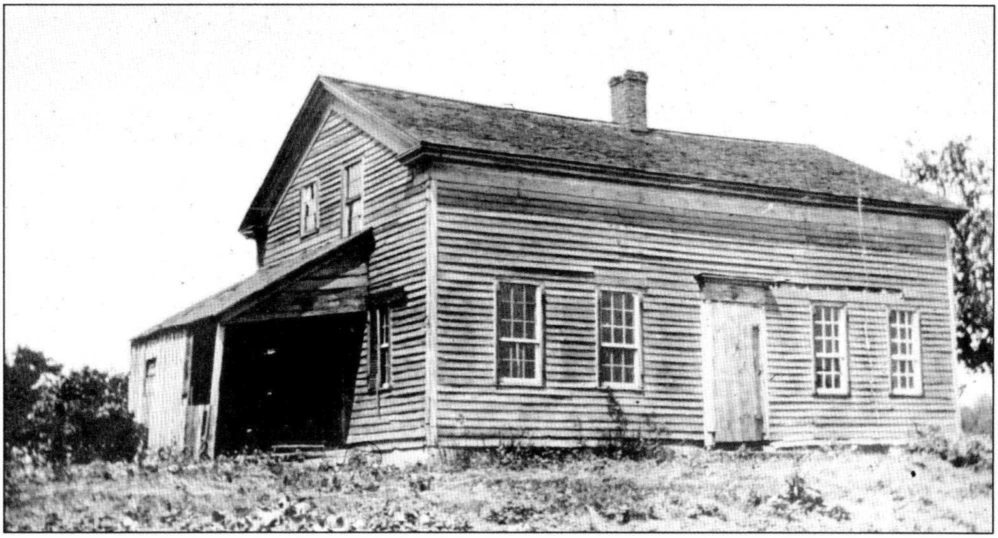

The original Jenkins homestead is pictured here. The Jenkins family was early settlers of Dover. The home was located on Root Road in what is now North Olmsted. (Courtesy of William Robishaw Collection, Westlake Porter Public Library.)

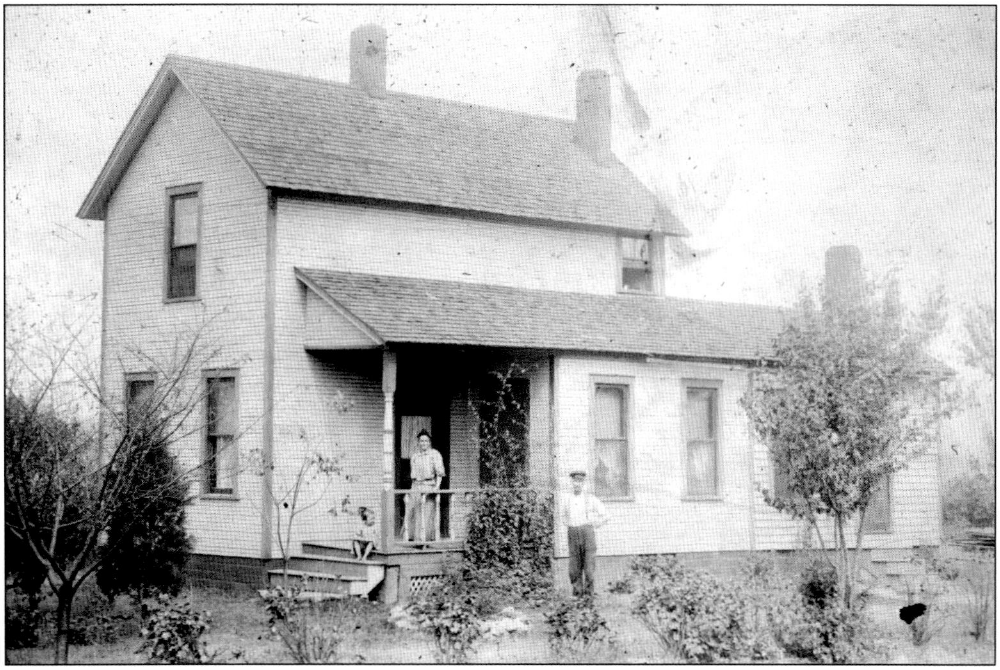

Jabez and Eliza Sperry Mitchell are standing outside their home on Clague Road at the northeastern corner of Center Ridge Road. Eleanor Horwedel MacAllister is seated on the steps. (Courtesy of William Robishaw Collection, Westlake Porter Public Library.)

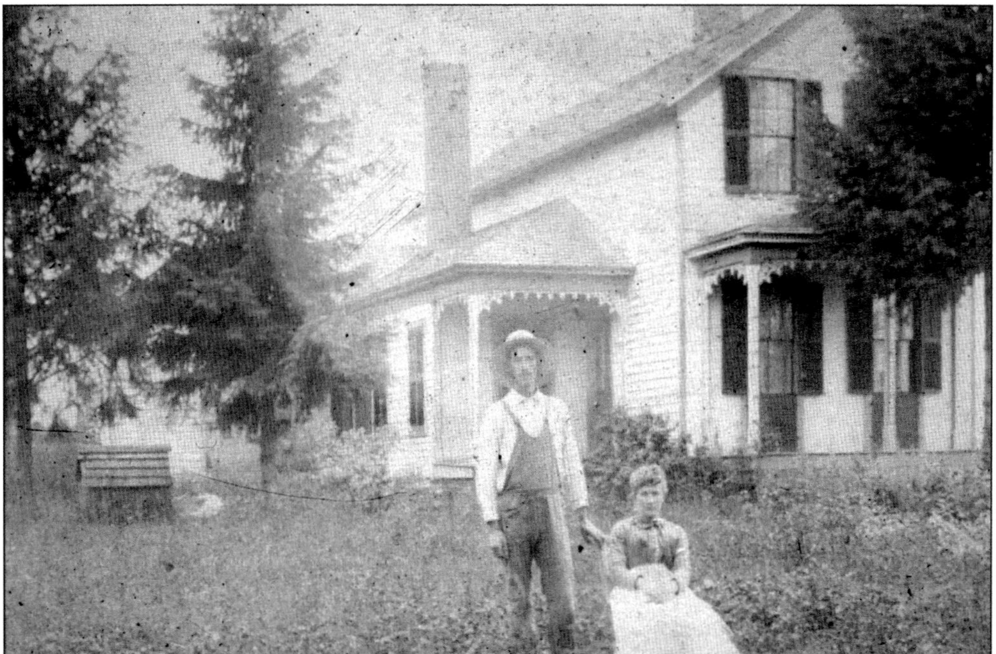

George Lewis and his wife, Eureka, pose in front of their farmhouse at 24629 Detroit Road around 1897. The home is no longer standing. (Courtesy of William Robishaw Collection, Westlake Porter Public Library.)

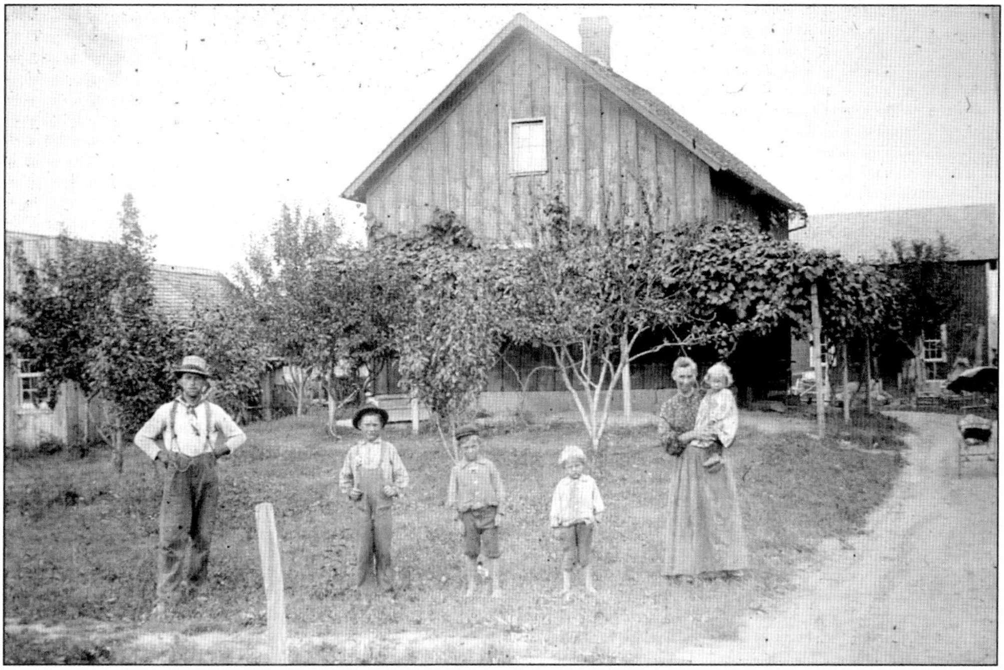

This 1886 photograph shows a farmhouse that was located at 1863 Dover Center Road near Hilliard Road. (Courtesy of William Robishaw Collection, Westlake Porter Public Library.)

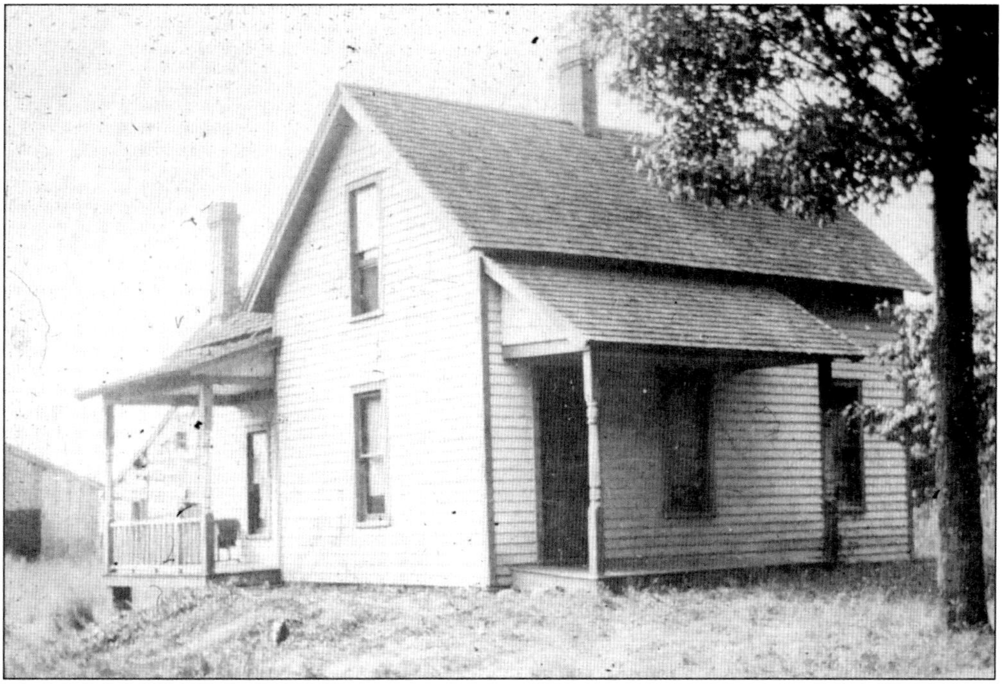

This home, built in 1874, belonged to Teresa Beardsley. The house was located on Dover Center Road and was later moved across the street and became the second house north of Rose Road on the east side of Dover. (Courtesy of William Robishaw Collection, Westlake Porter Public Library.)

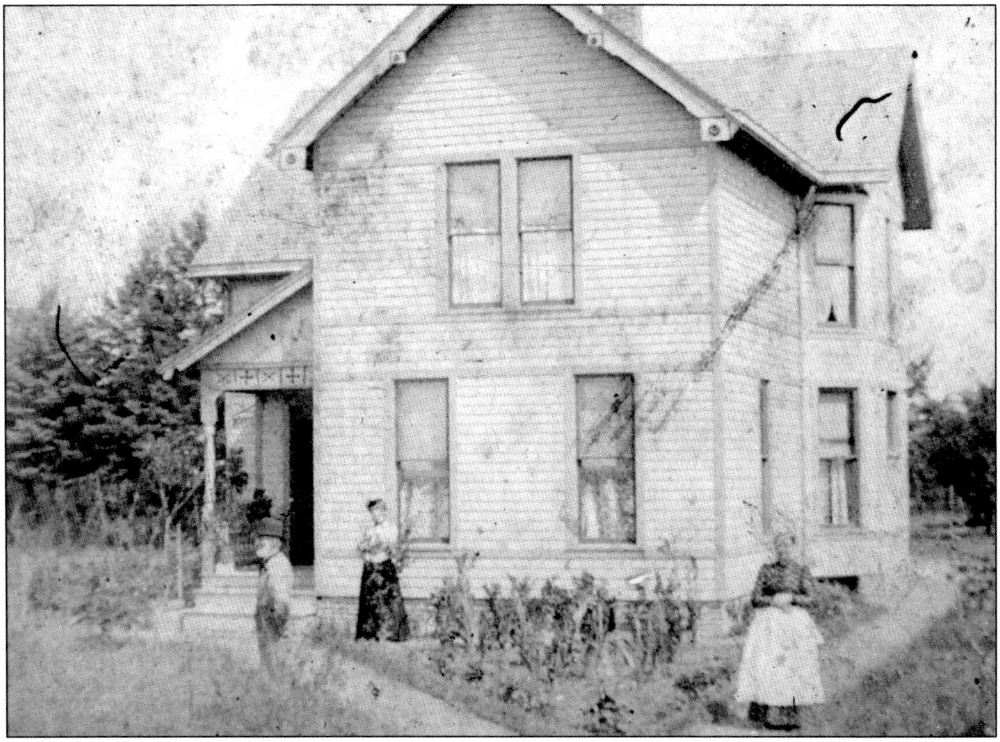

Born about 1872 and raised in Dover, Gustav Kluever married in the early 1900s. In this picture, he and Mary Kluever are shown in front of their farmhouse in early Dover. The vegetable patch along the walk appears to be ready to harvest. (Courtesy of William Robishaw Collection, Westlake Porter Public Library.)

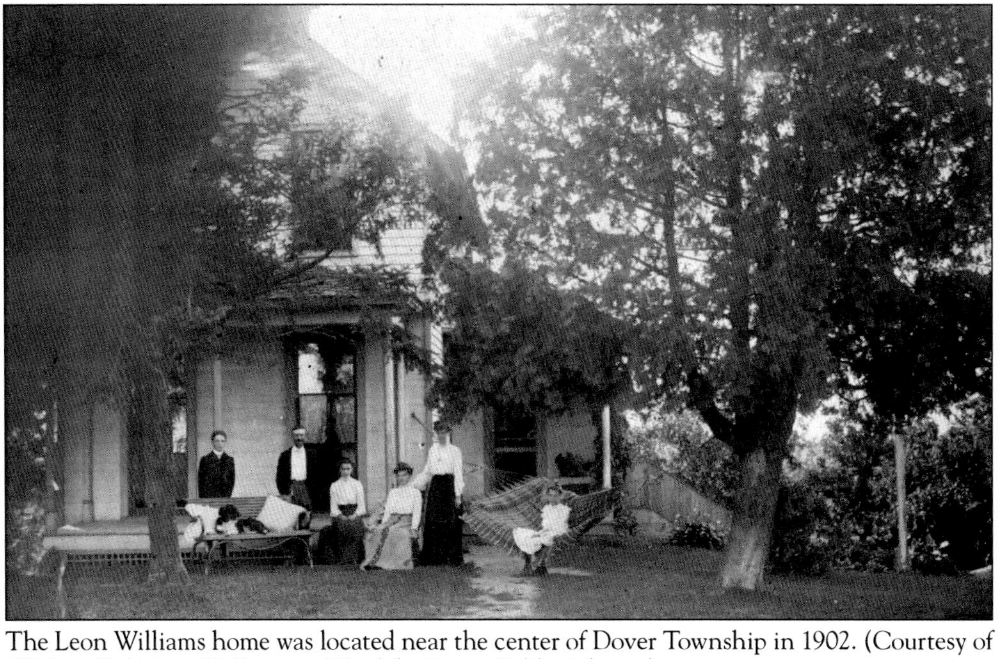

The Leon Williams home was located near the center of Dover Township in 1902. (Courtesy of William Robishaw Collection, Westlake Porter Public Library.)

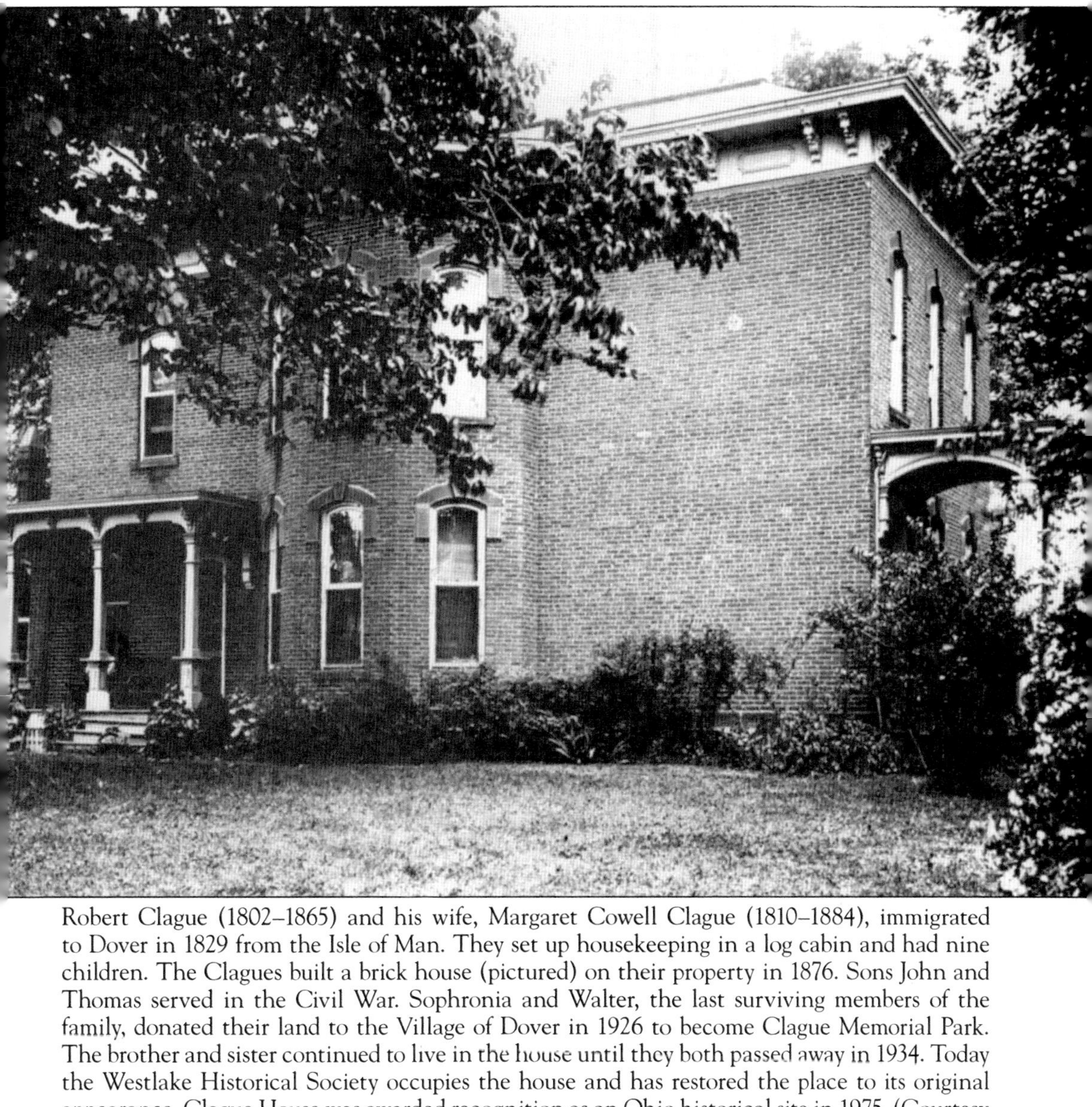

Robert Clague (1802–1865) and his wife, Margaret Cowell Clague (1810–1884), immigrated to Dover in 1829 from the Isle of Man. They set up housekeeping in a log cabin and had nine children. The Clagues built a brick house (pictured) on their property in 1876. Sons John and Thomas served in the Civil War. Sophronia and Walter, the last surviving members of the family, donated their land to the Village of Dover in 1926 to become Clague Memorial Park. The brother and sister continued to live in the house until they both passed away in 1934. Today the Westlake Historical Society occupies the house and has restored the place to its original appearance. Clague House was awarded recognition as an Ohio historical site in 1975. (Courtesy of William Robishaw Collection, Westlake Porter Public Library.)

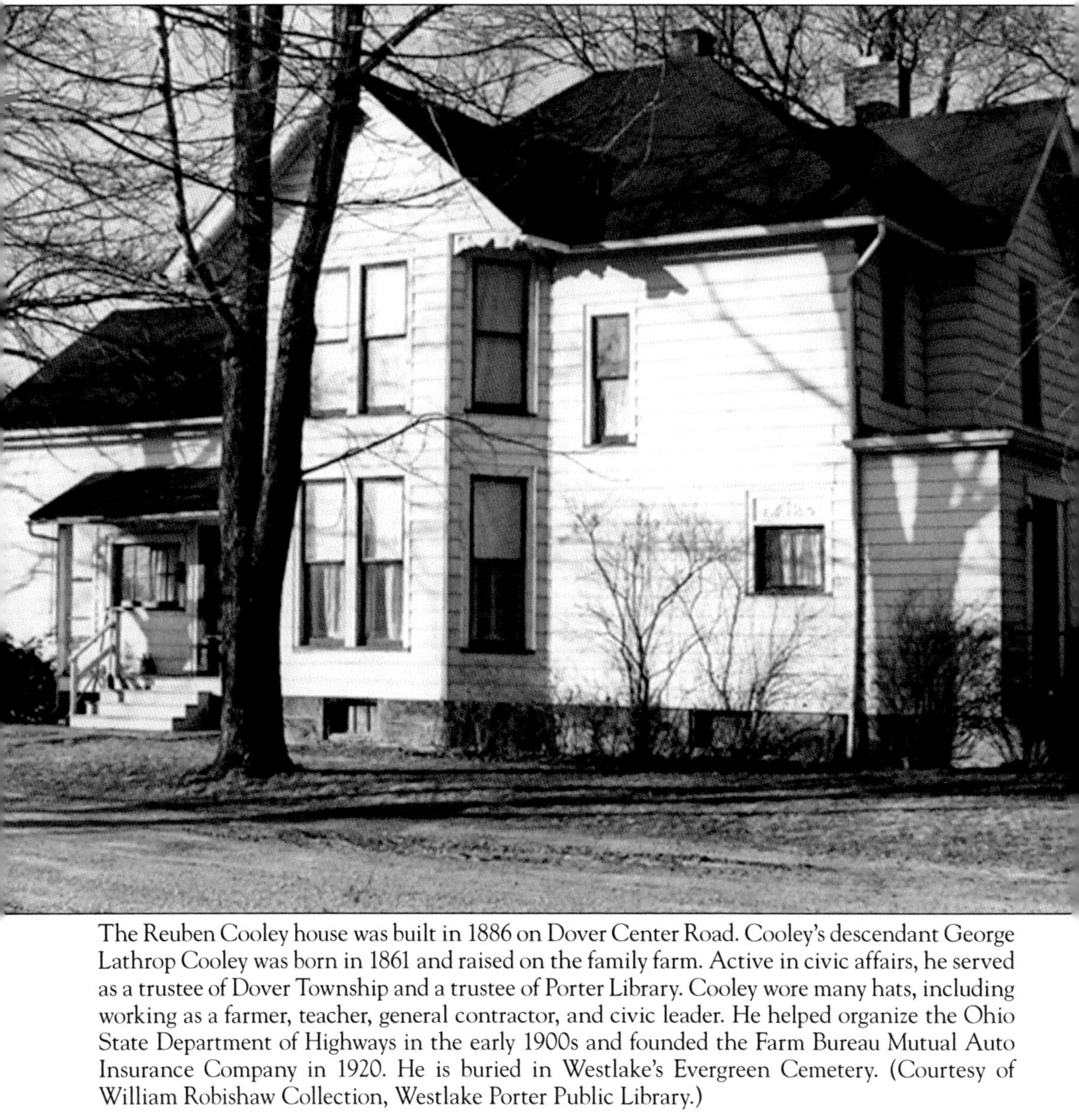

The Reuben Cooley house was built in 1886 on Dover Center Road. Cooley's descendant George Lathrop Cooley was born in 1861 and raised on the family farm. Active in civic affairs, he served as a trustee of Dover Township and a trustee of Porter Library. Cooley wore many hats, including working as a farmer, teacher, general contractor, and civic leader. He helped organize the Ohio State Department of Highways in the early 1900s and founded the Farm Bureau Mutual Auto Insurance Company in 1920. He is buried in Westlake's Evergreen Cemetery. (Courtesy of William Robishaw Collection, Westlake Porter Public Library.)

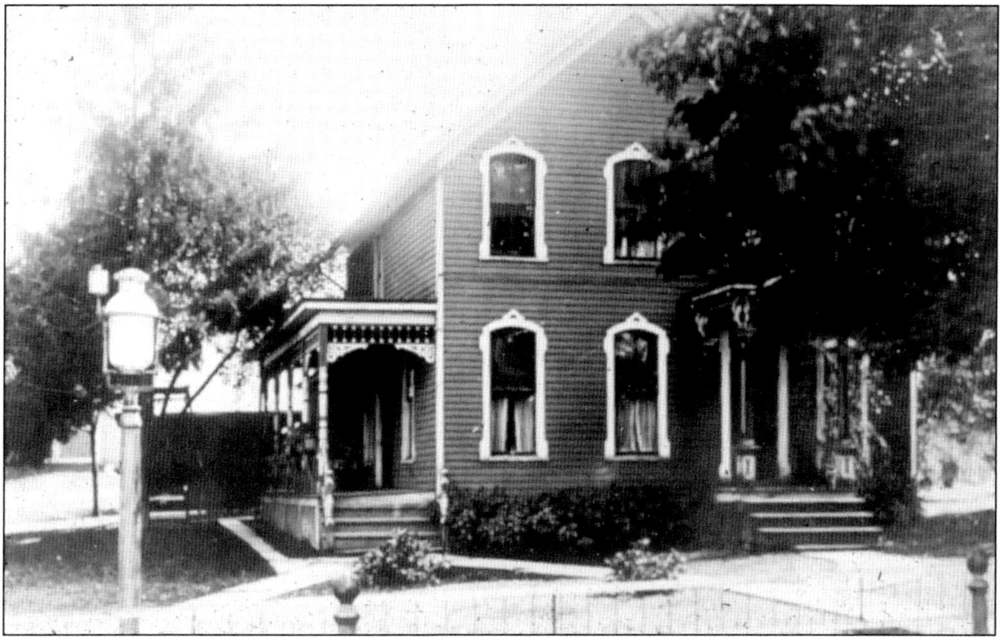

Dr. George Lathrop's home was located on Center Ridge Road just east of Dover Center Road near the center of town. Lathrop and his wife, Minnie, had two daughters, Josephine and Helen. (Courtesy of William Robishaw Collection, Westlake Porter Public Library.)

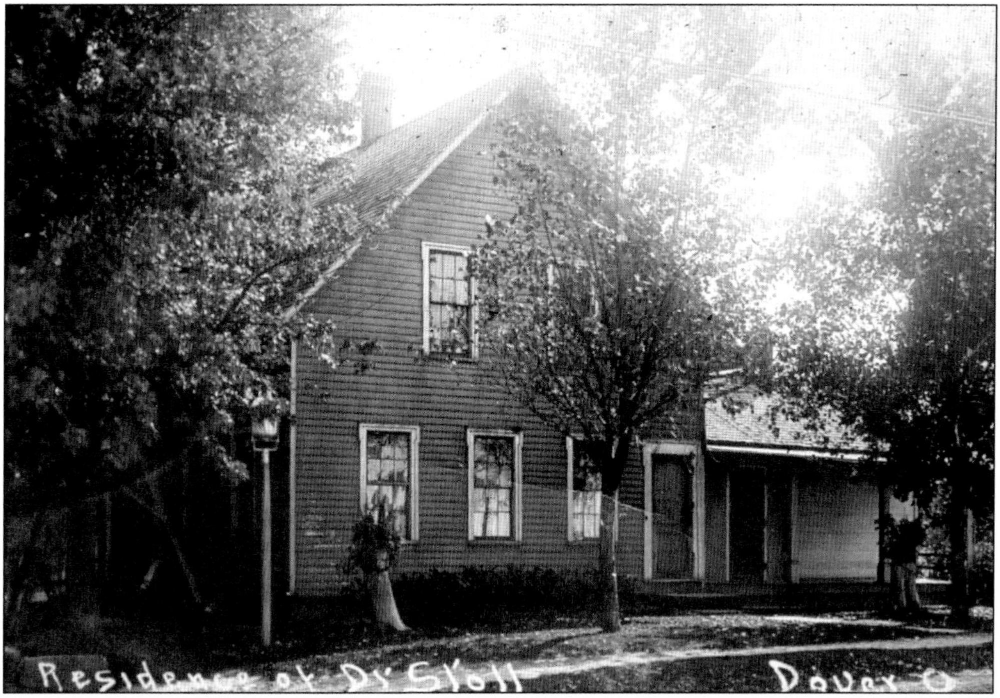

Dr. Christopher Stall's residence was also near the center of Dover. Stall (listed as Stoll here) and his wife, Eva, lived at 2543 Dover Center Road. (Courtesy of William Robishaw Collection, Westlake Porter Public Library.)

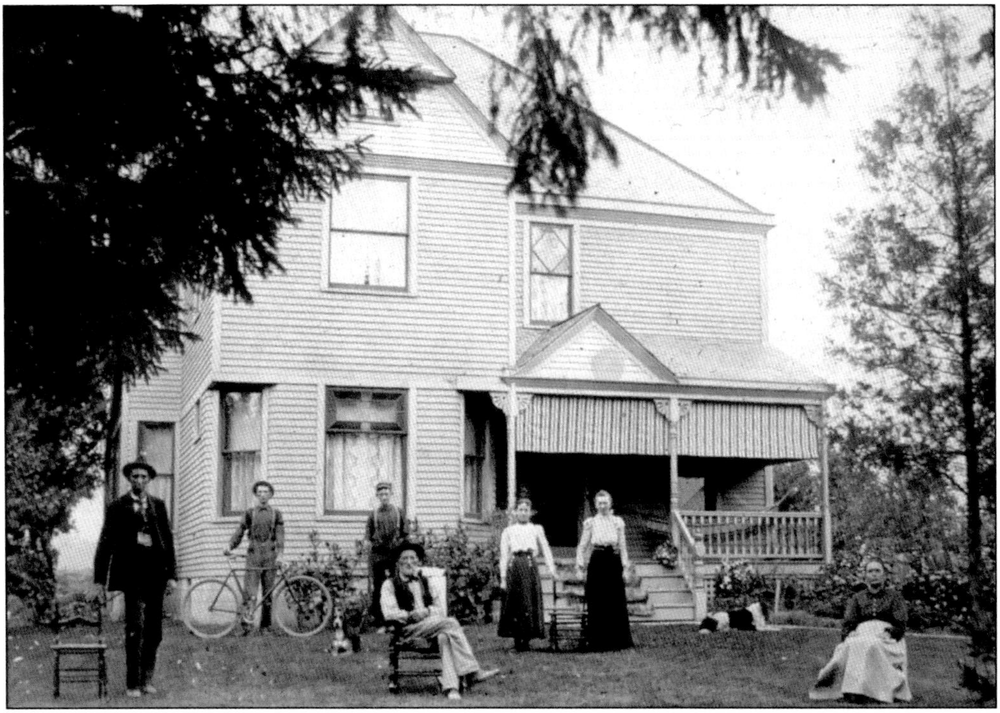

Pictured about 1905, the Wilbert family home was built in 1893 at 1793 Dover Center Road. (Courtesy of Westlake Historical Society Collection.)

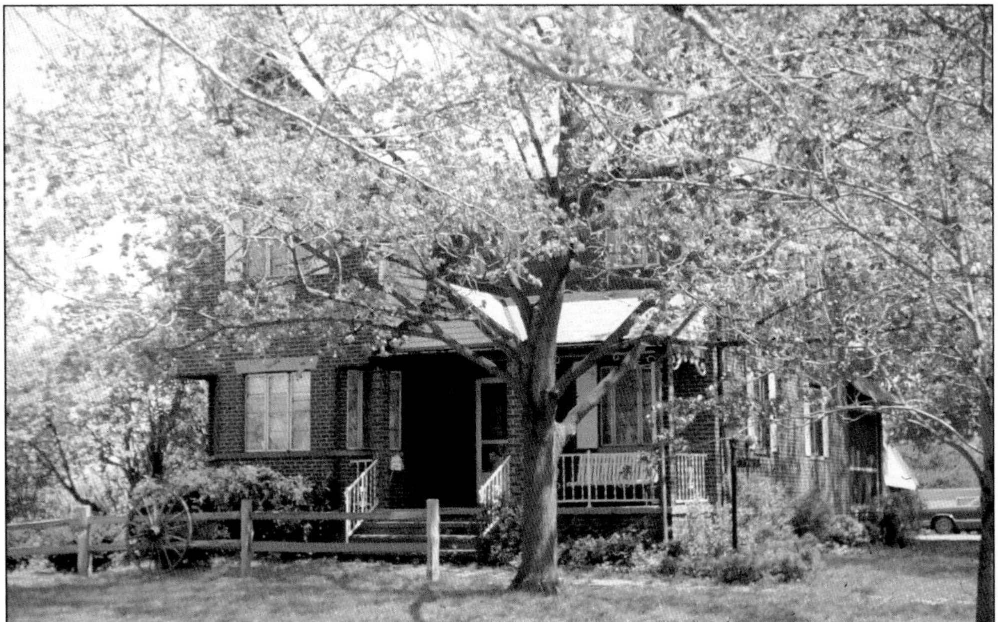

The same house at 1793 Dover Center Road is pictured in more recent years. (Courtesy of Westlake Historical Society Collection.)

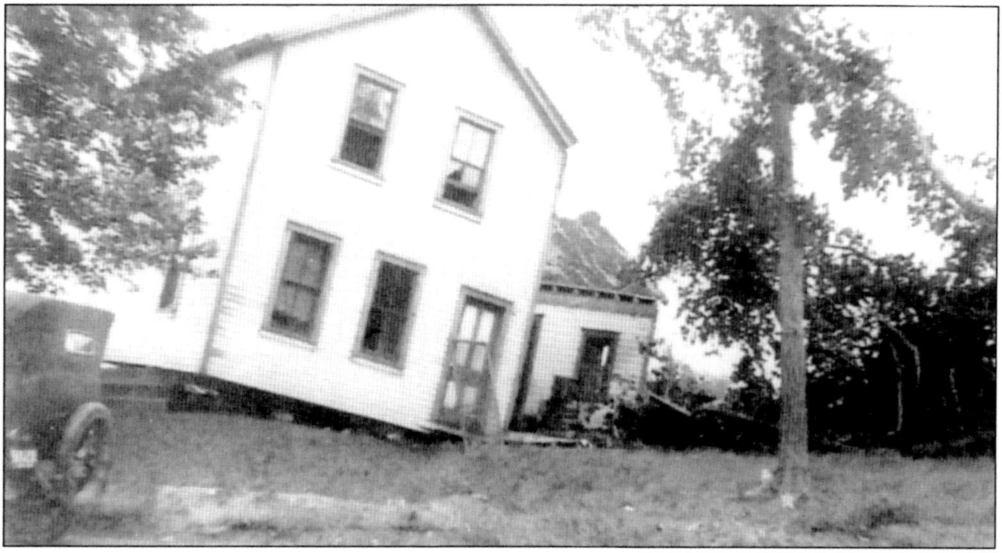

Bradley Road was paved in 1922. A storm struck the area on June 28, 1924, destroying the George Oster home. "A tornado blew every building down except the house which was damaged. All the trees were blown down," said Ann Dietz Surman. (Courtesy of Diane Oster.)

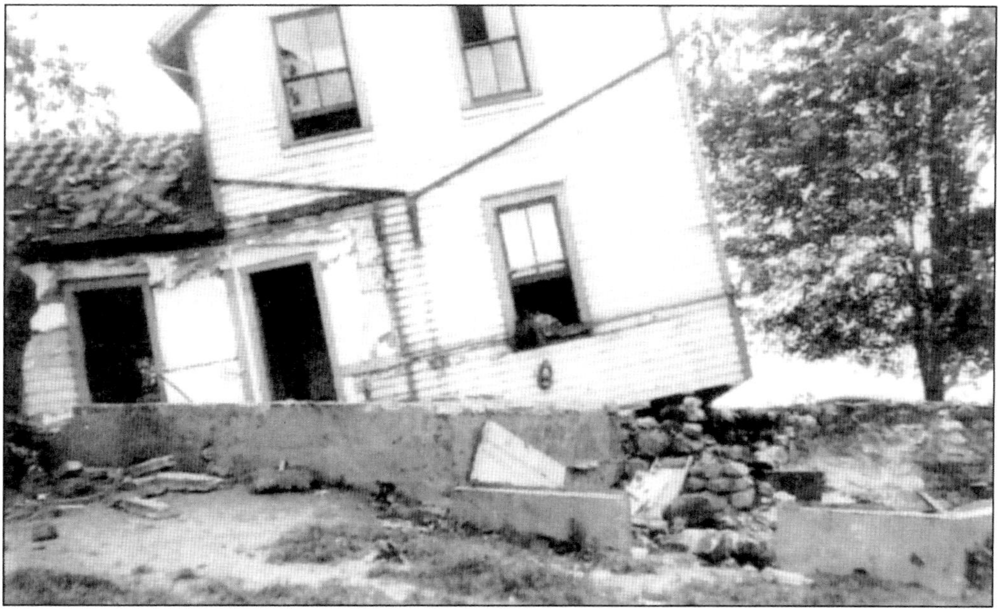

The number of fatalities from this deadly storm will never be certain, but an accepted figure of 85 dead included 72 in the city of Lorain. At least four tornadoes touched down. Wind and flood damage were widespread. (Courtesy of Diane Oster.)

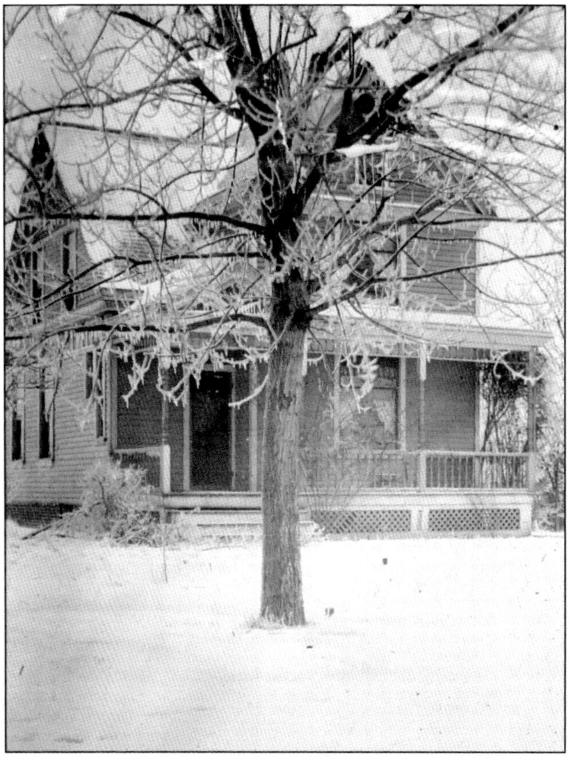

The Tanner home at 2339 Clague Road is pictured here in the winter of 1928. Alva Tanner died suddenly in 1929, and the Great Depression brought hard times to the family. After the Tanners lost the farm, Doris Tanner became an insurance agent for the Farm Bureau Mutual Auto Insurance Company. The company later changed its name to Nationwide Insurance. (Courtesy of William Robishaw Collection, Westlake Porter Public Library.)

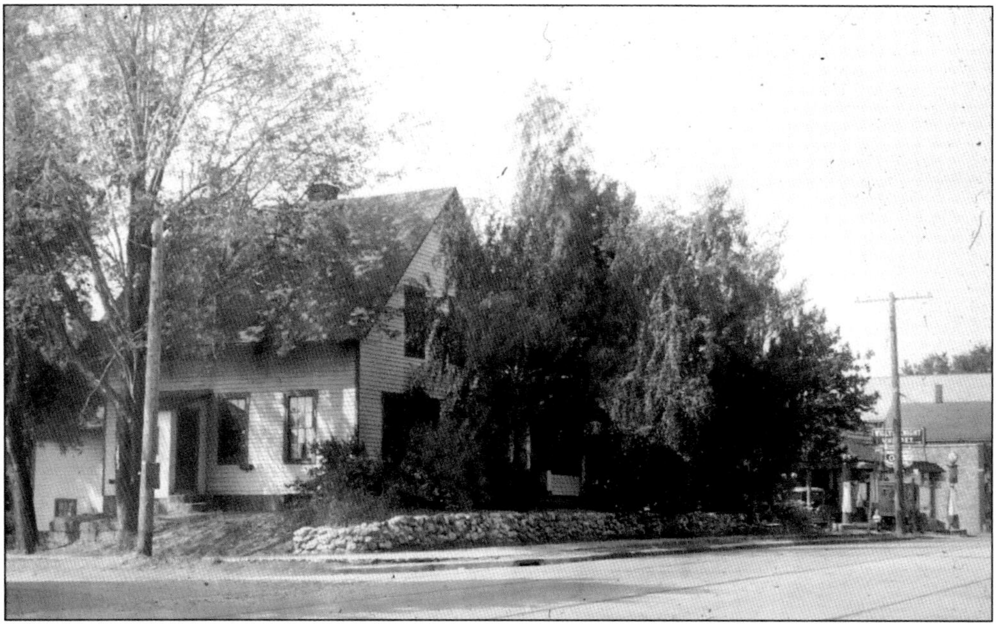

Frank Sauer's home was located on the southwest corner of Center Ridge and Dover Center Roads in what came to be known as Sauer's Corners. Sauer's businesses included the garage and machine shop, the Overland and Whippet-Willys Knight Sales and Service, and Sauer's Corner mower and garden tractor service and sales. (Courtesy of William Robishaw Collection, Westlake Porter Public Library.)

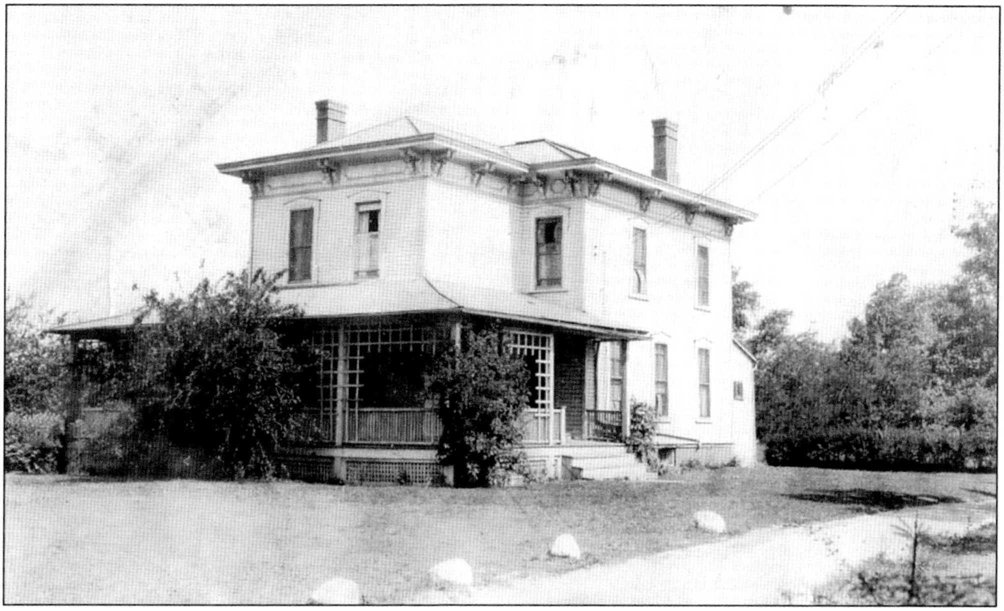

Henry B. Spencer built the house pictured here in 1870 in what is now Bay Village. He used the property for rental income. Leo G. DeWitt purchased the house from the Washington Lawrence estate in March 1929. (Courtesy of Herman and Susan Jachnick.)

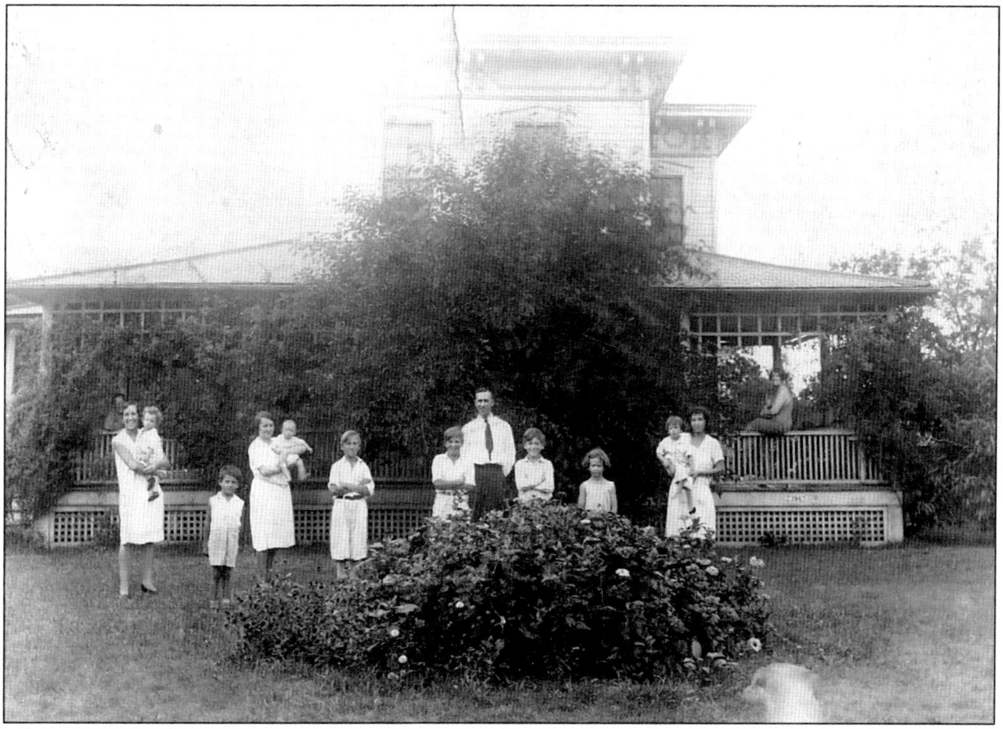

This photograph of the DeWitt family was taken by Leo W. DeWitt, 17 years old, in 1929. From left to right are Dorothy (holding Ray), Donald, Mary (holding Julian), Norbert, Aubrey, Leo G. DeWitt, James, Mary Jane, and Marcella (holding Rose Marie). (Courtesy of Herman and Susan Jachnick.)

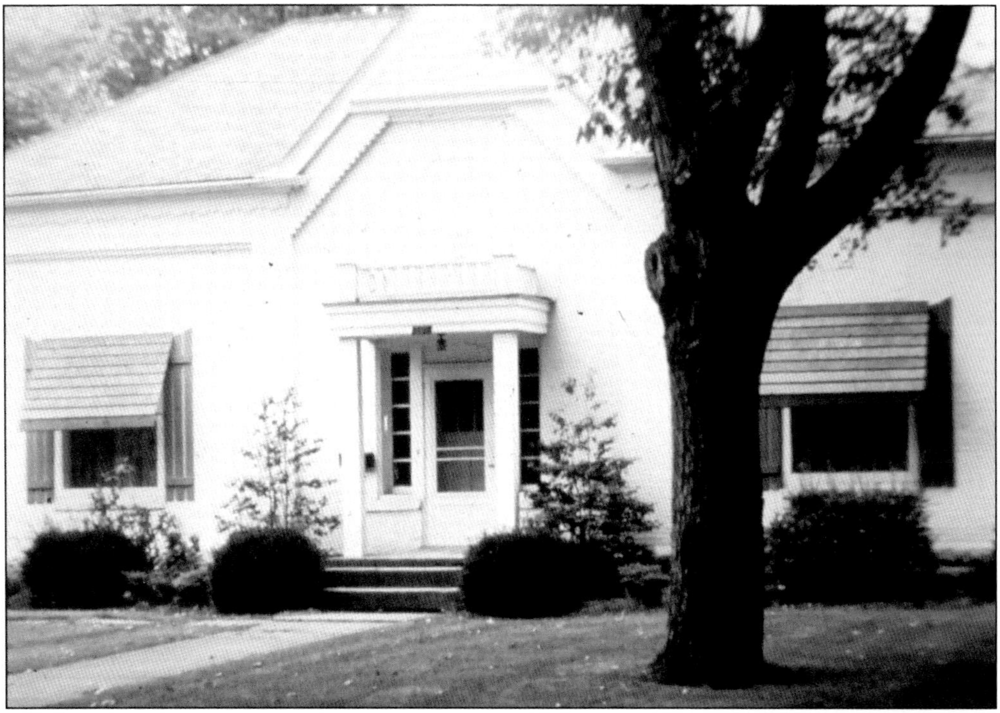

William Yaeger attended Depot School. He later purchased the school and made it his family residence. (Courtesy of William Robishaw Collection, Westlake Porter Public Library.)

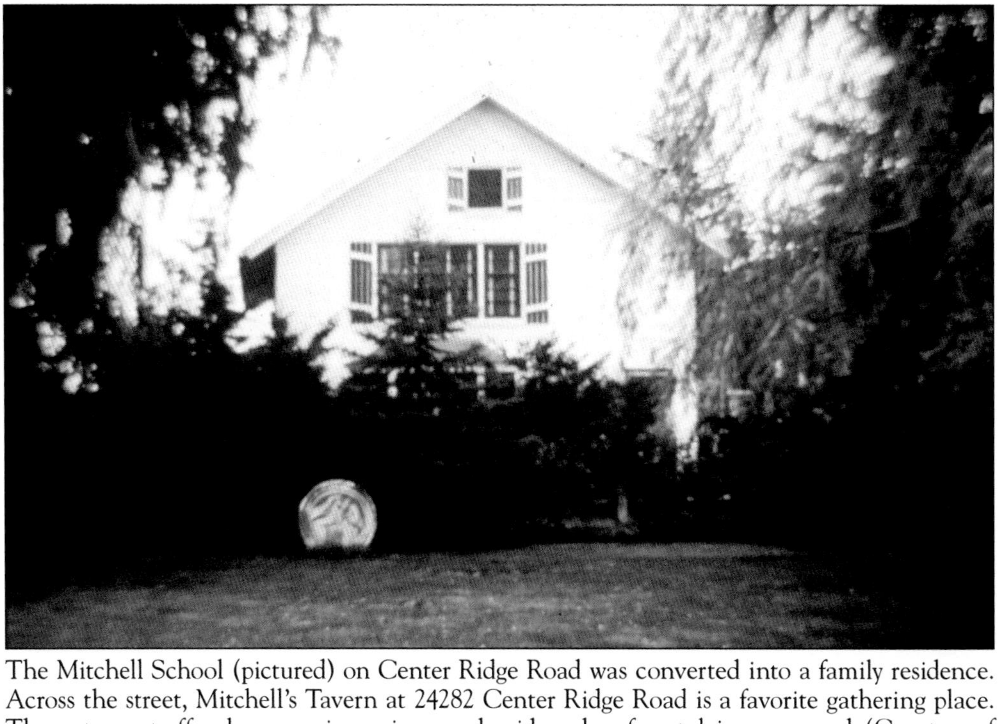

The Mitchell School (pictured) on Center Ridge Road was converted into a family residence. Across the street, Mitchell's Tavern at 24282 Center Ridge Road is a favorite gathering place. The restaurant offers burgers, pizza, wings, and a side order of nostalgia year-round. (Courtesy of William Robishaw Collection, Westlake Porter Public Library.)

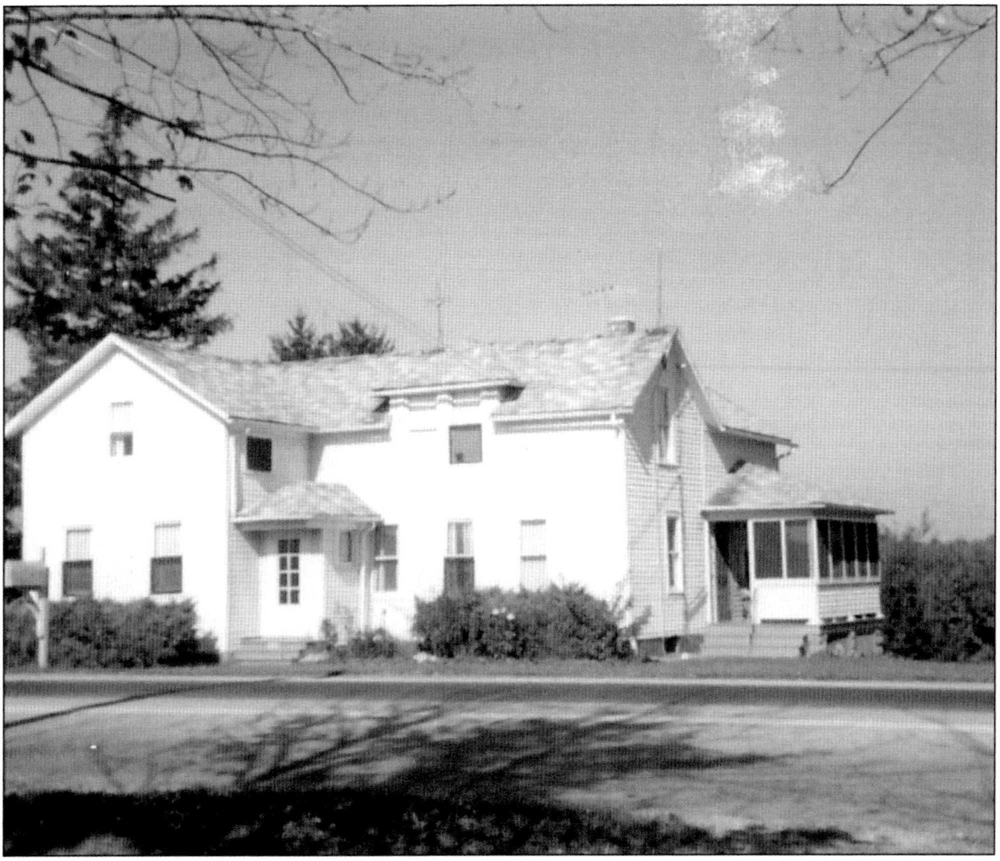

The Dorow home and farm were located on Detroit Road. (Courtesy of Ken Given.)

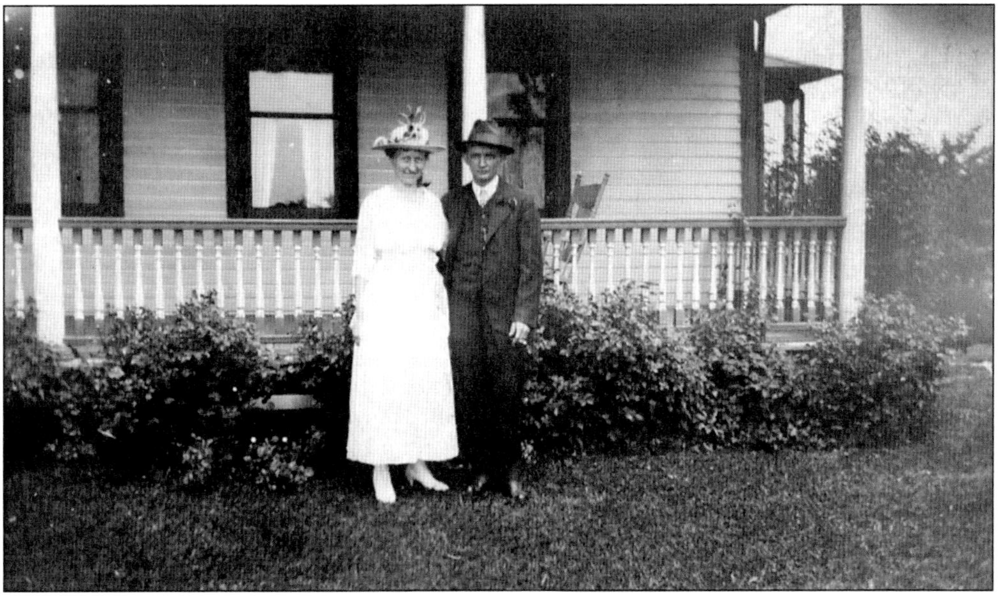

An unidentified couple smiles for the camera. (Courtesy of Ken Given.)

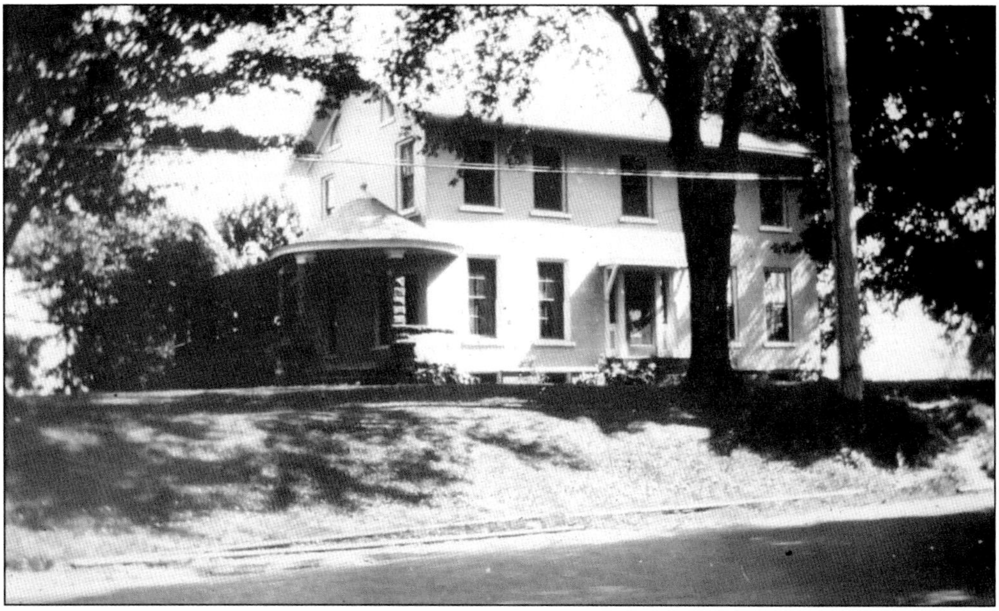

The Glendenning home is located at 28989 Center Ridge Road. In 1963, Alfred Glendenning, an officer in the Ohio Farm Bureau Association, recommended the formation of a farm bureau council to provide suggestions about subjects affecting the quality of living at local, county, state, and national levels. (Courtesy of William Robishaw Collection, Westlake Porter Public Library.)

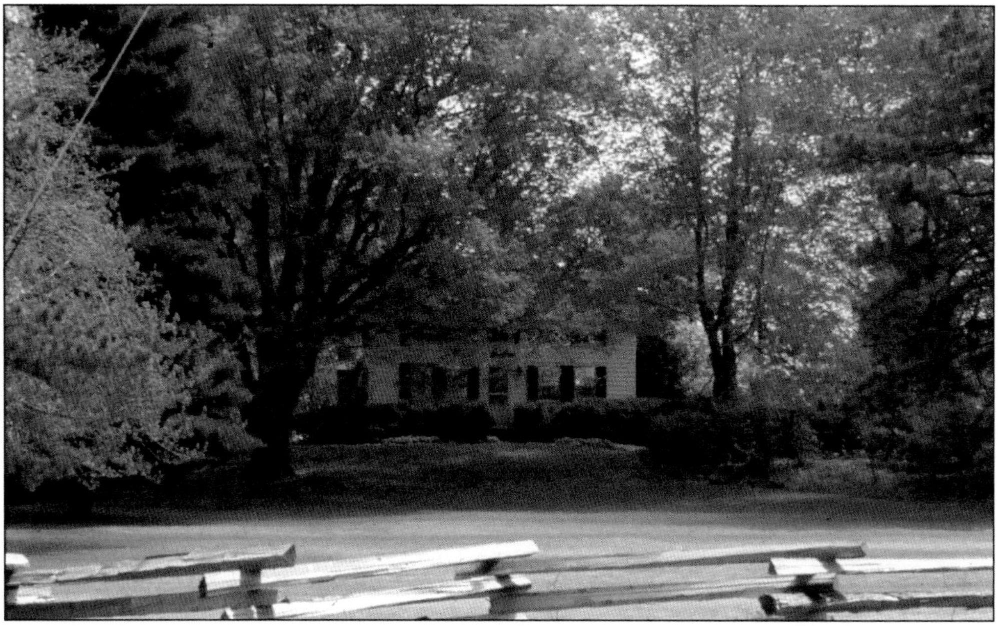

The Alexander century house located at 2639 Columbia Road is an example of the Cape Cod style. The three principal facades of the house have been a major factor in its preservation. Five single-hung windows are operated by sliding into a space concealed in the wall between the window head and the eave. The home is noted for period antique furnishings. (Courtesy of William Robishaw Collection, Westlake Porter Public Library.)

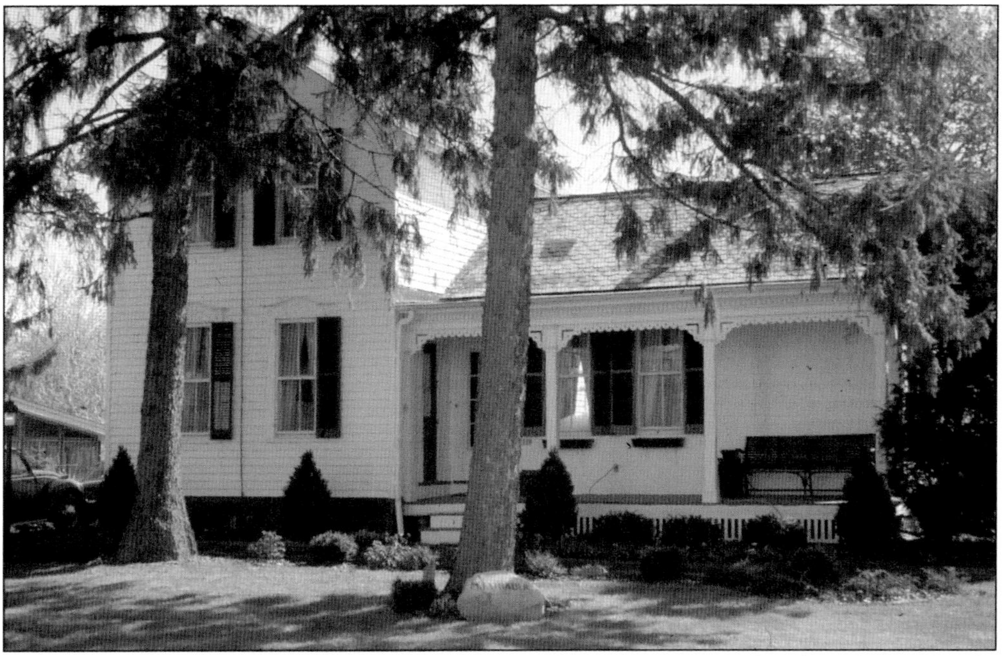

Built in 1853, this home at 1119 Bassett Road belonged to the Frederick Fathauer family. According to the Cuyahoga County recorder's records, Wilhelmina (Minnie) Fathauer sold the home to Robert and Laurene Deucher on March 26, 1969. Minnie is buried at St. Paul Cemetery in Westlake. (Courtesy of William Robishaw Collection, Westlake Porter Public Library.)

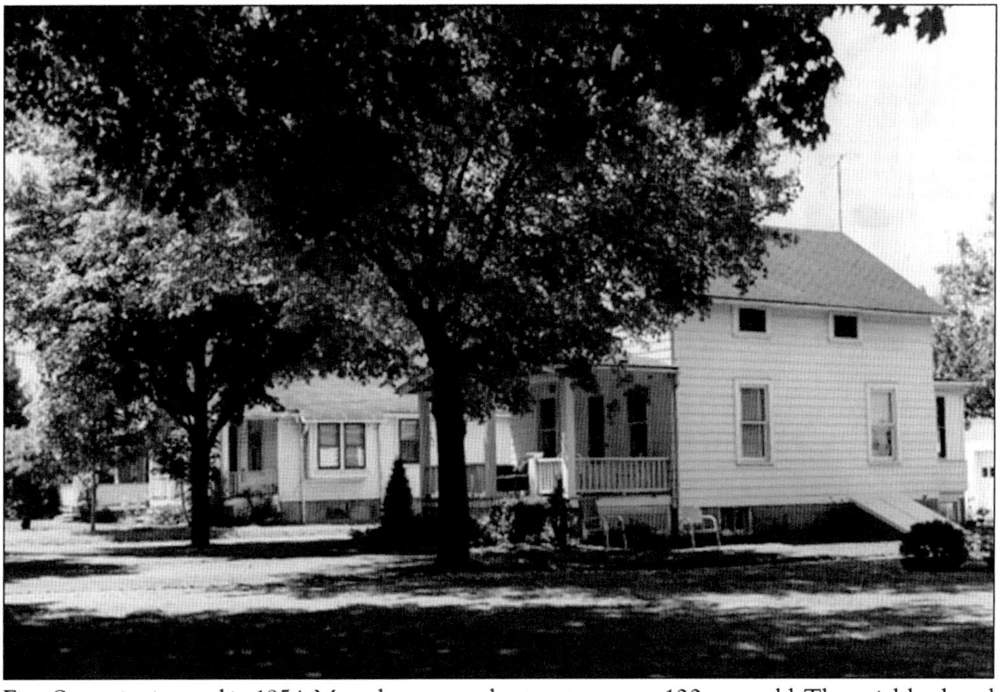

First Street is pictured in 1954. Many homes on the street are over 100 years old. The neighborhood is located in northern Westlake and borders Bay Village. (Courtesy of Cleveland State University, Cleveland Memory Project, Cleveland Press Collection, Joseph E. Cole, donor.)

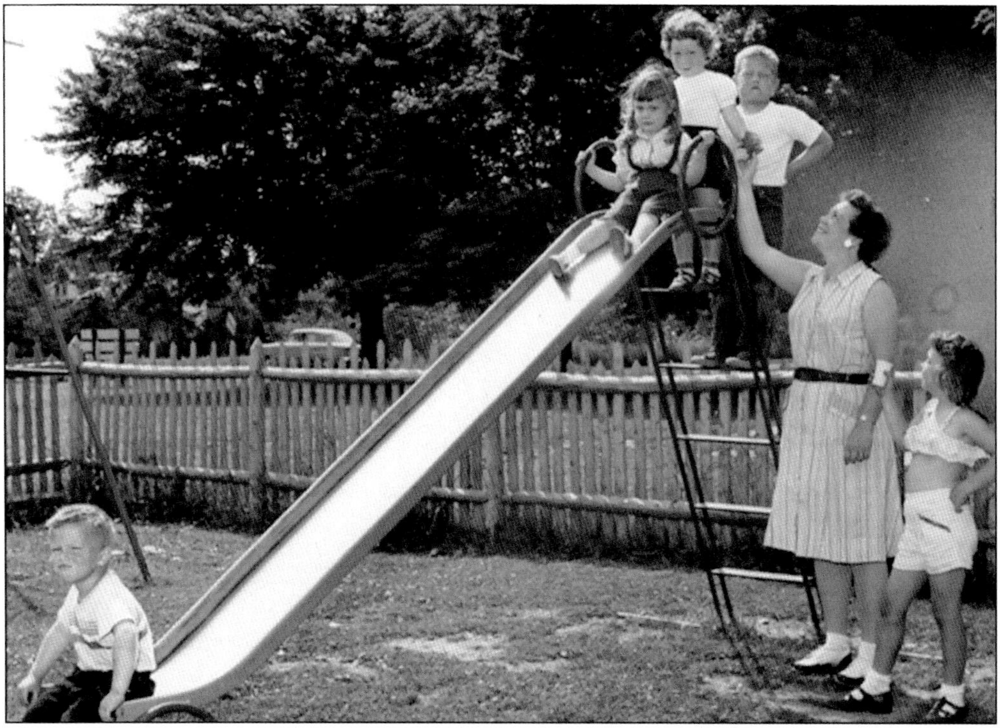

This backyard scene was featured in the *Cleveland Press* on June 1, 1955. Pictured from left to right are Peter Rock, Kate Zwierlein, Nancy O'Rourke, John Chindlund, Shirley O'Rourke, and Terry O'Rourke. (Courtesy of Cleveland State University, Cleveland Memory Project, Cleveland Press Collection, Joseph E. Cole, donor.)

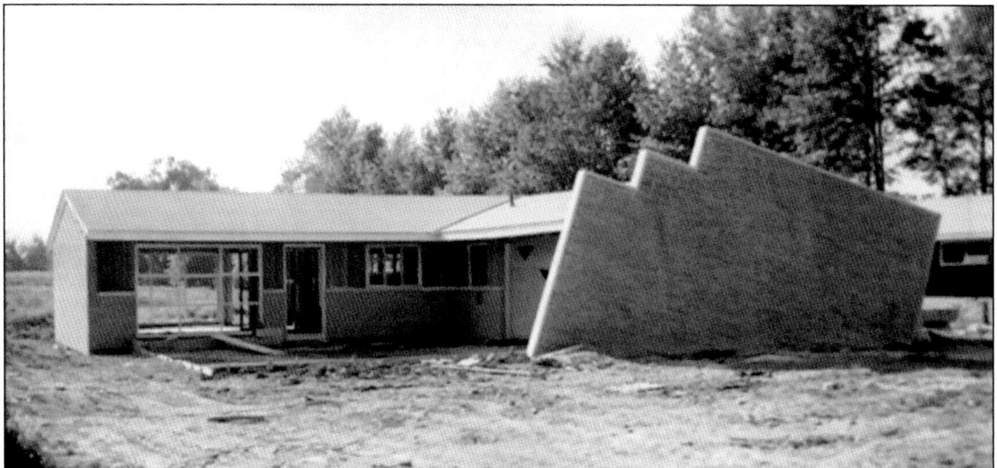

This photograph was taken on September 6, 1955. The back of the photograph reads, "Leaning wall is the unique feature of a ranch-style home being built at 2730 Walter Road, Westlake, and is not a construction mistake. Designer of the wall (and home) William Galick, got the idea when he saw a similar home in Florida. Builders say 40 to 50 motorists stop each day to stare and make such comments as 'When did the wall fall?' and 'When are you going to straighten it?'" (Courtesy of Cleveland State University, Cleveland Memory Project, Cleveland Press Collection, Joseph E. Cole, donor.)

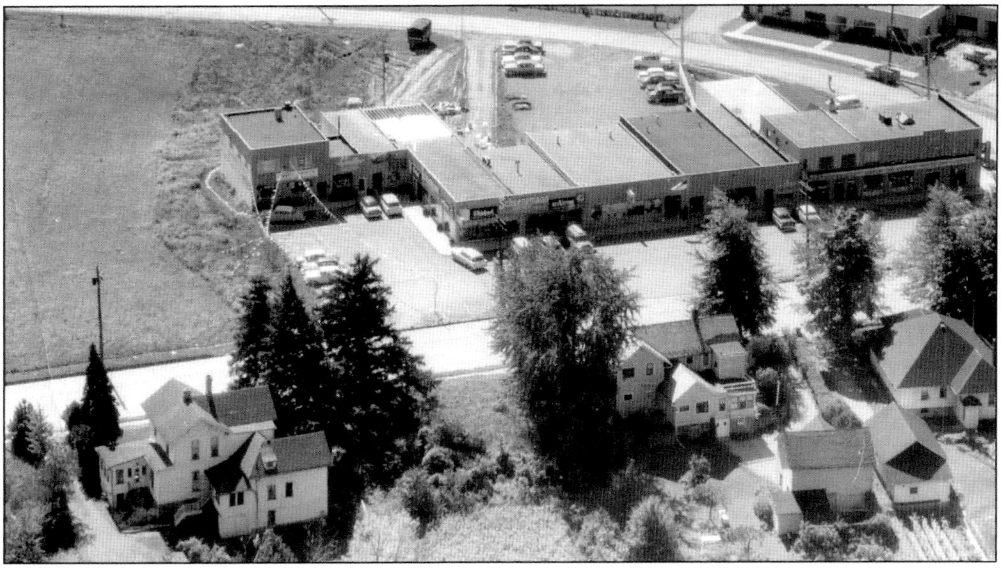

This 1956 aerial view of Center Ridge and Westwood Roads shows the home of Patricia Seggie on the far left. It is still standing today. The other houses pictured were demolished to build a shopping center. On the south side of Center Ridge Road, Schuenemann's appliance store advertised Whirlpool and RCA Victor brands. A grocery store and hardware store offered convenient shopping. Baluk's, at right, was a popular bookstore throughout the 1990s, serving the community with a wide assortment of books, magazines, and giftware. (Courtesy of Patricia Seggie.)

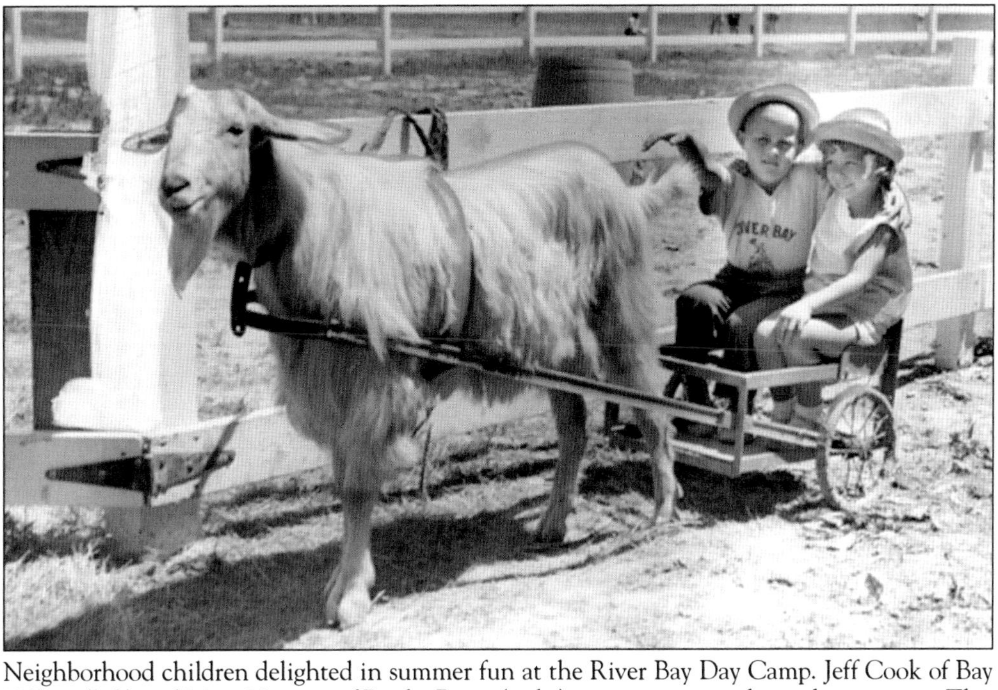

Neighborhood children delighted in summer fun at the River Bay Day Camp. Jeff Cook of Bay Village (left) and Mary Hegarty of Rocky River (right) are enjoying a ride on the goat cart. This picture was taken on June 26, 1957. (Courtesy of Cleveland State University, Cleveland Memory Project, Cleveland Press Collection, Joseph E. Cole, donor.)

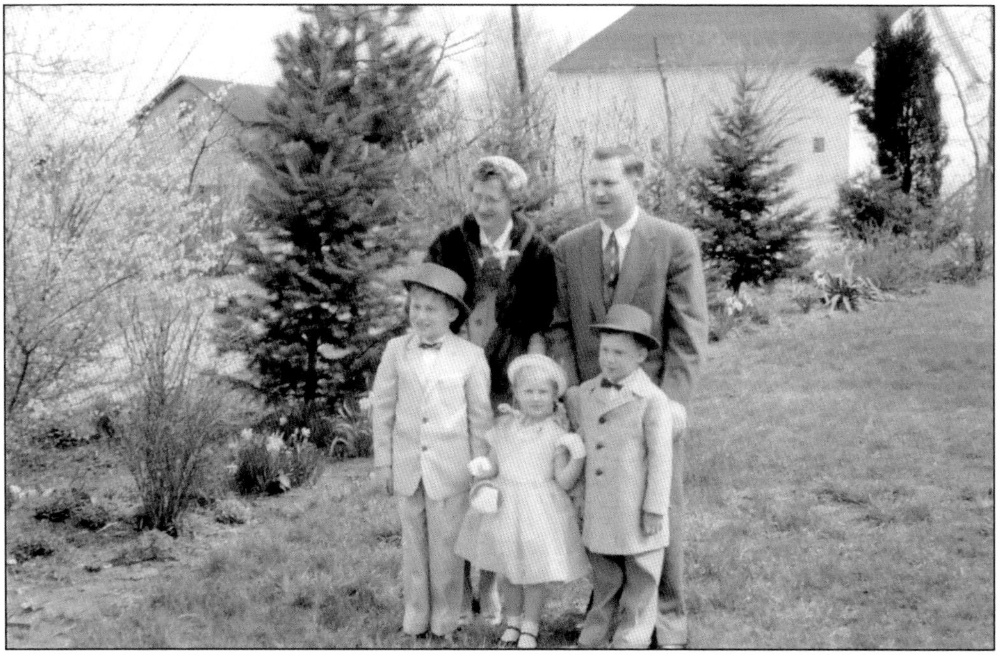

The Essig family is shown on Easter Sunday in 1957 in front of their farmhouse on Detroit Road. In 1942, Dora Essig (left) purchased 23 acres of land with her husband, Heinrich, to build a farm. Her granddaughter Barbara Essig Macy stands between her brothers in her Easter Sunday bonnet. (Courtesy of Barbara Macy.)

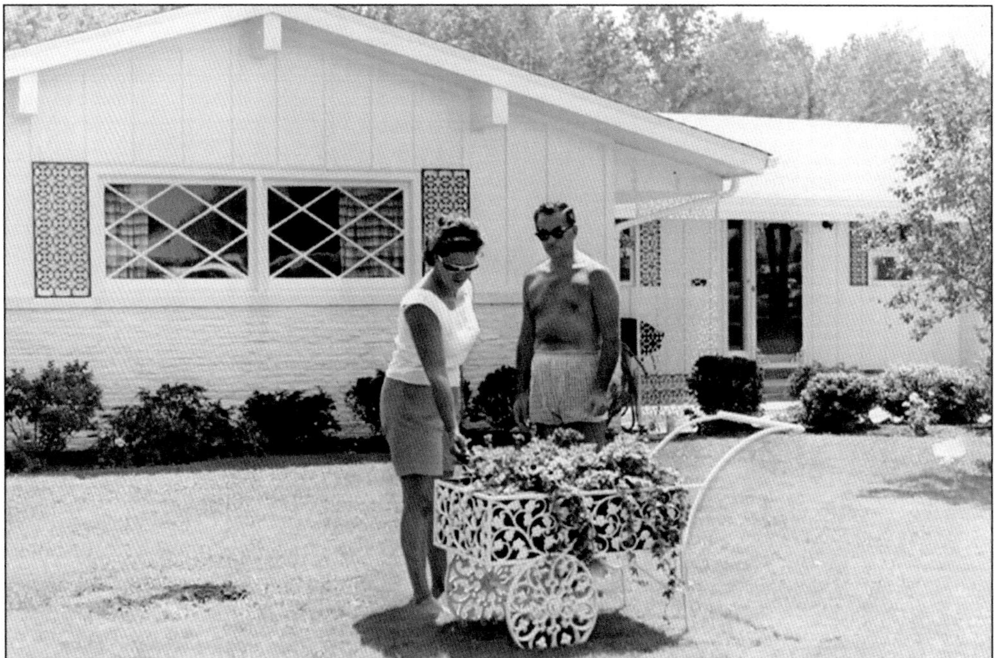

Don and Anne King are shown in front of their home at 24461 Westwood Road in Westlake on August 10, 1964. King was the owner of King Furniture. (Courtesy of Cleveland State University, Cleveland Memory Project, Cleveland Press Collection, Joseph E. Cole, donor.)

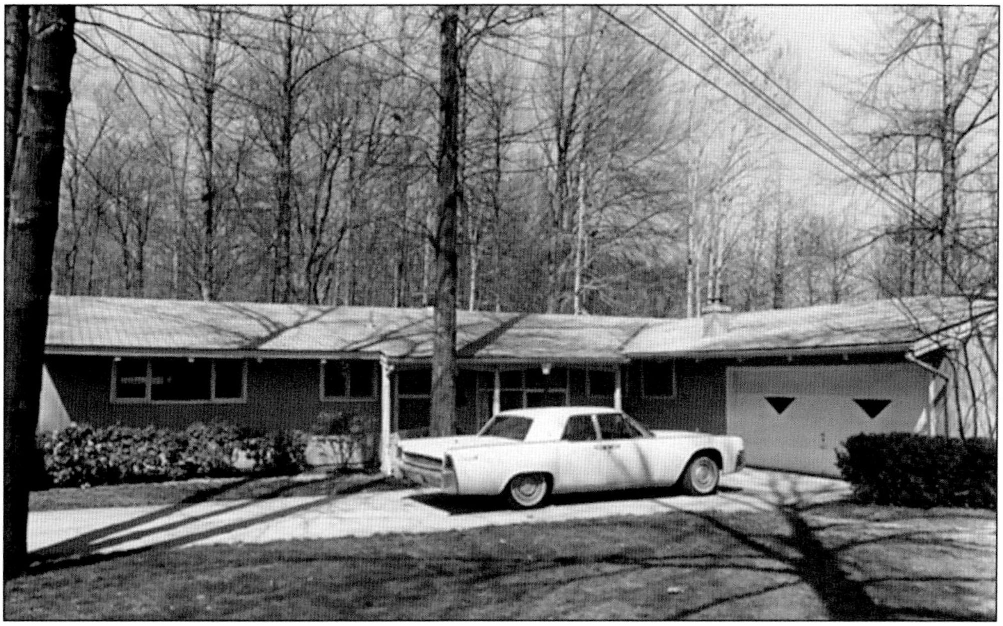

The front exterior of Westlake mayor John T. Kirk's residence is shown in 1964. (Courtesy of Cleveland State University, Cleveland Memory Project, Cleveland Press Collection, Joseph E. Cole, donor.)

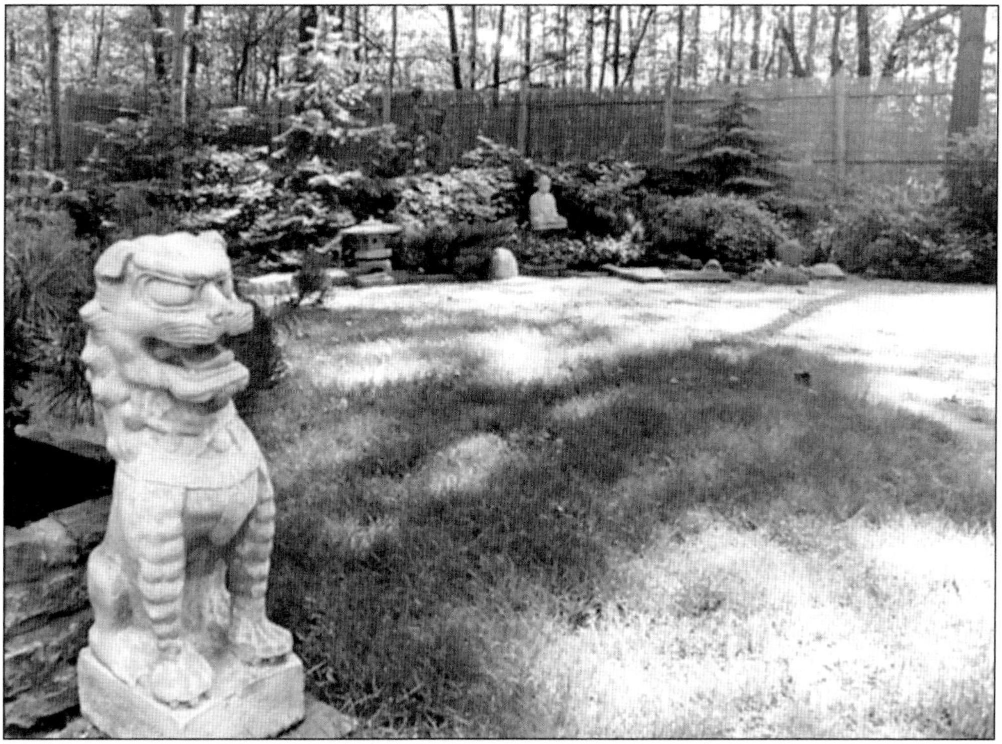

The back exterior of Kirk's residence features a Japanese garden and welcoming statue. (Courtesy of Cleveland State University, Cleveland Memory Project, Cleveland Press Collection, Joseph E. Cole, donor.)

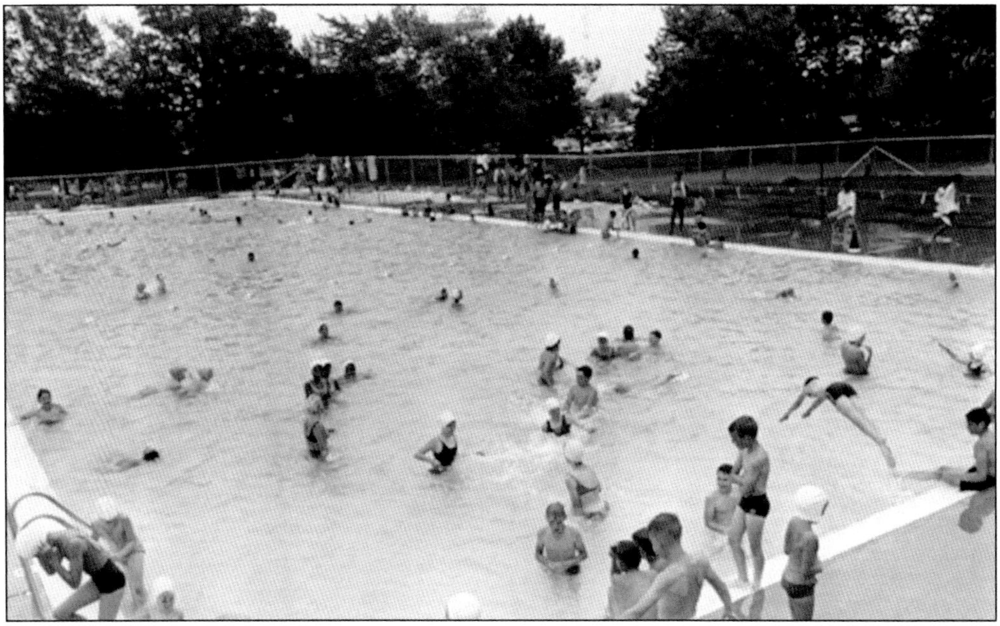

The opening of Westlake's swimming pool and children's pool on June 17, 1967, was well received by hundreds of youngsters and adults in the suburb. Although no count was made, there was a gratifying turnout, according to pool officials. The two pools were built through efforts of Westlake Swimming Pool, a citizens group formed to promote construction of the pool. The pools continue to be enjoyed by neighborhood children today. (Courtesy of Cleveland State University, Cleveland Memory Project, Cleveland Press Collection, Joseph E. Cole, donor.)

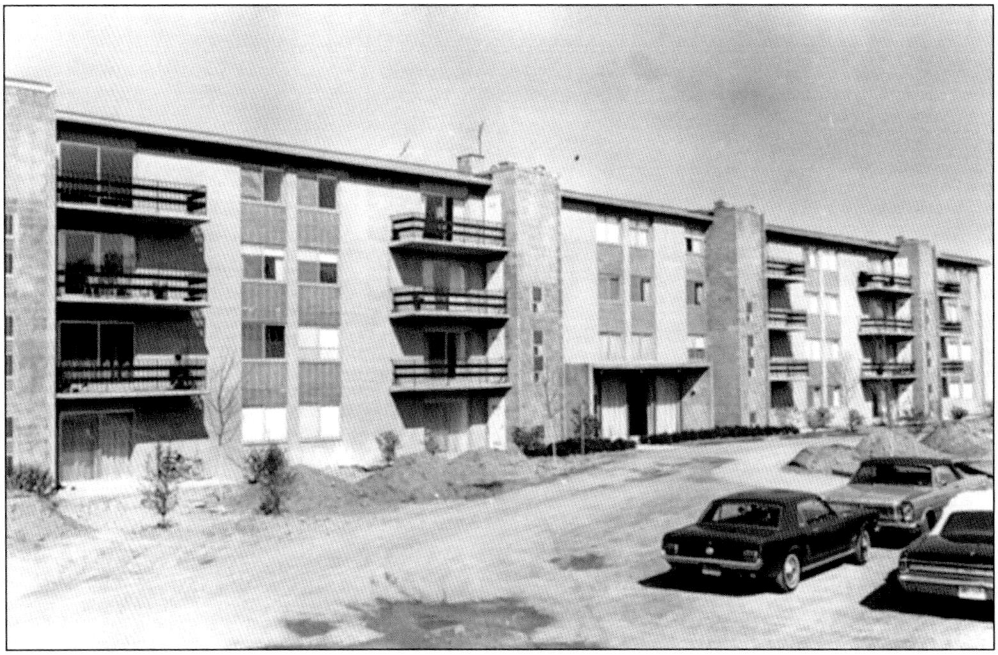

In 1968, the Westwood Meadows Apartments at Detroit and Cahoon Roads opened. (Courtesy of Cleveland State University, Cleveland Memory Project, Cleveland Press Collection, Joseph E. Cole, donor.)

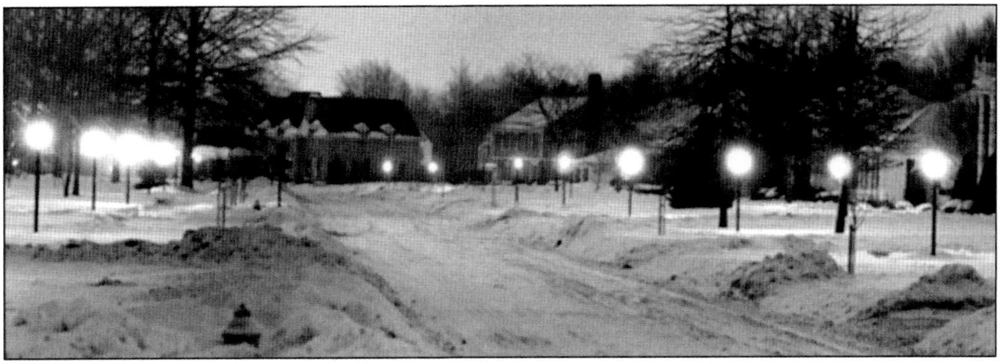

This peaceful winter scene shows Queen Anne's Gate in the King James Grants development. The picture was taken in 1977. (Courtesy of Cleveland State University, Cleveland Memory Project, Cleveland Press Collection, Joseph E. Cole, donor.)

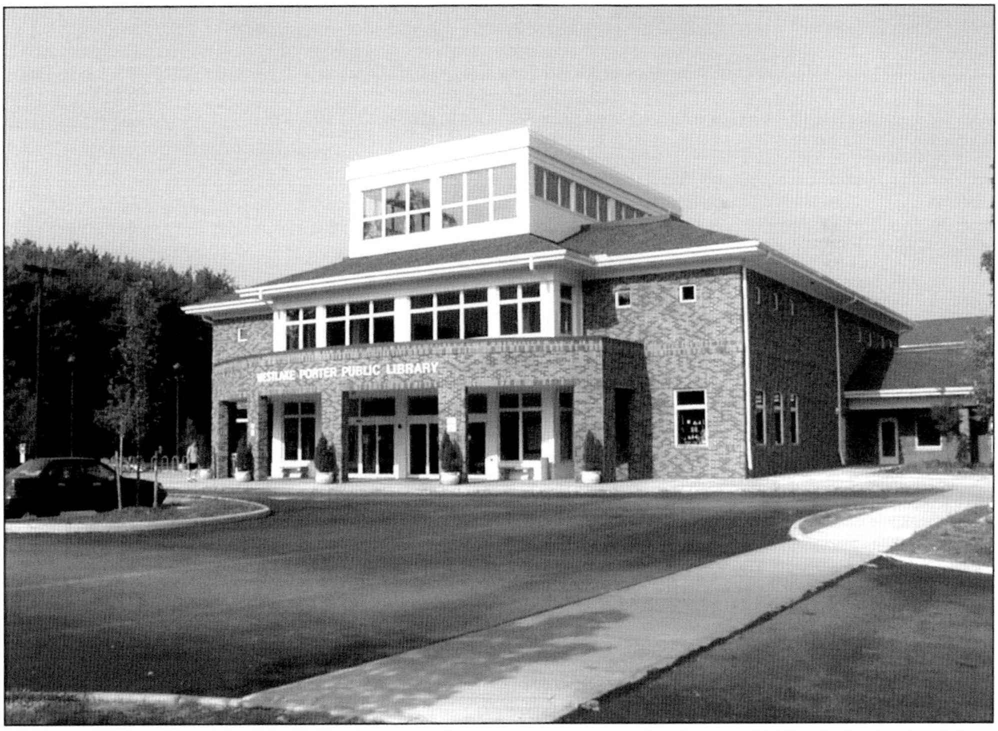

The Westlake Porter Public Library moved into a temporary facility in 1999 while the building expanded from 32,000 to 75,000 square feet. On July 22, 2002, the new library celebrated its opening day and cutting-edge features combined with enhanced traditional library services. Innovative designs upheld the mission of Westlake Porter Public Library, "to educate, empower, enlighten, and excite." (Courtesy of Westlake Porter Public Library.)

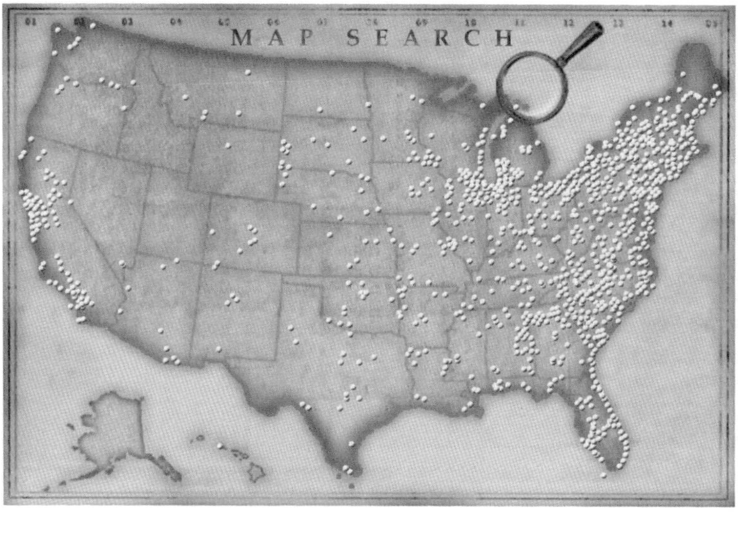
MAP SEARCH